D1598340

The Revelation of St. John

by

ABRAHAM KUYPER

Translated from the Dutch
by John Hendrik de Vries

WILLIAM B. EERDMANS PUBLISHING COMPANY
GRAND RAPIDS, MICHIGAN

PHOTOLITHOPRINTED BY CUSHING - MALLOY, INC.
ANN ARBOR, MICHIGAN, UNITED STATES OF AMERICA
1 9 6 4

FOREWORD

The Revelation of St. John, presented here in English garb, forms the greater part of the fourth and last volume of Dr. Kuyper's work: "The Consummation of the World." He calls it the Consummation first because the term is Scriptural (suntelias tou aionos, Matth. 28, 20) and also because of its wider scope from that of Eschatology. The latter's outlook is purely upon last things: death, judgment, heaven and hell. The former is both the backward and the forward look, and views last things in the light of things that are first; the end from the viewpoint of the beginning. I am Alpha and Omega, saith the Lord, and writes the author: "As the (Greek) alphabet forms one whole which begins with alpha and ends with omega, so the world had a beginning and a course of history, and shall only reach the Consummation when it shall have come to the omega of history; and that beginning *was*, that process of history *is* and that Consummation *shall be* of God."

Volumes I and II deal with the representations regarding the final outcome of things as they are found in the religions, philosophic systems and scientific conclusions of the world's life, as it is lived apart from the revealed religion of Old and New Testaments. In each of these the author points to the insufficiency of the result that is reached to meet the crying needs of the human heart.

Volume III starts out from the mother-promise of Gen. 3, 15 and from there on are traced the unfoldings of the outlook upon the Consummation of the world, as found in the Pentateuch, in the poetical books, in the historical and in the prophetical books of the Old Testament Scriptures. Prophetical Inspiration according to the author being "An action of the Holy Spirit upon the consciousness of the Seer, which leads up to a higher ecstasy." In this Dr. Kuyper marks three stages: (I) that in which by continued glorious action from Above the mind of the prophet has reached such a state of inspiration, that inspirational action amounts to no more than the incitement of this already inspired human spirit to action; (2) that in which the action of the human spirit more or less recedes, so that the action of the Holy Spirit preponderates, as when from the depths of sorrow the Psalmist mourns: "All thy waves and billows have gone over me"; and (3) that in which the human spirit becomes the passive agent, and the Spirit of the Lord speaks, testifies and writes through him, as when the Psalmist sings: "They part my garments among them and cast lots upon my vesture."

The fourth and last volume deals with the eschatological Discourses of our Lord and with the Revelation of St. John. And to show the Author's attitude and approach to this book, the reader is referred to Dr. Kuyper's treatment of the 22d Sunday of the Heidelberg Catechism, "E VOTO DORDRACENO" where, in connection with Chiliasm he describes the three methods of interpretation that have been applied to the Revelation of St. John, by which to reach a proper understanding of the same.

"The first method of interpretation virtually renders the book of Revelation meaningless to us, as it makes its visions to hark back to events that transpired in the early centuries of the Christian church, and its prophecies are said to be the products of human ingenuity and not of Divine revelation. So this can not detain us, and we turn at once to the second method which came into vogue by St. Augustine, was ably and inspiringly set forth by our writers of the marginal notes* and is adhered to by most of our orthodox exegetes to this day.

According to this representation this Book contains real prophecies regarding the course of the church's life from the destruction of Jerusalem to the return of our Lord. Thus not only are the return of our Lord and the events immediately preceding it prophecied here, but it also presents in highly-wrought visions an abridged church history. It foretells every heresy that will arise, every persecution that will break out, every hierarchy that would corrupt the church, and how notwithstanding all these menacing dangers Christ would yet maintain His church, and by means of the last judgment bring her to eternal glory.

The third representation takes the *ideal* way and shows how in the visions of Revelation whole series of mutually related

---

*Dutch: Kantteekenaren. Writers of the Marginal notes in the Dutch Bible translated by order of the States General. Tr.

pictures are presented, which successively depict all sorts of conflicts and results, to which—as in heaven so on earth, and as in the world of spirits so in the world of men—the main conflict between Christ and Satan, between the Mediator and the Antichrist shall lead; followed by a foreshadowing of the final unravelment in which this gigantic struggle shall terminate.

Yet even in these two representations we can not recognize the true method of interpretation. He who has made a serious study of the marginal notes of Revelation has been impressed of necessity with the uncertainty into which Augustine's method brings him. He is told again and again that this one finds this and the other one that in it. As the several figures present themselves the expositor can not make up his mind whether one king is meant or another, this pope or another, or whether the writer refers to a persecution of the past or to one that is still to come. Moreover it breaks the thread of devotional reading when the mind is continually diverted by historical and numerical calculations of dates, which as pawns on a chessboard are moved back and forth, and in any case lie outside the horizon of the devout among God's people· Again, this method of interpretation leads to results which reflect the time in which the expositor lives. S. Augustine, who knew nothing of the papal hierarchy, is reminded of the early persecutors of the church and of the great heresies of those early days, while the writers of the marginal notes, who were reared in the heat of the struggle with Rome, had in mind almost exclusively what had gone out from Rome's seat against God's counsel. All this breeds uncertainty and confusion. It turns exegesis into an artful play of ingenuity. And when men of such eminent piety as Bengel devote years of their life to the calculation that the final period was to begin in 1836; or locate the end of the world in a year that is long past; we realize that such exegesis can not meet what God's church expects from this particular part of Scripture.

Neither does the idealistic method of interpretation satisfy. We heartily agree with it for so far as it spares the devout the needless pains of following the course of vain calculations and questions of idle curiosity, in order at once to bring them face to face with the *spiritual* content of the Apocalypse. But yet even this in turn is too onesided and underestimates the altogether true element in S. Augustine's method, which has been followed by the writers of the marginal notes and most of our theologians.

It is both safer and more practical, therefore, not to adopt either of these two methods as such, but to combine what is of lasting worth in each. Thus we reach a result which is briefly stated as follows:

1. This Book is apocalyptic. The difference between prophecy and apocalypse is, that prophecy shows things to come, as they are in process of unfolding from things that are already present in the earth, while apocalypse does not borrow the images of things to come from earthly things, but from things that are in heaven, and pays no heed to the relation that binds these things to come to the present. Thus in prophecy the consciousness of the prophet is to a high degree co-operative, while in apocalypse everything comes to him as foreign substance from without. Prophecy moreover comes to us in imagery which is explainable by earthly conditions of things, while the heavenly visions of the apocalypse are clothed in forms which affect our consciousness in undefinable ways.

2. The main purpose of the Revelation of St. John is to comfort the suffering and militant church and to encourage her by directing her gaze to Christ, Who, as King of His church, shall one day gloriously triumph over all His and her enemies. But as this glorious final outcome already foreshadows itself in what precedes, is basic to all church history, and shall merely be the solution of that main conflict of spirits which went out from Paradise, and by the Incarnation of the Word has been marked as the decisive element in all the history of the world, yes even of the whole universe, in this Book we are shown successively a series of visions, in which the several parts of the struggle are imaged one by one. Each of these sketches or etchings is complete in itself, but is organically connected with the rest of the visions, and together with these is governed by God's counsel concerning His church both on earth and in heaven. So these separate visions or etchings are shown us in a symbolical grouping, *seven* seals, *seven* trumpets, *seven* vials, and everytime follows a new group of seven after the six that went before. A glorious interlinking which is indicated by the number seven, because it was thus linked by the holy will of God.

3. These visions, images or apocalyptic etchings are dioramically arranged. That is to say, they do not follow each other in

that order of a given time to which they should point, but each in turn indicates groups or factions in that mighty struggle, which far from being limited to one period of time, rather return in every period, and are ever the prototypes in which this age-long struggle is depicted.

4. The numbers and indications of persons in this Book are not actual but figurative numbers. There were more than seven churches in Asia Minor. The number 144,000 does not indicate the sum-total of all the saved. The 1600 furlongs of the pool of blood which reached unto the bridles of the horses do not measure a geographical locality. All these numbers are to be taken symbolically, according as they indicate the holy or the unholy, the fullness or a part, the break or the completion of a process.

5. From this follows that both S. Augustine and the Idealists were right in part. The Idealists were right in so far as these visions indicate the general types that play a part in the conflict between Christ and the Antichrist, and hence at no time refer exclusively to a particular event. But S. Augustine too is right, and our writers of the marginal notes are right when they claim that also in past history as well as in the history of the church and of the nations of our times these prototypes again and again repeat themselves and are continually recognizable.

6. The full meaning of the Apocalypse shall only be understood *"when all has come to pass"*. Then shall appear how accurately and truly the basic character of these struggles has been depicted in these visions. Then we shall learn in which part of history each of these prototypes expressed itself most clearly and most strongly. And then to the glory of God it shall be plain that even the particular features of these visions were chosen with far more accuracy and discrimination than now can be surmised. And all in accordance with the rule which Jesus laid down when He said: "And now I have told you before it would come to pass, that, when it is come to pass, ye might believe."

This prepares the reader for Dr. Kuyper's treatment of the Apocalypse from the viewpoint of the "Consummation."

It will interest the reader to learn that this four volume work on the "Consummation" was the last output of the author's pen. He began it when he was 76 years of age, and like most of his other works, it appeared serially in *De Heraut* (the Christian weekly of which Dr. Kuyper was the editor in chief for nearly 55 years) for about six years and did not come out in book form until after the author's death in 1920. So these studies in the Apocalypse were written when he was on the border of the other world, and may well be received as his Nebo-vision of the "things which must shortly come to pass."

Mr. Philip Mauro of Washington, D. C., who is himself a writer of many books, and to whom warm thanks are due for valuable assistance rendered in the preparation of the manuscript for the press, offers this comment: "I esteem it a great privilege that opportunity was given me to read in manuscript the English translation of Dr. Kuyper's great commentary on Revelation. Manifestly the author was a man specially fitted by rare and even exceptional endowments for the peculiarly difficult task of commenting upon and bringing to light (for apprehension by our occidental minds) the deep and rich spiritual content of the Apocalypse. His views as set forth in these pages are always deeply spiritual, frequently of the highest value and almost invariably worthy of serious consideration, even though the reader does not always agree with the interpretation. There is, in what this man of God has written, a sweet savor of Christ, and often besides a heart-warming mellowness that comes only as the result of a life-time of devout meditation in the Holy Scriptures."

Writes the Reverend Adolf Hult, D.D., Professor of Church History in the Augustana Theological Seminary, Rock Island, Illinois: "In the 'Revelation' studies of Dr. Abraham Kuyper we have a masterpiece of devotional literature. The deep congeniality of his soul with scriptural prophecy makes him fitted to interpret prophecy. His massive historical schooling as statesman, which he was in the Netherlands, and as a theologian, enables him to *think* prophecy without the fantastic sentimentality of many prophetic expositions. He also possesses a veritable genius for sensing the thought realities and life realities that are found in a symbolistic style of speech such as the Hebrew prophets employ. For to treat that style in the crude realism of Occidental mentality is to wreck both the literature as such and the thought which the prophetic Oriental mind seeks to convey. In fact, the lack of such a prerequisite in the interpretation of Hebrew prophecy has been the rock of destruction to modern interpreters. Doctor Kuyper works in a different manner.

"Amid all the welter of notional prophetic writing at present, the Kuyper work challenges the thoughtful and believing Christian to profoundest reverence for the message of the book of Revelation. It deepens his insight into this difficult work. The grand knowledge of human life and of the godly life removes the amateurish tone often noted in prophetic writings of our day. A great Christian man, statesman, scholar, theologian, spiritual genius and master of literary style and of religious expression has left the Christian church a legacy of which the future is bound to lay hold."

As a modest effort in this direction this volume is offered the English speaking Christian church by the

TRANSLATOR.

Old Saybrook, Conn.
May 8, 1935.

CONTENTS

CONTENTS
(Continued)

The Translator dedicates this book to
HIS WIFE,
who has been a constant inspiration to
him in his task of bringing the Great
Kuyper in touch with English readers.

The Revelation of St. John

I

THIS REVELATION VIEWS THE END.

*He which testifieth these things saith, Surely I come
quickly. Amen. Even so, come, Lord Jesus.* Rev. 22, 20.

In Holy Scripture the Consummation is not brought into full
view until account is also taken of the last inspired book, which
is the Revelation of St. John. On Patmos the Divine revelation
that is given to the church of Christ is concluded.

With respect to the future the Old Testament had first to be
examined in its historic and prophetic parts, until in Daniel,
which dates from the 5th century before Christ, it presents the
richest and most complete revelation. Shortly after this the Old
Testament revelation was closed by Malachi. What during the
four centuries that still preceded Bethlehem the Jews studied and
pondered was merely Jewish learning in the Scripture, and as
such has nothing to do with Divine revelation. This was only
revived again by what Christ provided during His life on earth.
and by what after His Ascension was added by His apostles, such
as St. Paul and St. Peter. But even this did not include what was
to bring the Consummation into full view, and only at the end of
the century that began with Bethlehem, a most surprisingly
copious revelation of what will come to pass at the end of the
world was given to the apostle John on Patmos. Hence if we
were to take no account of the Revelation of St. John, our study
of the Consummation would not be complete. And though no
exhaustive exposition can here be given of the whole Apocalypse,
as from now on we shall call the last book of the Bible, it will
not do to treat its rich content superficially. This may suffice
him who rejects the Apocalypse as a book of fiction, but is absolutely unwarranted on the part of him who accepts this last book
of Holy Scripture also as given us of God.

Yet this concluding part of our task is far from simple. The Apocalypse is in every respect extremely baffling. More than any other Bible book it abounds in images, and no book of the Bible has provoked such radically different interpretations as the Revelation of St. John. Not in the early centuries of the Christian era. At first the Apocalypse created a deep interest throughout the whole church and gave rise to few, if any, objections. And naturally so. In the early centuries after the Ascension the church of Christ lived almost of necessity in constant expectation of the immediate return of Christ. An insight into what afterward proved to be the case, namely, that the end of the world would be deferred for at least some twenty centuries, could in those early days not even be surmised. Only after the conversion of Constantine in the early part of the 4th century, and after St. Augustine's entirely divergent eschatological representations in the 5th century, did the future as it were begin to stretch itself and more and more reckoning was made with ever greater series of centuries. But when St. John on Patmos received his perspectives, the church, if we may so express ourselves, based her reckoning upon an extremely short term. No longer upon so short a period of time as the first Christians, who mostly lived in expectation of witnessing the end, but yet in such a way that this event was not deferred more than three or at most four centuries.

The Apocalypse of St. John occupies this viewpoint, and he alone who takes this into account can read aright and measurably understand what this mysterious book presents. The Apocalypse of St. John treats exclusively of what will come to pass when the ordinary course of things shall be broken up, and the concluding period of both the life of the church and the life of the world is ushered in. The case stands like this: After Jesus' Ascension there would first be a normal period, in which things would run their ordinary course, as has now been going on for nearly twenty centuries. The rise of the Christian church in the world had established entirely new and hitherto unknown relationships between herself and that world, but after the Ascension of Jesus into heaven and the passing away of the apostolate, earthly life anew became *normal*. That is to say, the course of the natural life, of the relation between heaven and earth and of the Divine action upon the same remained what after the fall it had always been. Life on earth went on as usual, the actions from heaven upon it bore their normal character; and there was no intimation of any miraculous, violent invasion upon the existing order of things, whereby everything would be changed. The parousia would bring the change, provisionally things remained as they were. Not spiritually. Spiritually the church, wherever she came, worked in every way an important change in the life of the nations, but this did not affect the outward life. Here indeed there were marked advances in every direction. Numerous inventions created different conditions of life, and man became more and more master over nature. Yet as regards *the common order of life,* century upon century things remained as they had always been, and there was no sign of the dawn of the Day of the Lord.

Question: Shall this go on until Jesus comes? In other words: Will Jesus come back unexpectedly and suddenly present Himself to His church, or will His return be preceded by a period of a modified, differently clothed worldlife? Will Jesus appear unheralded in the midst of our daily avocations, either in Europe, in Asia, or any other part of the earth, and will people everywhere be informed by telegraph of the stupendous fact that Christ is come to judge the world and is on earth again as He was before His Ascension? To this many reply that nothing uncommon will take place beforehand; that to the last moment things will go on as usual, and no preparatory signs will herald the event. Think of the disappointed people in Cape Colony, who had gone thither confidently expecting that within a few months at most Christ would make His appearance. They had no idea of any *transitional conditions* which would prepare the church for the Return of Christ. As life now is, it would go on to the end, and then suddenly and unexpectedly Christ would come down to earth and put an end to the present state of things and usher in the Consummation.

Yet the Revelation that came to St. John on Patmos utterly contradicts this view, as the Apocalypse teaches the direct opposite. It shows even at great pains that the Return of the

Lord will almost immediately be preceded by extremely important and very striking events. What is to take place in the opening of the *Seals* and the *Trumpets* and the *Vials,* with their attending woes and angelic appearances, will put an end to the
ordinary, normal course of the life of the world, and bring the
coming of Christ nearer, as it were step by step. So the whole
apocalyptic representation contradicts the false expectation of
those people and sects that deemed, or still deem, that the Return of the Lord will be so sudden and unexpected, that nothing
special or uncommon will herald its approach. The Apocalypse
of St. John holds the direct opposite before us. Not by a cursory
indication, but in a fully elaborated form, and even style, the
Apocalypse prophesies in detail a series of mighty events, which,
when the end is at hand, will precede and introduce it.

Naturally therefore the Apocalypse was hailed by the church
of the early centuries of the Christian era and was loved by it,
and only in later times, so to speak, did it pass into some dis-
credit. As is well known, Luther entertained serious doubts
about the genuineness of the Apocalypse. And since the days
of St. Augustine, Christian people at large scarcely reckon with
the Return of the Lord at all. Not that they deny it. They grant
that sooner or later the present state of things must and will
come to an end, but personally they take little interest in it.
In general preparation is made for death, but not for living to see
the parousia. After death one hopes to have a welcome at
heaven's gate, where everything will be so beautiful and glorious
as to leave nothing more to be desired. Assured confidence that
after death one enters at once upon the blessed state of the redeemed rendered the sick and dying practically indifferent to the
things that might come after. These are so dreadful and appalling, that one preferred to dismiss them from the mind. But
this was not so in the early centuries of the Christian era, when
gloomy uncertainty like a pall hung over everything, but dates
from about the 4th century, has gradually taken firmer hold of
the common mind, and now the greater majority of believers
almost never give the parousia a thought, and small sects and
individual persons, to whom this is still a matter of serious concern always lose themselves again in the expectation of a *sudden*
return of Christ.

Against both these forms of heresy the Apocalypse of St. John enters a direct protest. It declares dying and entering upon the blessedness of heaven to be merely *temporal* events, and makes everything that has taken place in the past and is taking place in the present culminate in that one mighty event, which by means of the parousia will solve all the problems of the life of the world and of faith. Again, by a circumstantial and minute account it shows how the transition from the ordinary state of the present life into that of the approach of the end and of the parousia of the Lord shall formally take place. Naturally all this was adapted to the order of the time when St. John was on Patmos, and was expressed in the ideas and forms of thought which were then in vogue. And so the apocalyptic prophecy was understood as referring to things with which believers themselves were in daily touch, and thus applied to their own times. In his Apocalypse St. John gave a minute account of the events that were to herald the parousia. They who imagined, as at the time the mass of believers did, that the parousia, if not immediately, yet was very shortly at hand, were thereby naturally tempted to apply the prophecies of the Apocalypse *to their own lifetime.* This is the more readily understood moreover when we think of the cruel persecutions which at the time again and again imperilled the lives of these Christians. These very persecutions were taken to be the beginning of the great things that would come to pass when the end of the world was nigh. So it was not strange that they should look upon the distress which according to this prophecy would precede the Return of Christ, as already realized in what they suffered.

The only thing that could modify this outlook upon what was prophesied was the lapse of time, and the attending changes in the general conditions of life. When persecutions ceased, and the passing centuries brought not so much as a hint of Jesus' return, the impression was bound to deepen, that the apocalyptic prophecies did not refer to the long period of history from the Ascension to the parousia, but dealt solely with the end of the world immediately preceding Christ's return. Only so a proper understanding of the Apocalypse was reached. The former impression, that the series of the Seals, the Trumpets and the Vials, together with what belonged to them, was but the rehearsal of what would immediately come to pass, of itself faded away, and it began to be seen more and more clearly that the Apocalyptic prophecies referred solely and exclusively to what would come to pass on the eve of the Parousia. The history of the world that was to precede the parousia formed no part of this. History was to be long and would run its normal course. And only when history shall have run its normal course, and signs of the parousia appear, can the things that were foretold to St. John be awaited. So the only proper conclusion is, that nothing of all this has thus far yet come to pass, that we are still in the normal period of history, and that the events which form the prophetic content of the Apocalypse shall only come to pass, when the end of the world is at hand.

Meanwhile, however, as really the Apocalypse gives no data with respect to history, but presents solely an account of the wondrous events that will herald the parousia, immediately precede it, and prepare the way for it, the church has not been able to give instant currency to this only correct understanding of the Apocalyptic prophecies. Even in Reformed churches, and elsewhere, it is still commonly held that what the Seals, the Trumpets and the Vials foretell simply refers to common historic events and occurrences. It scarcely could be represented in any other way, and even the translators of the (Dutch) Bible, as appears in their marginal readings, could not escape this deeply rooted and utterly untenable representation. Their extensive comments show how assiduously they apply the things which the Seals, the Trumpets and the Vials foretell, to the Turks, the Papists, and the events that in the course of presently sixteen centuries have disturbed the peace of Christendom. Especially in personal suffering and martyrdom, which the Reformation brought upon a large part of the Christian world, the thought that this distress and anguish had already on Patmos been foretold and mirrored, was very consolatory. Yet the church has rightly almost never attached any value to this, and later exegesis has more and more detached itself from this mistaken view.

Thus only during the last one hundred and fifty years have our ways been mended. Both the profane and sacred history of these almost twenty past centuries are now set apart from the Apocalyptic prophecies. It is realized that what here is prophe-

sied can and will be fulfilled only when the end of the world is
at hand and the advance signs appear on the horizon. For these
Apocalyptic prophecies do not refer to the past, they are no
history of the past twenty centuries, but forecast *what is to come
at the beginning of the end*. When this will be, how many years it
will take the Seals, the Trumpets and the Vials to fulfill themselves, we do not know. Nothing prevents the quick succession of
one upon the other. It might not cover more than the space of
a single year. What we must insist upon, however, is, that
what from chapter seven the Apocalypse records has not yet
taken place, neither has it yet transpired, but is still to come and
thus awaits fulfilment. So only can the Apocalypse be understood, and so only does this representation correspond to the
perspectives that are opened up before us.

II

THE APOCALYPSE IS FOR THE CHURCH
OF ALL TIME

Write the things which thou hast seen, and the things
which are, and the things which shall be hereafter.
Revelation 1, 19.

If thus the Apocalypse of St. John is a prophecy of things to
come when the Consummation is at hand, in the nature of the
case it impressed those to whom it first came differently from
what it impresses us now. When on Patmos the apostle received this prophecy, as well as during the early centuries of
persecutions, the Christians, so to speak, fairly longed for the
coming of the end. So at first no distinction was perceived between the history of State and Church and the parousia. It all
seemed close at hand. It reads so plainly (Rev. 1, 3): "Blessed
is he that readeth, *for the time is at hand*". In those early centuries, and especially when St. John was in exile on Patmos, it
seemed that the parousia would immediately occur. But the
further the course of centuries advanced, the more it began to
put on a different aspect. Century came, and century went, and
still the parousia tarried. This affected the outlook however but
little so long as persecutions were continued. The main feature
of this period was the deep longing for the end. It was when
persecutions ceased and under Constantine the church came more
and more into power, that longing for the end perceptibly moderated and gave place to the inclination to postpone the same
and to extend the dominion of Christendom over the life of
the nations both extensively and intensively. This was chiefly
supported by the saying of Jesus that the end would not come
until the Gospel had been preached to all nations of the world.
While thus in those early centuries the longing for the end
had been the Christian inspiration, with Constantine it all
changed, and now the conviction rather gained ground that there
was by no means yet any immediate prospect of the end and

many centuries were likely to precede the same. Then for a time it was deemed that the end would not come until the expiration of the 6000 years after the creation. This however was held by but a part of Christendom, and life at large was lived from one century to the other as though for long ages to come the world would not come to an end.

In the further study of this matter distinction was then made between the historic centuries that would normally precede the parousia and the short period crowded with miraculous occurrences which would only begin when the parousia is at hand. So of itself there arose the clear-cut distinction between three periods. The first period extended to 325, and included the persecutions which Christendom had to endure first at the hand of the Jews and then at that of the heathen State. The second period would run from Constantine to the beginning of the Consummation, now already 16 centuries long. Only then would the third and last period begin which would consist exclusively of those extraordinary events which shall usher in the parousia and bring the Consummation to perfection. The prophecy of St. John mainly treats of that short, last period. Wondrously constructed it gives the image of the first period of bitter persecutions, but what the series of the seven Seals, the seven Trumpets and the seven Vials prophesy has nothing to do with the history of the 16 intervening centuries, but deals solely with the approaching parousia.

The Apocalypse of St. John does not really begin with chapter I, but with chapter 4, and more particularly with chapter 6. In verse 1 of chapter 6 Christ begins the opening of the seven Seals. Verses 1-12 deal with six of the seven Seals, when a state of things ensues which is so wondrous, that "the sun became black as sackcloth", that "the moon became as blood, and that stars of heaven fall unto the earth." Hence it can not be said that only the Trumpets, the Vials, the woes and other angelic actions introduce what is wondrous and abnormal. Chapter 6, 12-17 shows the contrary. In these last six verses of chapter 6 we already face an entirely abnormal state of things, which is utterly unlike that of our ordinary history. Not only later, but already in chapter 6 which marks the beginning of these prophecies, the state of the world is so radically affected as to put an end to all ordinary history. Hence these six verses must be taken literally, lest we be misled by appearance. Look at the condition of things which according to chapter 6 shall immediately ensue. There shall not only be a great earthquake, but the sun shall become black as a sackcloth of hair and the moon as blood. The stars of heaven shall fall unto the earth, even as a fig tree casteth her untimely figs. More still. The heaven shall depart as a scroll when it is rolled together. All mountains and islands shall be moved out of their places. Yes the condition shall at once become so terrible, that the kings of the earth, and the great men, and the rich men, and also every bondman, and every free man, shall hide themselves in the dens and in the rocks of the mountains, crying: "Fall on us, and hide us from the face of him that sitteth on the throne, and from the wrath of the Lamb: For the great day of his wrath is come; and who shall be able to stand?"

Thus at the time of the Consummation the dreadful commotion shall not begin only with the Trumpets or with the Vials, but with the first miraculous signs, that is, with the Seals; and already in chapter 6—that is to say, in the first chapter that treats of coming events—prophecy does not deal with normal historic affairs, but with entirely abnormal events which, only when normal history is ended, shall usher in the tremendous change, and with it the end of all things. Chapter 1, which is introductory to the whole Apocalypse, is preparatory to this. Verse 3 of said chapter states, that what St. John is to convey to the church does not refer to things that have taken place, but is prophetic of things to come. It says that the things which he must write down are actual *prophecies,* and in v. 7 that *prophecy* is directly connected with the Return of Christ upon clouds. "Behold, he cometh with clouds; and every eye shall see him, and they also which pierced him: and all kindreds of the earth shall wail because of him. Even so. Amen" (v. 7). Thus the approach to the parousia, or, if you will, to the Consummation, is direct.

If it is asked whether then indeed the Apocalypse has nothing to say of the historic centuries of the past, the first chapter shows that it would not be right so to represent it. Verse 4 of said chapter expressly states that St. John writes this book to the seven churches which are *in Asia.* In this same chapter these seven churches are called by name: "Ephesus, Smyrna, Pergamos, Thyatira, Sardis, Philadelphia and Laodicea." Note also that here we have to do with the number seven. In all Scripture "seven" is the sacred number, and it will not do to take this in the literal sense. Think what a literal interpretation of this number here would imply. Every thoughtful reader will admit that this wondrous prophecy was not addressed to the seven churches in Asia-Minor exclusively, and that the prophecies of the Seals, the Trumpets, the Vials and visions of angels also concern us, and carry a direct message to us, and in general are designed for all Christendom, yes for all peoples in all the world. All the same, according to vs. 4 and 11, St. John addresses these letters exclusively to these seven churches in Asia-Minor, only one of which at most is still of any account. This would signify less, if St. John alone had thus expressed himself. But even this is not the case. Not John, but Christ speaks in v. 11 and commands, saying: "Write this in a book, and send it to the seven churches which are in Asia."

He who consults the book of the Acts realizes that the choice of these particular churches would be inexplicable. Take the church of Iconium, which was founded by St. Paul. Not only is it called by name in the New Testament as often as seven times, but is there to this day, yet does not appear on the list of churches given here in the Apocalypse. Thyatira appears on this list, though it is but once referred to in the Acts, and then merely in connection with a woman named Lydia, a seller of purple in that city (16:14). The same applies to Ephesus. Of the church that once flourished there no trace is left. In my book of travels 'Around the Mediterranean' (Om de Oude Wereldzee) I described what I saw at Ephesus as follows: "Here in Ephesus history alone is vocal. The city presents a scene of beautiful ruins, but can not be rebuilt, as the harbor is filled up with sand which renders all approach from the sea impossible. The leading object of interest there of course is the great temple of Diana, but of this celebrated sanctuary also almost no trace is left. In 1876 the foundations have been unearthed by Wood, yet these are not the foundations of the Diana-temple in the days of its glory. In 356 B. C. Herostratus set fire to the temple of Paionios, which was the last temple built by Democritus, and even this temple was destroyed by the Getae (Getes) in 262. The foundations of the several successive temples have been discovered again, the oldest of which dates back as far as Croesus, but only a few are in sight. Extremely impressive however are the remains of the old theatre that was built at the foot of Mount Pion, as the side of that mountain provides seats for 50,000 spectators. The stage and its adjoining rooms are still intact and present glorious architectonic beauty."

Less well preserved, yet still in the old lines, is the Odeion, partly built into Mount Pion, with its seats and stage with its three doors still intact. Near by is the so-called "prison of Paul", back of which are the remains of the ancient city-wall. Everything is beautiful as a mass of ruins, but the church of Christ is gone. He therefore who takes the language here employed in the literal sense, faces an insoluble problem. As said before, we accept as fact that St. John sent copies of his Apocalypse to the seven churches enumerated in chapter 1, 11. We see no reason why he should not have done so. Yet this does not say, that these seven churches in Asia-Minor here should have no symbolical significance. The prophecies that came to St. John on Patmos are of general significance *to all Christendom*, and by no means exclusively to a small company of Christians in one corner of the world. "After this I beheld, and, lo, a great multitude, which no man could number, *of all nations, and kindreds, and people, and tongues,* stood before the throne, and before the Lamb" (Rev. 7, 9). This shows conclusively that the prophecy of St. John directs itself to Christendon *in all the world*. How then can it tally with this, that St. John should literally have been charged to address his glorious prophecies exclusively to the seven churches in Asia-Minor, all of which, save one, have passed into oblivion, while other churches there which continue to this day are not included.

Thus we conclude that, while this prophetic revelation came to St. John, it can not have been intended as binding in that literal sense. The number seven appears here, as elsewhere, to have been used as the mystical number, and the address of the prophecy to Asia-Minor must be accounted for by the fact that Patmos was located in its proximity, and that probably in the later years of his apostolate St. John had intimately been connected with these churches. Presently it would appear that, rather than these churches in Asia-Minor, the churches which St. Paul founded in Europe would be the exponents of the future of Christendom. Yet this might readily have been foreseen even then, and that these seven churches in Asia-Minor, including the church of Thyatira, should be the permanent foundation of the church of Christ, can not at the end of the first century so much as have suggested itself to St. John. And as this can not be doubted, neither can it be accepted that with respect to such weighty prophecies as those of the Apocalypse, Christ could have given currency to such a representation. The very fact that only seven churches are called by name, when at the time there were certainly more than one hundred, shows, that what is presented here can only be taken in a symbolical sense. The Apocalypse addresses itself all along to the Christendom of all ages. Hence a really intended limitation of Christendom to seven churches in a given region is out of the question. Moreover what the ever mystical number seven indicates is confirmed by all the other parts of the Apocalypse. These seven churches of Asia-Minor are taken simply as an example of division, and what is really imaged thereby is the whole church of Christ in all the earth.

This symbolical note in the Apocalypse is still more strongly evident, when chapters 2 and 3 are more closely examined. They describe these seven churches more minutely. St. John is told to write to these seven churches, and also here misunderstanding has crept in. These seven letters of St. John have fairly generally been taken as almost valueless to us. It is deemed that they were significant at the time, when all sorts of abuses abounded in those churches. If we admit that before St. John died these letters had had so desirable an effect upon these seven churches as to have put a stop to what is here said by way of reproach or warning,—they had soon served their purpose, and thus ceased to be of significance. Other Christian churches, shadowed by similar abuses, might consider themselves as warned by them, but they could not be of further use than this. Even then this would always be the case very indirectly, since it is not likely that what these seven churches are reproached for, will present itself again, save exceptionally, in that form. The matter however assumes an entirely different aspect, when we dismiss the idea that these letters of Christ were addressed exclusively to these seven parishes, and adopt the entirely modified interpretation that these seven churches merely serve, symbolically to describe the peculiar character, in which the churches in all the earth would expose themselves to the danger of being poisoned and contaminated. Not that there is any arbitrariness here at play. We must admit that what in these seven churches was praised or censured, at the time presented itself in a more or less striking manner. But this did not prevent the writer from grouping these severally named churches together, in order to set forth the characteristic sins which in all ages would very distinctively mark the churches, and hold them up before all Christendom to the end of time as a warning.

In such a connection we commonly speak of types, and in this instance also we reach the view which is most correct, when we admit that in these seven churches Jesus has indicated the seven types which in the course of centuries His churches in the earth would severally exhibit. So the names of Ephesus, Thyatira, are secondary. Seven such types of churches were just as likely to be found in Greece or Italy. Not the names, but merely the seven *types* here count. We must admit that at the time these types must have developed themselves very strongly, or at least fairly clearly, in these seven churches, even though it be granted that by no means every one who was in close touch with these seven parishes would at once have recognized equally clearly all the features of this type. Wherever Christianity becomes established, the churches readily assume a modified form, subject to climate, manner of living, national disposition and racial distinction. These dispositions and conditions create a distinct manner of existence, and what is peculiar about it is, that this sort of types forms itself into one crystallized whole and, when all these variations are taken together, is always recognized again.

It is noteworthy and deeply interesting that Christ, who knew these variations and these types, has grouped together just such a series of churches as together exhibit the fundamental varia-

tions. Jesus did not choose these seven churches arbitrarily, but
in such a way, that together they present the main types in which
the Christian life could develop itself, both in laudable and censur-
able directions. Whether such a church goes by the name of Ephesus or Thyatira, makes no difference. Our duty is to see what type
is most strongly evident in our own church, that we might heed
the warning that applies to our own organization. And this is not
all. From what Christ in these seven types holds before us follows, that we should not demand that all churches in the earth
shall be like our own in type, nature and character. Especially
missionaries in foreign lands are so readily tempted to commit
this fault, and thereby invite failure. A mission in China or
Japan which merely strives to reproduce in those foreign countries a copy or an imitation of our churches at home, must always
end in disappointment, because it does not count with the peculiarity of such a nation and with the variation of the national
type. This makes the letters of Jesus to the seven churches in
Asia-Minor so richly instructive. They contain a direct hint for
Missions, and every Mission that does not count with this, fails.

III.

THE MYSTICISM OF NUMBERS

The Revelation of Jesus Christ, which God gave unto him, to shew unto his servants things which must shortly come to pass; and which he has sent by his angel and signified unto his servant John. Revelation 1, 1.

With the fourth, or rather with the sixth chapter of the Revelation of St. John the Consummation begins, and the prophecies which then follow refer, as appeared above, not to the course of history, nor to the world empire, nor to the church of Christ, but gives the prophetical perspective regarding what, when the Consummation begins, in connection therewith shall come to pass. Yet this does not say that the Apocalypse has nothing to do with the preceding historic course. It does refer to this, but merely in chapters 2 and 3, which contain the seven letters of Jesus to the seven churches in Asia-Minor. These seven letters have no bearing on the Consummation, but deal with the history of the church of Christ prior to the approach of the Consummation. It already appeared that this would cover a period of some twenty centuries. St. John and his contemporaries however knew nothing of those centuries, and Christ gave them no instruction regarding them. Rather it must be said that the Apocalypse as a whole is calculated to prepare believers for a prompt and speedy coming of the end. This would not have been possible if the plan of the Apocalypse had been based upon an idea of numbers, and at the hand of these numbers had aspired to indicate the course of things to come. On the contrary the Apocalypse breathes a prophetical atmosphere, and Old Testament prophecy ignores the reckoning of years by numbers, and deals merely with the essential relation. Not, of course without some exceptions, as when Isaiah foretells the coming of Cyrus, and as when Micah refers to Bethlehem as the birthplace of Jesus. For the rest all prophecy links itself together by the essential relation and not by that of time. Only in Daniel, who was the last of the prophets, was there a turn in this. From of old every prophecy lost itself in the indefinite. It was a sheer reach into the future. Only rarely did the prophet introduce anything more definite. Yet this could not go on for ever, and in Daniel we find the change.

That in the Apocalypse St. John almost entirely ignores this time-relation of centuries, years and months is obvious already in the first verse of the book. It reads that the Apocalypse is a "revelation of Jesus Christ, which God gave unto Him, to shew unto His servants things which must *shortly* come to pass." The word *shortly* is emphasized in v. 3 by the clause: *For the time is at hand*. If we were to write the Apocalypse, we would not put it this way. We would state the fact that a long period of some twenty centuries would precede the appearance of signs that would mark the beginning of the end. We must not slight this difference between what we think that it ought to read, and what it does read. It must become clear to us why it is not as we, who count with the historic course of the centuries, think that it ought to be. For the difference is so great that without further explanation we seemingly face an insoluble mystery; as indeed all too many already, because of this discrepancy, have flatly denied the genuineness of the Apocalypse. So this point of difference must not be slighted. It must become plain to us why and in what sense it could so emphatically be said, there would *shortly* come to pass, and "the time is at hand" of what after these twenty centuries still suffers delay. Even a cursory reading of the Apocalypse would impress one with the fact, that what is prophesied here could not possibly be consummated in a short space of time. The content of the Apocalypse is far too rich for this, is of too varied a character, and divided into too many periods. It must therefore be well understood that what here indicates a speedy and immediate consummation, can have no temporal but a spiritual significance.

To understand this fully the fact cannot be stressed too strongly, that from beginning to end the Apocalypse is not cast in the ordinary chronological mould. In Holy Scripture we continually find a mysticism of numbers, and so we find it here. This is particularly obvious in the use of the number *seven*. Seven is three plus four, in which combination *three*, as a mystical number, re-

fers to the threefold fulness of God, and four to the creation
which the Triune God called into life. Call to mind the four
points of the compass. And so three, in connection with four
refers to the counsel of God with an eye to the creation. So we
have seven week-days, which are reckoned after the creation, and
the constant use in Scripture of the number seven, when it must
be noted that we are not to count with our calendar centuries,
years, months and days, but with the relation between the divine
disposal of all created things and the signs of it that show themselves in the creation. We should make a careful study of this,
because we, Westerners, know nothing of these mystical representations which are common in the East, and can only faintly
visualize them. Hence we must heed the fact, that in the Revelation of St. John seven is a fixed datum, which governs the entire
representation. How important a role this mystical number seven
plays in the Apocalypse is shown by the fact that its use there
occurs no less than about fifty times. Twice in chapter 1, 4 and
again in verses 11, 12, 13, 16, and six times in verse 20. In
chapter 4, v. 5, in chapter 5 in vs. 1, 5, and three times in v. 6.
It occurs once in chapter 8, v. 1, twice in v. 2, and twice in
v. 6. In chapter 10 in v. 3, twice in v. 4, and once in v. 7.
In chapter 12 twice in v. 3. In chapter 13 it occurs but once
in v. 1. It does not occur in chapter 14, but in chapter 15 no less
than eight times in vs. 1, 6, 7 and 8. Chapter 16 has it three
times in vs. 1 and 17. Chapter 17 has it eight times in verses
1, 3, 7, 9, 10 and 11. And in chapter 21 we find it three times
in v. 9 and once in v. 20. Thus in this book of but 22 chapters
the number seven occurs almost fifty times, which fact must not
be overlooked. It shows that the relations that are dealt with
in this last book of Holy Scripture are governed by mystical data
from above, and that in this book the connection and the coherence of things are not under the control of earthly chronology,
but under that of the mystical regulation of the relations that
emanate from God.

Necessarily use had to be made of numbers, because without
them we can neither represent duration nor relation. But one
would gravely err in his understanding of Holy Scripture, including the Apocalypse, if he were to apply the same meaning

to these numbers, as is done in common life. This does not imply
that exact numbers do not occur even several times in Scripture,
but we must not forget that such numbers can not be applied
with any accuracy to the eternal, and therefore must carefully be
considered. The like phenomenon presents itself in Genesis I.
Hence the wide difference of opinion regarding the length of
these days, between their evening and their morning. In our common speech we deal similarly with the numbers three and ten.
When we say: You must do this in a trice, we mean that it must
be done at once, or as quickly as one can count *one, two, three.*
When we say: He can not yet count ten, it is not the number
ten that counts, but the limited development of the child. With
us however such use of numbers is mainly by way of exception.
But in Eastern languages, and hence also in Holy Scripture, and
more particularly still in the Revelation of St. John, the use of
number *seven* is so very great, that it must be regarded as of
special significance. And this significance is, that this prophetical
book does not take its cue from our ways of expression, manners
of speech and representations, but is governed by what in the divine representation, which is always mystical, has another than a
chronological meaning.

The right understanding of this removes all ambiguity which
in the direct reference to the coming end affects one so un-
pleasantly. For then it is plain that there are two ways of viewing things and their mutual relation, one of which is our way,
and the other the *Divine* way. According to our manner of representation we could not have stated things as they are stated in
the Apocalypse. If then we discard our way of viewing things,
and adopt the Divine way, not only is every objection and difficulty obviated, but we realize that of necessity things had to be
presented in the way in which they are. In our study of the discourse of our Lord in Matthew 24-26, we indicated the same
difference, but the radical difference between the ordinary human
manner of speech and the Divine way of viewing things, as
observed in St. Matthew, is still more strongly evident in the
Apocalypse. There as it were it strikes the eye. There he who
takes pains to squarely face the difference, yes the antithesis between the human way of representation and the Divine way of

viewing things, no longer encounters any difficulty. He feels that so it *had* to be represented and could not possibly have been done otherwise.

What then is the difference, yes the antithesis between the human and the Divine representation? The answer to this is obvious. All we can do is to take the chronological course of things at a given point, from which to trace the historic line, and only when we have reached the end of that line can we speak of the Consummation. When someone from abroad sends us the seed of a choice plant, which we have never seen and know nothing of, we put it in the ground, and watch the growth of stalk and bud, until we see the flower bloom in all the fulness of its development and enchanting beauty, for then it has come to its Consummation. This is our way of doing things, but this cannot possibly be God's way. God did not somewhere come across the seed of a choice flower, which He planted to see how it would unfold, but His all-seeing eyes saw first the flower that was to be, and from this was inferred what the seed had to be, from which so choice a flower could germinate. With us beginnings are first and endings later, but with God the result which He plans is first, and from this is inferred what the beginnings must be. Thus the reverse order. And such is the case here. We reckon from the Ascension of Christ across a lapse of many centuries till we come to the Consummation, but God considers first the final outcome, and when this has been determined and the process of its unfolding has begun, every requisite to bring about the intended result follows. Note this with special care. With us the outcome of things is the result of preceding data. With God first the end is determined, and only then do the data arise which must eventuate in this outcome of things. The same principle that operates in art, operates in this. He who is creative in the world of thought, feels himself suddenly apprehended as it were by a striking idea or noble form of art, and only afterwards does he look for the necessary data that will embody the same.

Members of Reformed churches have unquestionably taken but little interest in the development of art, and he who knows the world of art at close range can not but concede that Calvinists, by their withdrawal from the world of art and its sensual pleasures, have escaped some things that are detrimental to the higher life. Yet the willful closing of our eyes to what God has given us in art, would be an entirely unwarranted under-estimation of one of the most glorious revelations in God's creation. In art there is an inner compulsion that is almost divine. This is specially evident in the spontaneity, the of-itself-ness which in art plays so mighty a role. In our processes of thought idea follows upon idea, as in life event upon event, but in art the things that will presently take shape and form are already beforehand a part as it were of the root of our inner life. The genius, the real artist feels what he shall presently produce take hold of him as an unseen power, and while he does not understand it, it overwhelms him. He draws no sketch of it, makes no calculation regarding it, he does not piecewise bring it together, but there it is, there it stands out before his mind's eye even before he realizes what it means, as a coherent whole that overpowers him, and selects him as the worker to bring it out into the world. And prophecy is part of the world of art, the Apocalypse has its place in it, together with public worship and all the riches of mysticism. We were bound there-fore in this connection to refer to the art-idea, to make the irresistible allurement of the Apocalypse to be felt. And this al-ready measurably takes hold of us, when we let the murmur of the two apocalyptic currents make itself heard.

The world process, that began with Jesus' Ascension and shall end with the last judgment, forms in the Divine view of things one coherent whole. God did not first wait to see what course the twenty centuries history of the world would take, in order only at the approach of the end to take active measures to usher in the Consummation. No, in God's sight all this forms, if we may say so, one great, coherent whole, though divided into three or four acts. So God does not discover the great tragedy only when the last act is on the boards, but from the outset He sees the sacred tragedy in course of process. A tragedy can have a prologue, and there is a prologue here. Jesus' passion, death and resurrection preceded His Ascension. But the direct action upon mankind and upon our human life only began on the day of Pentecost, with the mission of Pentecost, and with what took place on Patmos. Since then the several acts of the sacred tragedy have been played in course towards the end. So the sacred tragedy was not merely a part of the last act, but began in the first act, immediately after the introductory prologue. When therefore a tragedy is to be presented on the stage, it will not do to say: Call me in time for the last act. To understand the last act, one must be present when the first act begins. So the warning is in place: Be in your seat on time, that you may see it all.

And such is the case in hand.

In the sight of God everything forms one whole, and this whole includes not merely the beginning and the end, but is from the outset adapted to the end. There is no futile haste, but orderly process. This process begins with the first change that God works in the existing state of things, and from which every subsequent change spontaneously emerges. It is not a tragedy that is only transacted during the play. Before the prologue begins the whole tragedy is a finished product, and the first act sets the pace for the whole course of the play, as in the several acts it is to be unfolded. The beginning and the ending are inseparably connected. When the first note is struck, all the rest is certain. It is with this as with an alphabet. When A has been said it runs of itself on to Z. So here the very beginning at the same time indicates the moment when the final scene shall be applauded. There is nothing added to it later on. Rather of itself the one scene emerges from the other. It is one sacred tragedy, each part of which of itself merges into the other.

Bear in mind that we reckon with *time,* and God does not. With Him a thousand years are as one day. With God there is transition from one thing to the other, but what with us in such transitions is chronology, is not so with God. God is eternal, and the characteristic of the eternal is that the beginning and the ending melt as it were into one. It is with this as with our election and salvation. With us these two are separated by the years of our earthly life, but with God the one includes the other. In so far as we are bound to separate these two by the difference of time, in the great plan of the whole course of our world there are two data which should not be confused. One is the normal course of the world's history from the days of Paradise to the last judgment, and the other is the entirely abnormal series of events of Divine origin and ordering, by means of which out of this lost world to save a new humanity. The latter began with the promise in Paradise, anchored itself in Abraham's call, with the consequent rise therefrom of the Israel of God. Israel at first was a united people, but has long been scattered among all the nations of the earth. So now the Israel of God is that part of Adam's posterity that has been elected of God out of, and set apart from, all mankind. This part of our human race is now in its last act but one, and presently for this part of mankind the final act shall usher in the Consummation. This separated part of the human race pursues its course from Jesus' Ascension and from the day of Pentecost to the Consummation, and this was prefigured when to St. John on Patmos was laid bare what course in this sacred process God would take. The world of the lost stands outside of this, but God's people who already now have joyous foretastes of their salvation are included in it. To the part that is to be saved a twofold existence is assigned. They are to live their life in the world, and at the same time in entire separation from the world live a life of their own.

This separated life is in God's hand. It began with the Ascension and more particularly with the rich revelations of St. John on Patmos. The sole object that engages all the attention of God's people's life in the earth is the end, the parousia, the last judgment. What in connection with this separates the starting point from the point of arrival is the eternal, in which time has no count. He therefore who lives in close fellowship with Jesus is not concerned about the things that must precede the Consummation, because he is keenly alive to the fact that the parousia of Christ can await him at any moment. Morning by morning and evening by evening his expectation is the appearing of his Saviour. Hence that in the Apocalypse time is almost put aside. Hence the saying in Rev. 10, 6: "That there should be time no longer." Necessarily therefore from the first all Christendom had to be advised by the message from Patmos that already now the Consummation is at the point of arrival. This could differ in fact according to one's life in the first or in some later century; but to all of us of every age it must continually be the deep conviction in the heart, not only that He comes, but "He comes quickly." And therefore, O my soul, continually await Him with the prayer: "Even so, come, Lord Jesus, yes come quickly."

IV

THE SEVEN CHURCHES

The mystery of the seven stars which thou sawest in my right hand, and the seven golden candlesticks. The seven stars are the angels of the seven churches: and the seven candlesticks which thou sawest are the seven churches. Rev. 1.20

The Apocalypse divides itself very unequally into four parts. The first part is chapter one. Upon the introduction in chapter one follows as second part the seven epistles to the seven churches in Asia Minor, and is continued in chapters two and three. Then follows the third, which is by far the greatest part, from chapter 4, 1 to chapter 22, 7. And the fourth part is chapter 22, 8-21. Four parts in all; (1) the introduction; (2) the historic part; (3) the apocalyptic part; and (4) the short close. The historic part in the seven epistles to the seven churches is dealt with first. This is no general survey of the Christian church in Asia. These seven churches were not far distant from one another. It does not say that the church in Asia is staged apart from that in Europe and Africa. It merely deals with a small group of churches, close by one another, with which St. John had most been in touch, especially during the latter part of his ministry. They were, if we may say so, Johannine churches, and not far distant from Patmos. Moreover according to vs. 4 and 11 of chapter one, a literal interpretation would make it seem that the revelations to St. John on Patmos were solely intended for this small group of seven little-known churches.

In that case it can be taken to mean that these seven churches are held up to the churches of all time partly as examples worthy of emulation and partly as warnings, whereby at least in part they would appear as types; but then they ought at the time to have been of greater significance. St. Paul's account of his stay in the church at Ephesus is deeply interesting and fully portrays its condition. St. Paul's leave-taking of the elders of

41

Ephesus on the seashore is a tenderly affecting scene. But we have no intimation of St. John's ministry to the seven churches that are addressed from Patmos. They are evaluated, praised or censured by Christ from on high, but all we have of St. John's preaching in their midst are mere generalities. Strangely enough the great offenders only in these churches are called by name. Nothing is said of the holiness of these churches, nothing personal of St. John, in short nothing again but generalities. Naturally this has often supplied antagonists of the genuineness of the book with a weapon with which to combat it. Yet this objection to the genuineness quite loses its significance when the concrete and personal interpretation is set aside, and it is taken in the sense, that Christ sees in these seven churches *the seven sorts of ecclesiastical conditions* which were bound to show themselves not only there but everywhere, not only at the time but at all times, and that the conditions that are here described naturally follow upon the impact of the ecclesiastical life upon the social and national data, which in every way present themselves in given regions.

That this states the case correctly is more fully realized, when we examine each of the seven churches by name. For then we learn that only two of these seven churches are mentioned elsewhere in Holy Writ, namely, Ephesus and Laodicea. Neither the Acts nor the Epistles have anything to say of the other five. Save in this instance Sardis, Smyrna, Philadelphia and Pergamos are not mentioned in Scripture. And while Thyatira is spoken of elsewhere in Scripture, it is not, as said before, to tell us anything of a church in that place, but merely to say that Lydia, a seller of purple, was of that city (Acts 16). Thus we learn that Ephesus and Laodicea alone occur elsewhere in Scripture. As to Laodicea however, this means almost nothing. A church was founded there at an early period, but St. Paul was never there, and there is no mention of further contact with the Laodiceans. The church in Ephesus alone was eminent at the time, as it was the largest of them all, and not only St. John, but also St. Paul chose it as the center of his activity. But in this connection note well, that Ephesus has many centuries ago been utterly destroyed. In our travels there, as said before, no trace of any Christian church was found. Nothing but the site of the celebrated temple of Diana is left. The magnificent ancient library, which at great cost was constructed entirely of white marble, is the only building of note that still survives. Also the hill on which stood the theatre, the courthouse and other public buildings, and the place where early Christians endured their woes.

If then we commit what here would be the unpardonable fault of taking the Apocalypse as a common apostolic writing exclusively addressed to the members of the seven churches that are here called by name, it would make it a document that would long since have served its day, insomuch as these churches have tracklessly disappeared centuries ago. Not of course as though epistles that were addressed in the long ago to the churches in Rome, Corinth, etc., could not be of interest to us, but because this is a writing that, while it is presumed to be directed exclusively to the seven churches of that day, contains prophecies the fulfilment of which still tarries, while almost no trace of these churches is left. A more drastic sobering would not be conceivable, and as a sample of miscarried prophecy the Apocalypse would prove valueless. Hence the necessity of showing the absolute untenability of the representation, that the Apocalypse applies to these seven churches alone. Hence also the necessity of emphasizing the mystical significance of the number seven, and of making it clear that these epistles must not be taken as applying locally and exclusively to these particular churches, but to the *types* of the churches in all the earth and in all ages, of which these seven churches were the prototype. And although we, Westerners, may find it difficult to appreciate fully such a mystical expansion of a given thought, to the Asiatic of Semitic origin and to the Easterner in general it is perfectly natural.

This is the more binding as these seven epistles are not the product of St. John's pen, nor of that of any preacher of that time, but are original with Christ Himself. Chapter 2 begins with the order that is given St. John: "Unto the angel of the church of Ephesus write; These things saith he that holdeth the seven stars in his right hand, who walketh in the midst of the seven golden candlesticks." The very form of language here is

already athrob with heavenly mysticism. It is not the apostle
who speaks, but the voice comes from heaven, where Christ is
seated at the right hand of God, and now lives to intercede for
us. Thereby everything receives metaphorical heavenly names.
The pastors are called heavenly stars, and the churches to which
they minister are introduced as golden candlesticks. St. John had
already observed those seven stars and those seven candlesticks
in the sacred vision. As Rev. 1, 20 reads: "The seven stars are
the angels of the seven churches; and the seven candlesticks which
thou sawest are the seven churches"; and now follows the saying
of Christ, who sits at the right hand of God, that He holds the
seven stars in His right hand, and that He walks in the midst of
the seven candlesticks. If in spite of your Western inability you
try to picture this to yourself, you must realize at once that
what here follows can not possibly refer solely to this small group
of churches in Asia-Minor. Christ, who is seated at the right
hand of God, can hold *more* than the seven stars of this small
group of churches in His hand, and dwell among *more* than these
few churches in Asia-Minor. Christ is Head of all His churches
in Europe, in Africa, and wherever else they are found. Before
Him the pastors in all the churches are as stars, and churches
in all the earth are to Him golden candlesticks amongst which He
walks. So whatever is here said refers indeed to the churches of
Pergamos, Sardis etc., but not to these seven churches alone, and
it is impossible that it should not apply to the more than one hundred churches which already then were found elsewhere. This
appeals more strongly yet when we call to mind that more than
ten centuries ago all of these seven churches but one have disappeared from the face of the earth.

Thus (1) what would apply to all the churches in all the earth
Christ Himself here applies to the seven churches called by name;
(2) these seven churches are taken as types, because St. John was
intimately acquainted with them, and thus could understand what
was said of each of them; and (3) the several characteristics of
these seven churches present the different tempers, or if you will,
the different types which to the end of time would characterize
life in the different kinds of churches. Hence it makes no difference where these churches were located. Christ could just as well
have taken seven churches from other parts of the world, pro-

vided in their mutual relation and in their character-traits they presented equally well the seven fundamental types. Our Saviour's main purpose was to take a group of churches by way of example, and as conditions were in the example of His choice, so they would be in general. All the apostles save St. John had suffered martyrdom, and quite naturally Christ took the example or type from those churches to which St. John was specially related, and in which he so recently had labored.

When these churches are examined at closer range, it is self-evident that the number seven corresponds to the way of Divine doing. It had pleased God to found this solidary group of churches in Asia-Minor, to further their development and, as at other times, to apply the sacred number seven. This was not accidental, but result of the fact that God had put this group of churches together and had committed it to the care of St. John. It is noteworthy that in each of these churches we face conditions which are far from interesting and pleasing. The first church here mentioned is that of Ephesus, and there is much for which this church is commended and praised. "I know thy works," says Christ, "and thy patience, and how thou canst not bear them which are evil; and thou hast tried them which say they are apostles, and are not, and hast found them liars." More still, for the Lord goes on to say: "Thou hast borne, and hast patience, and for my sake hast labored, and hast not fainted." A gracious testimony. But this is not all. While everything in Ephesus had been most promising, ere long things had begun to wane and the church had denied her first love. She must therefore repent anew. And unless this were done quickly, Christ would remove her candlestick out of its place. The church of Smyrna was more favorably conditioned. Suffering and persecution awaited her, some of her members were to be thrown into prison. There would be a tribulation of ten days (naturally again a mystical number). But not one word of rebuke. She had been faithful, and if she would continue so she would obtain the crown of life. In fact this is the only church that survives unto this day. The other six have long since ceased to be. The church of Smyrna still prospers, and she alone was above reproach.

In the church of Pergamos things were very different. It is definitely stated that there was the throne of Satan. And that this church had resisted the advances of satanic propaganda was indicative of spiritual power. Only, moral life had suffered loss. Some were followers of Balaam, others made common cause with the Nicolaitans. We would say: Orthodoxy had stood its ground, even martyrdom had been endured, but spiritual purity had sustained loss and moral power had been broken. Thyatira also could boast of lives of heroic faith. Love and faith and patience abounded, and best of all the last love was greater than the first. Seemingly there was nothing there on the down—but rather on the upward grade. Yet alas! faith was ineffective. Jezebel, the blasphemous woman of corrupt morals exerted baneful influence. This shameless woman had openly defended the most flagrant fornication; and while the Lord had given her space to repent, she had not repented. Actually this church had been divided thereby into two factions, one of which fell into sin and went from bad to worse. Hence persecution could not be averted. But the Lord would preserve the small company of believers. They that had not known the depths of Satan would be given the power over the heathen. Upon them the morning star would rise.

The church in Sardis was in a still much worse plight, as she had a name of being alive, and was dead. So she must repent, lest Christ come to destroy her. Yet a few faithful ones were left, humble believers who had not defiled their garments, and who presently would walk with Christ in white. The church in Philadelphia is highly spoken of and like the church in Smyrna was famed for sanctity. The church was not large. She had 'a little strength', but had kept the word of patience, and by reason of this faithfulness the Saviour would "keep her from the hour of temptation, which shall come upon all the world, to try them that dwell upon the earth." And lastly there is the church of the Laodiceans which, while she had not wandered off in the ways of Satan, had suffered her faith to grow faint. There was no action there. No one could accuse her of positive wrongs, but there was no evidence of life in her. So the Laodiceans also must repent. Unless they repented, their destruction was certain. Yet the Lord had not given them up. He stood at the door and knocked, and if they would hear that knocking and open the door, Christ would come in to him that had wakened from sleep, and

would sup with him. In Laodicea the case was not hopeless, but
its barrenness needed the infusion of life. So in some of these
churches the life of faith was lived nobly: three were perilously
near the dangerpoint; what the last two lacked, was life and
action. In keeping with these strongly marked differences the
sacred watchword of Christ is sounded again and again: "He
that hath an ear, let him hear what the Spirit saith unto the
churches"; and this with the 'churches' always in the plural,
which clearly shows that it was not a matter that concerned these
seven churches in Asia-Minor alone, but that the Lord in these
seven churches dealt with His whole church of all time in the
earth.

This ends the historic part of the Apocalypse. It shows
that under the effective rule of a holy life of faith the churches
of Christendom would not present an aspect of unity. A many-
sided difference rather was to characterize the history of the
churches of Christ. This began to show itself already during St.
John's lifetime, as grievous unfaithfulness, apostasy and demoralization marked the comparatively small group of churches that
had been under his charge. Christ Himself had testified all this
to St. John in unmistakable terms. Some members of these seven
churches were of Jewish, and some of heathen origin. Some were
of the Eastern-Asiatic, and some of the European-Germanic type.
They were anything but uniform. So these seven churches
present the main types which would show themselves in the
church of Christ in every age, in all lands and among all nations.
What these seven churches were, such would be the life of the
church until the Consummation. And it is noteworthy that
Christ does not describe these several types of churches system-
atically, but as exemplified by these churches indicates them as in
life itself. When therefore in chapters 2 and 3 one merely reads
what applied at the time to these seven local churches, he does
not appreciate the meaning and significance of what here is revealed, which is merely ecclesiastical history until the dawn of the
Consummation. This history is outlined, as it were, in seven
types. Like all history it would run its own course and cover its
own period of time, but would have no count with respect to
the unfolding of the life of the Kingdom of God. It was entirely
an aside, a something strictly apart, and what would quickly,

and almost without count of time, and as with a leap of centuries hasten forward from Patmos to the parousia, is what from the temporal would lose itself in the eternal, and be consummated not in an earthly, but in a heavenly way. Of this the end ever was and is at hand. So we too leave this historic course of the centuries aside, and turn to the prophecy of what the end shall bring. This begins with chapter four.

V

THE TRANSITION TO THE PROPHETICAL
PART

*After this I looked, and, behold, a door was opened in
heaven: and the first voice which I heard was as it
were of a trumpet talking with me: which said, Come
up hither, and I will shew thee things which must be
hereafter.* Rev. 4. I.

Chapter four has nothing to say about events that were to
mark the passing of the second, third or any later century, but
deals directly with those mighty happenings which Almighty God
will bring to pass when history shall end and the Consummation
be at hand. It makes a giant leap across what in no case could
be less than twenty centuries. Thus what precedes and what
begins with chapter four are two parts of Revelation which have
nothing to do with each other. The historic part in chapters 2
and 3 gave the sevenfold type of all history in the earth, but with
chapter 4 we come to the short and last period in which the conditions of the world's life shall give place to that entirely new
state of things, which shall be ushered in by the parousia. Even
in the form of the narrative therefore, St. John entirely separates what now comes from what had gone before. So without
any suggestion of connection he writes: *"After this* I looked, and,
behold, a door was opened." Thus what preceded and what now
follows are two entirely different matters, between which there
is no coherence, each standing by itself alone. Not to have duly
noticed this is the great fault, which alas has too long prevented
the proper understanding of the Apocalypse. So we urge our
readers to look away from what has gone before, not to expect
the narration of historic events, but as by one leap, so to speak,
to make the great transition from the days of St. John's exile on
Patmos to the early eve of the Consummation, and the appearance
of Christ upon the clouds.

In this striking transition the apostolate played the leading part. In His epistle to the church at Ephesus, Christ indicated that there would be a false apostolate. "1 know, that thou hast tried them which say they are apostles, and are not, and thou hast found them liars." There was nothing surprising in this saying. As the church of Christ came into three continents at once and exerted such power as to fairly turn the world upside down, she was bound to create endless confusion in our world of sin. With an eye to this, and in part at least to avert this menacing danger, Christ had instituted *the apostolate*. The apostolate was by no means an ordinary pastorate. Already long in advance Christ had chosen His twelve; and for their first mission in Israel had equipped them with special gifts and powers (St. Matth. 10). His constant care had been the training of these twelve. Finally they were officially instituted into a special ministry, and when Jesus went up into heaven, these twelve apostles were charged to shepherd the church in her initial activities, and to establish her in the intended form of life.

In keeping with this, the apostolate had been inspired by Christ in a twofold way. In the first place by an entirely independent inspiration of the Holy Spirit, by which to bring the nascent church into the knowledge of all necessary truth and to establish her therein; moreover in the man of Tarsus a special and potent reinforcement had been added. The period of the apostolate has been absolutely indispensable to the church of Christ, not merely with respect to that particular time, but even more specifically with respect to the church of all succeeding ages. In the face of widely diverging opinions and insights that were to spring up among the nations as truth, a fixed standard of doctrines that were to be preached was absolutely indispensable to the church of Christ, and also in the face of the widely diverging types of churches believers should know which type to retain. The Old Testament could not supply this measure of spiritual leadership. Even what the Gospels provide is of too general a nature to throw sufficient light upon the many difficulties which presently were bound to present themselves in the life of the church. Hence the apostolate was by no means instituted for the sole purpose of planting churches and of making them live according to a given form. No, the apostolate was commissioned no less to lend to the newly established churches, in their distinction from the synagogue, a form of their own; a proper form of government; and in connection with this in the epistles to create a literature which should govern the life and the official functions of the churches until the end of time. As after the patriarchs Moses was raised up to impart form and stability to the life of the Israel of God, so after Christ it was the sacred calling of the apostolate to guide and direct the church in her efforts to attain her independence.

So only in Jesus' work of preparing those who after His Ascension would in part have to take His place and carry on His work of redemption in the world, can one understand the supreme importance of the apostolate. Imagine for a moment that there had been no apostolate, and you realize how inextricably the church of Christ would have become entangled in the mazes of endless error. All unity would have been lost, every group of believers would have stood by itself alone. Confusion worse confounded would soon have put an end to all coherence and unity. Even in spite of the apostolate, and the apostolic warnings against this evil, confusion has become unspeakably great. But what would have become of it all, had there been no apostolate, first by word of mouth, and afterward by epistolary literature, measurably at least to counteract this evil. The high calling of the Christian religion is to bring Salvation to a deeply sinful and erring humanity. But almost everything was bound to oppose and counteract the truth. Hence for the maintenance and propagation of the true revelation at least some guarantee was absolutely indispensable. And the great means to this end has been the institution and the ministry of the apostolate; and according to Gospel records this apostolate has not been planned by man, neither has it been instituted by man, but entirely apart from human purposes and intention the apostolate has been planned and instituted by Jesus Himself, and by reason of this the apostles have not been entrusted merely with the correct doctrine of the truth, but have also been accorded the power, in a striking manner, to work miracles; and over and above all this, in an entirely special sense to the apostles has been given a dispensation of the Holy Spirit,—that is, a holy inspiration.

Immediately connected with this is the origin and gift of the Apocalypse to the church. Though it is difficult to state the exact number of years in which the apostles, one by one, were removed by death, mostly by martyrdom, the general consensus is, that at the time of St. John's exile on Patmos he was the last surviving apostle. Thus his death would imply the end of the apostolate. It had always been the comforting thought to the other apostles when dying, that St. John was still left to represent the same. But when all of them had departed, St. John realized that he alone was left, and that in view of his advancing years his own departure was at hand. As he wandered about on Patmos, he must have been impressed with the fact that presently with him the apostolate would pass away. After him no apostle would be left. The persecution of which he was one victim must have brought the imminence of his end still more closely home to him. So he must have asked himself : When I am gone and with me the apostolate is ended, what will become of Christ's church? First Christ Himself had founded the church. After His Ascension the apostolate had fulfilled its entirely unique mission. And during the fifty years after Pentecost the church had wondrously become established in already three continents. Such had been the success of the apostolic labors. But when presently with the demise of St. John the apostolate would end, what would happen then? What was to become of Christianity as a whole? Would it all be doomed to end in dismal failure? Or would there be a future for the church which by means of the parousia would fulfil the rich promise of prophecy?

Only by inquiries such as these can we understand the indispensableness of the last book of the Bible. The passing away of the apostolate demanded a further supplementation, which would form the transition from what had been given in the apostolate to what was to be awaited in the parousia. Surely, by the ministry of the prophets, of Christ and the apostolate everything had been prepared to bring about the reversal of the life of the world, so that now the end could be awaited. Yet one more link between the apostolate and the parousia was missing, and the special revelation on Patmos to St. John, and through him to the church of all time, supplies this link. It was known that everything

would end in the parousia. There could be no doubt about
Christ's return. Things could not go on as they were. With the
new order of things that had come in, the end was now at hand,
but as the inspired prophecies of the Old Testament had preceded
Bethlehem's crib, so now there was need that the morning star
should become visible above the horizon and the future of Christ's
return should beam, as it were, from afar upon the church. The
expectant mother well knows the pains that await her; yet she
takes pleasure in the sight of the cradle from which her babe
shall presently smile at her. Such was the case here. The passing
away of the apostolate was to create a hiatus in the representation
of Christ's church. She knew that the end would be terrible, she
also knew that this sorrowful end would be the only means by
which the Consummation could be ushered in. And on this account the darkness in the perspective was lifted, and after
the apostolate, in the far distance the morning star began to
glisten. Recall the promise (2,28): "And I will give him *the
morning star.*"

Thus it betokened wondrous grace to His church that, before
the death of St. John put an end to the apostolate, Christ opened
this glorious perspective to the last apostle in his exile. If at the
close of the apostolic ministry the church had merely been given
an anticipatory summary of ecclesiastical history of all time,
it would have been but a pitiful narrative of ecclesiastical misery.
But now, as it were, this whole record of the centuries is screened
from sight. Attention is diverted from it, as though the Lord
were saying to His people: "Do not blind your eyes in gazing
upon this distressing scene, which in the course of time my church
shall present, but look up, peer into the heart of the perspective,
which yonder discloses itself to you, and let the profound seriousness, but yet glorious outcome of this perspective enthrall and
grip you." To this end Christ makes the approaching parousia
glisten as it were before the eyes of the last surviving apostle,
not by just one indication, but in broad detail and in intensively
elaborated perspectives, and charges him to image this glorious
perspective and to write it in a book, that it might be until the
end of time a strong consolation to His struggling church in the
earth.

Thus clear light dawns upon the whole apocalypse. Christ could not possibly allow the apostolate to pass away, without in conclusion granting us a clear, surprising view of the final issue of things. How distressing a sight ecclesiastical life presented even in its earliest stages, was a matter of common knowledge. In the epistles of chapters 2 and 3 we found only two churches whose Christian character was fairly pure, and how within so short a time as 50 or 60 years after the Crucifixion all sorts of degrading practices had crept into the other five, combining worldliness and shameful denial of the truth with godliness. There was no secrecy about all this. One church knew it of the other. Read what Paul was forced to write to the Corinthians. Oh, it was so deplorable that already within seventy years after Jesus' Ascension the spiritual decline had assumed such proportions as to darken, as with thick clouds, the ecclesiastical horizon. And so by the gift of the Apocalypse Christ caused a gleam of light from afar to shine down upon the future of His church, by which then and throughout all time to rouse new zeal in the mind of believers and every time again to instil fresh courage. True, the Apocalypse accomplished this purpose but in part. When in the first Christian century persecution became more and more violent, the Apocalypse worked wonders, and the church of Christ drank from it as with deep draughts cupfuls of new zest for holy living. The Apocalypse was read, thought and meditated upon. Ownership of a copy was treasured and appreciated. Deep spiritual joy was derived from it. Its genuineness was not doubted. The last Bible book had the preference, from which pulsating life was drawn.

But this did not last; especially since the days of St. Augustine the Apocalypse has been relegated to the background; it is little read; in its threatening tendency it is rarely understood, and consequently no longer enjoyed. The morning star is no longer seen glistening in its sky. That one perchance might live to see the Return of the Lord is no longer an arresting thought. In the main the common outlook is toward the Father's house of the many mansions, and with an outlook such as this who can still derive comfort from the representation according to which believers are to be called away again from their heavenly home back to this earth and summoned to the judgment bar of their King, which standing there can scarcely be otherwise than with great shamefacedness.

Yet, this is a regrettable darkening of our Christian life. Whatever may overtake us here on earth, the end always portends the parousia again, and he who calls himself a Christian, is in no safe way, so long as to him the Return of his Saviour is not as a shining light that beams upon him from afar, and prophesies to him the fulfilment of every holy desire that God has implanted in his breast. Hence that to so many people in our churches the morning star does not shine forth from the Apocalypse, must be mourned as a spiritual loss, and the gain for the Christian life will be great, when also the grave effects of the world war, under the weight of which the whole civilized world still totters, renews in us more strongly than in the past the expectation of spiritual encouragement from what in the Apocalypse Christ gave us.

VI

THE ELDERS

And hast made us unto our God kings and priests; and we shall reign on the earth. And I beheld, and I heard the voice of many angels round about the throne, and the beasts, and the elders: and the number of them was ten thousand times ten thousand, and thousands of thousands. Rev. 5, 10 and 11.

We now come to the main part of the Apocalypse, which begins with chapter 4 and goes on to v. 8 of the last chapter,—that is, the actual writing of St. John, in connection with which all the rest serves as introduction and conclusion. In the nature of the case the difference between the several expositions of the Revelation of St. John, especially when it comes to chapter 4, is heaven-wide. If like to most expositors we take this chapter as the continuation of the historic review, so that here we have the beginning of the history of the past twenty centuries, chapter 4 must refer directly to the events that followed immediately upon Jesus' Ascension, or if you will, upon Pentecost. But here we find no trace of this. The fourth chapter transports us from the earthly into the heavenly; but in the heavenly the difference is wide between what it was when Jesus returned thither and what it will be when He leaves it again in order here to consummate the final separation between believers and unbelievers. The very grave antithesis between these two representations must be clearly visualized. If one adopts the most widely accepted representation, chapter 5 follows immediately upon Christ's arrival in the heavenly sanctuary. But if one adopts the more recent interpretation, chapter 3 at once ends the historic narrative, and with chapter 4 the Revelation to St. John immediately passes on to the approaching parousia, and introduces the Consummation that is at hand. The question is, which of these two representations is not only commended by what we read, but justified as the only accurate one.

And then first of all the fact is emphasized, which arrested our attention above, namely, that up to this time the apostolate had borne supreme rule in the churches, but that with the revelation of Patmos this apostolate entirely disappears and what now is revealed to St. John does not join itself to Pentecost, when the apostolate really first began to function, but on the contrary starts out from where the apostolate ends. St. John was the only surviving apostle and he was near the end of his days. Moreover he, by his exile, had been doomed to inactivity. So it can be said in the first place, that after the Ascension of Jesus and after Pentecost the apostolate took up the work of founding the church of Christ in the earth and of bearing rule over it until the end of time, and in the second place, that when the Revelation came to St. John on Patmos, this apostolate had reached its end, and that with this an entirely new state of things began. And when one feels that this presentation of the case can not be gainsaid, he at once faces with it the question: Whether after the disappearance of the apostolate again a predominating revelation has come down from heaven, or whether the life of the church entered upon its ordinary trend, and that new events, such as will again mingle the heavenly with the earthly, are only to be looked for at the end of the world preparatory to the parousia. He who in spite of everything that diametrically opposes it, still wants to hold to the first representation, must needs interpret mere ordinary, normal events as heavenly actions. While they who feel that this will not do, must needs accept with us the second view, to-wit: that with the disappearance of the apostolate the church began her ordinary and normal ecclesiastical life, and that, uninterrupted by any new revelation, this will go on until the Lord's Return for judgment. If this view is correct, there immediately follows from it, that what chapter 4 introduces has nothing to do with the ordinary course of church history, and only begins with what at the end of time shall announce the approach of the parousia.

In this connection one communication in chapter 4 specially appeals to us. You find it in the last three verses, where we learn that *the elders* also play a leading part in the choir of heaven. More still. The presence of these 24 elders in the heavenly choir

is noted as of so great importance that the whole introductory
4th chapter makes it its main theme. The rest of the chapter,
which deals with things relative to the glory of the divine heavenly life, is not surprising. Already in Ezekiel several things had
been revealed, that give an idea of it. But neither in the vision-
call of Isaiah 6, nor in the Ezekiel descriptions of the heavenly
life was anything said of the "elders". Note well that "elders"
here does not refer to chosen laymen, who serve under pastors
as officials of a second rank, but that in the New Testament
"elders" refer first of all to pastors, and centers the main attention upon them.

Of these "elders" in this sense the following is told in vs. 9,
10 and 11: "And when those four beasts give glory and honor
and thanks to Him that sat on the throne, who liveth forever
and ever, the four and twenty elders fall down before Him that
sat on the throne, and worship Him that liveth forever and ever,
and cast down their crowns before the throne, saying Thou art
worthy, O Lord, to receive glory and honor and power: for
thou hast created all things, and for thy pleasure they are and
were created." Note that as a matter of fact these three verses
constitute the content of this entire chapter. The content of
vs. 1-8 was in the main well known from the Old Testament. It
may here be described somewhat more in detail, but it is not
new. He who is versed in Isaiah, Ezekiel and Daniel, is quite
at home in this representation, at least as regards the fundamental lines. But without precedent the 24 elders are here
introduced for the first time, and this is something entirely new.
So all the rest merely seems to serve as introduction, and that
these 24 elders are mentioned only at the end of the chapter
makes them appear as the main factor that counts. It is also
surprising with what minute detail these "four and twenty elders"
are here spoken of, and how they are said not only to be in
heaven, but that they offer the Almighty richest and highest
homage. The four beasts also laud and praise God's holiness,
but reading the account makes one feel that their homage is by
no means of as high an order as that of the 24 elders. It even
seems that this fourth chapter as a whole, and the insight thus
granted us into the heavenly life, mainly intends to bring out,

in as inspiring a manner as possible, the predominating fact of
the elders' song of praise, and to put it to the fore.

Wherever somewhat allied insights into the heavenly divine
life occur in Isaiah, Ezekiel or Daniel, there is not only no
mention of such a role, but of no chief role of the *Presbytery*
as such, as we will mostly call these "Elders" from now on by
their Greek name, as with us the idea of "Elder" has become too
greatly modified. The New Testament speaks repeatedly of
"elders" even of the Jews; but more generally of "elders" of
Christian churches, when this almost never means assistants to
pastors exclusively, but implies them both. When Titus went
from town to town to ordain elders (1, 5), it did not mean
elders in our current sense, but pastors as heads of congregations.
The title of "elder" does not occur in the Old Testament at all.
The reference there is exclusively to what our translators rendered by the word "eldest" and more directly by "the eldest
in Israel." But these "eldest" were not the same as our Presbyters
or elders. At that time the "eldest" were appointed to be assistants to Moses in the administration of civil affairs, and in
juridical functions. Moses could no longer carry these responsi-
bilities alone, so these "eldest" became his aids or coadjutors.
Their duty ended with civil and political economy, and they had
no part with Aaron in the spiritual ministry of Israel. How
then in the throne room of the Almighty could these civil
adjuncts be ordained to the holy function of playing in the heavenly spheres the leading and highest role in the worship of the Holy
God? In the nature of the case this is out of the question.

The case assumes an entirely different aspect, when we take
these Presbyters to be the representatives of the collective churches
of Christ in the earth. There was no such church yet under the
Old Testament, and hence in Isaiah, Ezekiel and Daniel we do
not become aware of the presence of such Presbyters in the
throne room of the Almighty. With the transition from the Old
into the New Testament, however, it had all become different.
The Jews as a people and nation had lost their former position
of glory. Aside from what the future holds for them, with the
passing away of the apostolate toward the end of the first century the Jews had disappeared from the sacred stage, to give
place to the people of the Lord, who had made choice of the

Christ of God, and already in three continents had secured for
the church of Christ her rank and standing in the midst of the
social and political life of the world. So the church was an entirely new element in the holy, which in advance even came to the
front and in the worship and glorification of God had to play
a chief role. So it became by degrees in the earth, and so it is
in the throne room of God. For Christians in the hour of death
do not lay aside their Christian character, rather only in the
Father's house were they privileged to attain unto their perfect
Christian, and with it spiritual, character.

So everything proceeds in its natural order. With Christ's
Ascension and the great event of Pentecost the apostolate, and
presently through the apostolate the Christian church, takes its
rise as an entirely independent phenomenon in the life of the
world. That Christian church becomes the revelation of the
Kingdom of heaven. They who belong to it become in a narrower
sense one with Christ, and after death believers enter upon the
glory of the Father's house; in the throne room they occupy the
highest place, and in rendering praise and honor and worship unto God and His Christ take the leading part. Hence
in referring to the glorious life above, it did no longer suffice to
point to God's throne and His majesty, or to the four beasts, but
it was of main importance to refer to the redeemed in
glory. The disciples and followers of Christ, who in the courts
of blessedness had reached the state of just men made perfect,
came to stand in the front rank; and while all the other inhabitants of heaven glorify the Triune God, the Mediator with His
redeemed host needs most occupy the foremost place. Thus in
the description in chapter four of the throne room of God, attention must chiefly be centered upon the representatives of Christ's
church, which Presbyters, as the official body of the highest rank,
offer honor, praise and worship to God.

And when could this Christian host occupy this illustrious
place of honor in the throne room of God? Of course provisionally only in part, but at the time of the end the role of the redeemed on High shall obtain its full reality.

Hence that here, where the time of the end is so forcibly
brought to mind, and at least the forecast of the end already in
every way announces itself, the blessed Christendom in heaven

could not fail of special notice; could not be counted second to the four beasts; but was bound in the worship of God to be assigned the first place of honor. Not that in the last days the number of martyrs would not be multiplied, and the heavenly host of the redeemed be considerably enlarged, yet the Revelation of St. John indicates again and again that in the latter days the earthly Christendom will diminish, rather than perceptibly increase in strength. If then we take what is further revealed to the last surviving apostle as referring to what shall immediately precede the Return of Christ, we get a perfect order. For then the redeemed Christendom, which presently on the new earth would constitute the new people of God, was practically already entirely assembled in the higher spheres of blessedness, and everything awaited but the end. So of all the creatures that were assembled in the throne room of God the sainted host of believers is naturally accorded the place of highest eminence. They were the body that would presently form the new humanity on the new earth, which would owe its origin to the parousia of Christ.

So we see how absurd it was to say, that twelve of these four and twenty Presbyters are of the "eldest" in Israel, and twelve of the leaders in the Christian church. This makes it twice twelve Presbyters, and it is not realized how impossible it is to put the social and political "eldest" of Moses' economy on a par with the spiritual representatives of believers in Christ, and to combine them in one spiritual unity. The "eldest" of Moses' economy and the "elders" in Christ's church are in no particular alike; so they can not be classed together. They are two distinct classes of men and bear entirely different characters. Thus the "four and twenty elders" or Presbyters, who at the time of the end are seen in the throne room of God occupying the highest seat of honor, must be the sainted host of believers in Christ, and more particularly the outstanding figures among the spiritual leaders in Christendom. That sainted host of Christians is the new humanity which shall presently dwell on the new earth; and while after Pentecost Old Testament saints have joined this company, yet these were never of the number of those who from the days of Moses were called "eldest". Moses and Aaron did not belong to the company of these "eldest", yet none will doubt that both are of the number of the redeemed that preceded Bethlehem. Or take the still more telling case of Abraham, the father of all believers, and who will class him with the "eldest" whom Moses instituted? So the four and twenty Presbyters can not be divided into twelve Old Testament "eldest" and twelve New Testament pastors, and the attempt to do so can in no way be justified.

To this must be added, that he who favors the division of the twenty four elders into twelve "eldest" and twelve Christian pastors, does not count with the fact that in the Revelation of St. John, even to the last chapter but one, everything Christian is clothed in the Jewish national form. Even the walls and gates of the new Jerusalem bear the names of Israel's tribal fathers. From first to last the book of Revelation wears the Israelitish garb, in order to make it very evident, that one heaven, one grace and one glory is the portion of all the blessed elect from Adam until now. It will probably never be ascertained with certainty, whether the doubling of the number twelve should be explained from the combination of the blessed from Paradise to the Parousia, yet suppose that this representation is correct, it does not hark back solely to the Jews, but to the two periods, one of which extends from Paradise to Bethlehem, and the second from Bethlehem to the Antichrist.

VII

THE FOUR BEASTS

And before the throne there was a sea of glass like unto crystal: and in the midst of the throne, and round about the throne, were four beasts full of eyes before and behind. Rev. 4, 6.

In connection with the Presbyters, special notice must be taken of what follows in v. 4, which reads: "And round about the throne were four and twenty seats: and upon the seats I saw four and twenty elders sitting, clothed in white raiment; and they had on their heads crowns of gold." Thus in the description of the glories of heaven they take the lead. They are the first to be brought to our notice, and only in v. 6 the four beasts are introduced. The high rank and supremacy of these Presbyters is also shown in what follows in chapter 5. There we read that when the book of the seven seals was seen in God's right hand, it was a Presbyter who first took notice of it. When St. John wept because "no man in heaven, nor in the earth, neither under the earth, was able to open the book," it was not an angel, nor anyone else, but a Presbyter who comforted him saying: "Weep not, behold, the Lion of the tribe of Judah, the Root of David, hath prevailed to open the book, and to loose the seven seals thereof." And only after this our attention is directed to the four beasts. Again and again these Presbyters are introduced throughout the Apocalypse, and every time the exalted highness of their rank in the sanctuary is indicated. Even in Rev. 19, 4, in the last judgment, when the Alleluiah is sounded in all spheres, we read: "And the four and twenty elders and the four beasts fell down and worshipped God that sat on the throne, saying, Amen; Alleluiah!" Here the four and twenty elders again are mentioned first, and after them the four beasts.

The crown on the heads of the 24 elders also deserves notice. The four beasts are not said to have crowns. The crown on the heads of the 24 Presbyters is the more significant, because with

it there is a throne. So we read: "And round about the throne
were four and twenty thrones" which were occupied by the four
and twenty Presbyters. So they are presented in every way as
occupying the first place in the throne room of God, and as
clothed with the highest possible creaturely honor. Around the
throne of God they sit on thrones, clothed with dominion, even
as conquerors who from the struggle on earth have made their
triumphant entry into heaven, and there enjoy honors that far
exceed anything that can be awarded a creature. Now bear in
mind that in the Apocalypse all numbers are symbolical, so that
the number of these Presbyters need not be limited to 24. In
this instance also the number 24 is mystical, and indicates two
categories of 12 each; while the number 12 in turn is the combination of the divine 3 with the earthly 4. The main point is that in
the realm above two categories of crowned and sanctified leaders
shall occupy the seat of honor. Hence our reference to the two
categories of triumphant believers, the one from Adam and
Abel to the call of Israel in Abraham, who is the tribal father
of the race from which in Bethlehem the Christ was born; and
the second coming after, and in the Christian church at length
spreading itself over all the earth. So there is nothing enigmatic
in this number 24, and everything indicates that the guard of
honor which these crowned Presbyters form around the throne
of God is made up of the redeemed from all nations and peoples,
as well of the first category from Adam to Bethlehem as of the
second which appears as "Israel" in purified form. even as also
St. Paul refers to this in Gal. 6, 16.

Meanwhile, before we go further, we must note the significance
of the four *beasts,* to which, not without emphasis now and
again, reference is made. Evidently these four beasts are far
inferior in order of rank and importance to the afore-named
Presbyters, and as will appear from a closer examination of the
"beasts" themselves, this inferiority of rank goes further than
superficially one would think. The word *beasts* in our Version
is a defective translation of the Hebrew and Greek words by
which they are designated in the original and in the Septuagint.
In Hebrew they are called *Chaioth* (Ezekiel 1, 20, and elsewhere), and the Septuagint translates this word by *Zoa.* Both
these words. the Hebrew as well as the Greek. mean "living

world". A plant is alive, but by its root is bound to a place, while men and animals can freely move about; and this free motion, as characteristic of a life of their own, is hereby expressed. This is done in four kinds. As freely moving beings are named: (1) Man; (2) beast of prey; (3) tame animal; and (4) the animal in the air. So we read of man, of lion, calf and eagle.

As is well known, in former times one was at a loss as to what to do with these four freely moving beings. Especially the classing together of man with wild beasts, cattle and birds affected one too strangely. St. Augustine made a figurative representation of this, and, as pure guesswork, inferred that the reference here is to the four Evangelists, as is held even to this day. Matthew is said to be the lion, Mark to indicate man, Luke the calf, and John the eagle. Others took these four beasts to represent the four cardinal virtues; others again the four main moments of the content of the faith; the Incarnation, the Passion, the Resurrection and the Ascension of Christ. All this however was pure guesswork and shows that, in utter disregard of the intent of Scripture, one has taken as purely figurative what, rightly understood, has a real and very important significance. That man here is named in one breath and thus as on the level with the beasts, and among them is not given the first, but the second place, was always an obstacle in the way to a right understanding of the being and significance of these "Zoa". Had the order been: man, lion, calf and eagle, it might have done; but that man was named after the lion was but the more confusing and misleading. Now that man, since the days of Linnaeus, is often reckoned among animals, be it as the most highly developed of them all, this representation might be more favorably received. But when in former times this numbering of man with animals had not yet come in vogue, for a proper understanding of these four "beasts" one had to do the best he could with a purely figurative interpretation.

But this figurative interpretation could not satisfy a more thorough investigation of Scripture. The Apocalypse does not introduce these four Zoa as mere figures, but as living beings, even as beings that glorify God and contribute to the glory of His majesty. As has been shown they are inferior in rank to the 24 Presbyters, and it will not do to name them with these in one breath. Yet they evidently have a calling of their own in the magnifying of God's name. This must not be overlooked. We have no right to make all this purely figurative. The order of rank with which they are credited in the Revelation of St. John is too constant and too high. From what is told of them in the Apocalypse it clearly appears that when these four Zoa are set aside an indispensable element is removed from what must glorify God's majesty, or, by making them purely figurative, as St. Augustine did, they are rendered utterly unrecognizable. Every attempt, therefore, to understand in a metaphorical sense what is here said of these four beasts, or to turn it into the figurative, must for good and all be put aside. What the Apocalypse has to say about them has evidently at first not been understood, one has not known what to do with them, and to escape from the dilemma one has made the most of a subterfuge which was without rhyme or reason. So we must for good and all break with these figurative interpretations. It must be understood that the order, rank and place of the Zoa in the Apocalypse are such as to make it impossible to put these beings out of existence; and we must not rest content until the purport of St. John, or rather the purport of what in the name and on the authority of Christ he wrote, is no longer set aside by such an illusive interpretation.

The more accurate interpretation is by no means so hard to find, provided one clearly sees that in God's representation, more yet than in ours, there is a radical difference between the original creation and what it has become by the fall of Satan and of Adam, and by grace has been restored in and by Christ. We do not say that the Mediatorial work of Christ merely restores what existed before. Were this the case, after the restoration another apostasy of angels would be possible, and consequently also another fall of man. He who understands anything of the great Mediatorial work sees at once that the restoration of mankind by Christ must at length lead to the existence and well-being of a new humanity on a new earth; and that relapse into sin and misery must needs be impossible. The Apocalypse, from first to last, tends to establish and make sure this mighty fact. In the end the Mediatorial work shall prove to have been entirely successful. What took place by Satan's fall in the world of angels, and as result of this in the earth by reason of satanic influence, shall not repeat itself. What in Paradise became the occasion for distress can only occur once. They who have continued to be subject to the influence and after-effect of that fall must end in what is satanic, and together with everything that shares this satanic nature must once face judgment and ruin in the weeping and gnashing of teeth.

But this does not alter the fact that nature, as God originally created it in Paradise, was radiant with a Divine majesty, which has uninterruptedly been operative in the glory of the angels who have continued in their holy estate. Thus as often as, even in the Our Father, we are referred to the angels as our example, it always implies a reference to the sinless purity in which God in Paradise created our race, and there surrounded it with everything that could enrich our existence. So when the Apocalypse presents again and again the distinction and antithesis between the 4 beasts and the 24 Presbyters, it but emphasizes the antithesis between the condition of the original Paradise and our present state of things. Our life is twofold. There is that which is ours by reason of our creation, and which has been vitiated by the fall, and there is the restoration of that original life which had been marred, defaced and plunged into misery by sin. Naturally this restored life is of a higher sort than that which was originally given us. As was shown above, the life that was ours by creation was susceptible of defilement and desecration, while the life that is restored by the Mediatorship of Christ not only excludes such backsliding, but even could not end otherwise than in perfect glory. Compare the four beasts or Zoa with the four and twenty Presbyters and the difference between what they respectively represent is perfectly plain. The four beasts simply point back to the creation and indicate how before the fall the glory of God's majesty was the radiance of Paradise. It glistened richly in the natural, but was liable to decline into the sinful and unholy. And over against this, as fruit of the Mediator's work, a second humanity had taken its stand, but of a much higher quality.

For now believing Christendom had come to represent a vast multitude of human beings, from all nations and peoples, which can no longer fall, which presently in dying would break with sin entirely, and be set free from sorrow and pain for evermore; and thus very far exceed in highness and spiritual nobility everything that Paradise had offered. That reborn, restored, reconciled and presently for ever glorified humanity found its model in the four and twenty Presbyters or elders, and consequently took the highest rank and celebrated its victory in the throne room of God. But over against this stands the original humanity of before the fall, as it had been in Paradise, but had not been able to defend itself against the unholy influence of Satan. And this original humanity is here represented by the four *Zoa* or beasts. This could not have been left out of the scene. Though grace brings man a perfect rebirth, in the state of grace he is and always will be *a human being.* As man he has a natural life, which is not his by reason of his regeneration, but which he has inherited from Adam, and thus from the original creation. So the regenerated man can never be explained from regeneration alone. His original existence as man is always his by reason of his descent from Adam, and thus from his first creation. The believer has this existence as man in common with the unbeliever, and it always constitutes the ground of his being. Both they who enter heaven and they who pass through the portals of the lost are and ever shall be *human beings;* the original creation of their common nature in Adam makes them *human.* With an eye to this, God in the Apocalypse accords the two elements severally a conspicuous place in His throne room; both our human nature as it originated in Paradise, and the reborn and sanctified man as product of regeneration. The four Zoa represent the original, the four and twenty Presbyters the renewed, regenerated, sanctified, man.

Naturally therefore the original Paradise-man here appears as the lesser, as of lower standing and of inferior order, and then, as distinguished from him the regenerated man, the believer, who is redeemed by Christ. The latter is of much higher standing and is the product of a grace that scintillates only in the mediatorial work, and has achieved a much higher result. The original man is hardly comparable with the regenerated man. Regeneration is so striking a renewal of fallen man, that at times it seems as though the old man has ceased to be, and has become a new person. Of course this is not so. He who was lost in wickedness and sin and by regeneration has become a new creature in Christ, is and always will be the selfsame person. He is renewed, but he is still a child of Adam. After his fall he must needs be exiled from Paradise, but when regenerated a renewed Paradise awaits him which in every way so far excels the original as can scarcely be compared with it.

To bring this difference and antithesis into view the entirely natural relation of the original Paradise is recalled. Bear in mind that animals and man were created on the same day, except those animals that make their home in the waters. They were created on the fifth day, from the whale to the smallest fish, and with them the winged creatures of the air· (Gen. 1. 22.) But on the sixth day, as we are told, the earth brought forth living creatures after their kind, cattle, and creeping things, and beasts of the earth after their kind; yet the creation of the beasts of the earth did not bring the sixth day to a close. There followed on that same day the chiefest product of the whole creation, for we read that God said: "Let us make man in our image and after our likeness." In consideration of this Rev. 4, 7 states that at first there were three kinds of beasts, lion, calf and eagle, and that under this category and connected with it man also was created. The order of succession is not entirely correct, and in Gen. 1, 21 birds also had been mentioned separately, yet we can fully understand, why with the Zoa that hark back to the creation in Paradise, man is named in one breath with the rest of living beings. On the sixth day man and animal were created. The sixth day was the great creation day of living creatures, among which animals came first and man came after. Hence the apocalyptic representation of the same.

VIII

THE SEVEN SEALS*

And I saw when the Lamb opened one of the seals, and I heard, as it were the voice of thunder, one of the four beasts saying, Come and see. Rev. 6, I.

If in the foregoing chapter the significance of the elders and beasts has been explained, it will not be difficult to show that the content of Rev. 5 refers directly to the time of the end, and not to the age-long history of the church of Christ in the world. It begins with the story of a book which is in the hand of God. It is not a book that has only just been written, but one which has ever been in God's hand and contains His eternal counsel. So it is merely figurative speech. There was no book there, but something in the form of a book, because as a rule we commit to writing both what we are sure of and is also of concern to others, as for instance our last will and testament. So the two great revelations from God are known as the Old and New Testament. What in daily life must be kept account of in an orderly manner, we write in a book; as to our finance in our cashbook, as to our life in our diary, and for giving out of orders we use bulletin-boards. In short, the things in which others are concerned, and which insure the fixed course in life, even after our death, are committed to writing; and by the printed page are brought to common knowledge. Quite naturally therefore the fixed decrees of God, which are to dominate the final outcome of things, are presented in the form of a book; and to make sure the provisional secrecy of the same, in the form of a *sealed* book.

This book was not newly written, since the decrees of God are not of recent origin, but date from all eternity. But these decrees had never been revealed to men. God had determined these

---

*In the original "The Seven Seals" cover chapters VIII and IX.

decrees, but only at a later date could they be revealed. Thus while these decrees were known to God, to us they formed a secret. Consequently the book that held the record of these decrees, was sealed; which of course implies that they were secret to us, until God Himself would break the seals and make the contents known. Again the statement that there were seven such writings, bound in one volume, can not be taken literally. As everywhere else the number seven in this instance also is used symbolically. There is not only one decree, but there are several decrees; and while they come to us from the sanctuary, they are summarized in the sacred number seven. But apart from this the attention here is centered on the fact that a volume of seven written rolls, which up to this moment had been closed, and sealed, will now be opened. The call for this does not go out from any man, but from the world of angels. The world of angels is always presented in Scripture as being exceedingly interested in what befalls believers in the earth. They are separate from the fallen angels which under Satan have conspired against God. Good angels stand diametrically over against demoniac angels. And since the break in the world of angels had also worked havoc in the world of men, naturally the world of men, as reflex of the higher world, is of greatest interest to good angels.

And the good angels had as little knowledge as we of these decrees of God concerning the future, they even shared our ignorance of the fact that there were any such decrees at all. Only now they learn of their existence, and that they are recorded in the book that is in God's hand. But that book is sealed with seven seals. How can they fail of being curious in a sacred sense to know what that book contains? And "a strong angel" is their spokesman, who cries "with a loud voice", which made the heavens tremble: "Who is worthy to open the book and to loose the seals thereof?" To understand what this means, note what v. 11 tells about the angelic hosts. There we read that "the number of them was ten thousand times ten thousand, and thousands of thousands," which means several hundred millions in addition to almost endless millions more. And this innumerable multitude of angels is deeply stirred by what now they see and hear. They see the book of God's decrees regarding the things to come. But it is sealed with seven seals. Who now would open it? The tension is very great. The longing to know what the book contains is well-nigh irresistible. And nothing brings relief. For as we read in v. 3: "No man in heaven, nor in earth, neither under the earth, was able to open the book, neither to look thereon." This affected St. John so deeply that **he** began to weep, yes *to weep much.*

But upon this weeping follows the comforting. One of the 24 Presbyters says to him: "Weep not, behold, the Lion of the tribe of Judah, the Root of David, hath prevailed to open the book, and to loose the seven seals thereof." And at these words St. John saw Christ come forward from the holy circle around the throne of God, from the midst of the four Zoa and of the 24 Presbyters, even in the form of a Lamb. In v. 5 He appears as the Lion, but here in the form of a Lamb "having seven horns and seven eyes," which together were to image "the seven spirits of God, that were sent forth into all the earth." Thus in no respect is the action here limited to the Jews, or to Jewish converts. The action here goes out to the church in all the world. As in v. 9 the anthem reads: "Thou hast redeemed us to God, even bought us with thy blood *out of every kindred, and tongue, and people, and nation".*

This would be utterly unintelligible if it could, or might refer to the early Christian church. Rather the opposite appears to be the case. The representation here warrants but one explanation, namely that what is here dealt with immediately precedes the end of all things, the coming of the antichrist and the Return of the Lord. That at first this book or Testament was hidden indicates this. He who prepared such a writing of what is to come, and sealed it and kept it in a secret place, does not show it openly except as the end is at hand. Only the nearness of the end renders further secrecy unnecessary. Such a written disposition is made with an eye to the end, and until the end is at hand is kept out of sight. Only now, when all is done, and the end is at the door the document is produced and is made public. The will with respect to this matter is naturally nought else than the will of God. God did not write this book, as with us wills, as a rule, are drawn up, only when the end of life is felt to be near. With God there is nothing new, and nothing new comes up in time. God's counsel and thus likewise His decree regarding the end of things is fixed from all eternity, only it was kept secret, but now that the end is at hand it is disclosed to us.

This book, this sealed volume, this sevenfold roll is not the same as ordinary revelation, but is radically different therefrom. God's ordinary Revelation began already in Paradise, has accompanied believers in every age, has ever increased and become more rich, and as time went on has never been taken away from the faithful. That Revelation has never been sealed, but has always been open. Its appeal is to every one of us, and all through life it stays by us. The Revelation in question here however had not been sent out into the world, but had been kept hidden in strictest secrecy. It was purposely kept secret, for it was thickly covered, altogether mysterious and sealed with seven seals. In Revelation everything is urge that everyone shall know it; in this mystical volume on the contrary it was meant that no one should have a glimpse of it, until the time of the end is come. The absolutely untenable representation that this sevenfold volume was to be unsealed and made public at the outset of the career of Christ's church in the world must therefore resolutely be set aside. Rather, the church of Christ must first have finished her course. It plainly reads, that the Gospel of Christ must first be preached "to all nations and kindreds and peoples and tongues, before this book could be unsealed." Even as it reads in Rev. 7, 9: "I beheld a great multitude, which no man could number, of all nations, and kindreds, and peoples, and tongues, standing before the Lamb." Here the Consummation is at hand, and unless this is clearly kept in view, the Apocalypse as a whole remains unintelligible.

With what the Apocalypse reveals, we are at the end of things. The church of Christ in the world will then in every respect have been perfected. And with the end the destruction of the world is at hand. For the antichrist cometh. And this is what the Apocalypse holds before us.

Bear in mind that the seven seals embrace the whole. Though the trumpets come after the seals, and the vials after the trumpets, yet all this is but the further effect of the seventh or last seal. From the seventh seal proceed the seven trumpets, while the woes attend them all, but the book with the seven seals is always the secret record in which everything was prophesied in advance. So it will not do to imagine that after the first or second seal is opened the book were laid aside, and only after a century or more were taken in hand again. He who remembers how St. John wept, as he called for the opening of the book of the seven seals, must admit that the seven seals were opened successively and without a break. It will not do therefore to imagine that there were great pauses between the opening of the several seals. It is also worthy of note that Rev. 8, 1 reads: "When the seventh seal was opened, there was silence in heaven about the space of *half an hour.*" Even this can not be made to mean exactly thirty minutes. Such references were common in prophecy from of old, and also in the Apocalypse must be taken as indications of a more general character. But here at least it must be borne in mind that the reference is to a very short, quickly passing course of time, such as is common in the examination of ancient records. A keeper of archives, who has seven or more records to examine, is apt to take a half hour recess before he goes on again. Yet it certainly would be foolish, if after he had carefully examined the first six records he were to put off indefinitely the examination of the seventh, especially when this was supposed to contain the most important directions of all.

Moreover the seven parts that were bound together in this book of the seven seals were evidently not large. If each of them consisted of 50 pages, the reading of them all, especially if the script were small, might take several weeks. But such was not the case. It even seems that this book contained pictures and figures, rather than writings, at least the first four parts. For the story of these first four parts is told in the opening eight verses of chapter 6, and all that is seen in each of them is *a horse.* These four horses differ in color and significance and each is briefly described, but the main impression is that these four horses indicate what the prophecy means to convey. It does not state the time when these prophecies shall be fulfilled. Room is left for the ages that will presently come and go until the time of the end, but the parts themselves merely indicate what will come to pass at the end of the world, while nothing is said of what will precede the end.

At the same time it is remarkable how prominent a role the four beasts or Zoa of Paradise play in it all. Right here at the time of the end the reference is again and again to the creation and paradise. So in every way we are made to feel that what here is dealt with is no middle period, but the conclusion of the whole creation. Verse 1 of chapter 6 reads: "And I saw when the Lamb opened one of the seals, and I heard, as it were the noise of thunder, one of the four beasts saying, Come and see!" And more! When it comes to the second seal, we read again: "And when He had opened the second seal, I heard the second beast say, Come and see!" So it goes on with the third and fourth seals in vs. 5 and 7. With each of these four seals one of the Zoa takes the lead and addresses St. John, inviting him to see what comes. This does not repeat itself with the three remaining seals. But with each of the first four seals there is a voice that, as it were, comes out of Paradise, and points to the conclusion of the world's life, and so directs St. John's eye to the final event by which, what began in Paradise and corrupted itself, now ends in glorious restoration. Nothing is said however, of a period of time between the opening of the several seals. They are opened one by one successively and without a break, and can not be said to refer solely to events of common historic life. Read verses 12 and 13. At first it seems that we are still in the midst of common life. There had to be a connection between ordinary life and the new that was to come, but already in vs. 12 and 13 we read that "the sun became black as sackcloth of hair, and the heaven departed as a scroll when it is rolled together; and every mountain and island were moved out of their places." Here we are already entirely outside of ordinary life, and have entered upon the great change that is to come both in the life of nature and of man.

In connection with this the great things which with the first four seals became visible, are merely introductory. In the lead is the appearance of the Christ. The session of Christ at God's right hand to intercede for us (Hebr. 7, 25) is now ended. As victor and as the-of-God anointed and crowned King, Christ ushers in the time of the end. St. John sees Christ advancing seated on a *white* horse as a victorious hero rides when he makes his triumphal entry. Also here Christ is no longer *the Lamb,* but wears the *crown,* and so He goes forth conquering and to conquer, that is to say, to consummate His final triumph. Next to the white horse of the conquering Christ comes the *horse that is red,* even red as a sign that there would be a war in the earth greater than had ever been before. Of him it is said that he shall "take peace from the earth." So his signal is a *great sword.* Result of this is dreadful misery among the children of men in the earth, which misery is indicated by the third, which is the *black* horse. Now famine breaks out in the earth. There is no wheat for daily bread, oil becomes scarce, and there is no more wine to cheer the heart.

Yet this is but the beginning. When the fourth seal of the book is opened the *pale* horse comes, "and his name that sat on him was death, and Hell followed with him". Death and Hell now attack human society, and the great destruction sets in, the first effect of which is bewilderment and general havoc, as a fourth part of the inhabitants of the earth is destroyed by the sword or by starvation or by deadly disease or by wild beasts. A terrible state of wretchedness, and a loss, according to our reckoning, of some 400 million lives. Naturally in the days of terror such as those of the great world war, reference was made to this "black horse". And though now the number of those who have shaken off all seriousness of life, and feast on plays of a frequently immoral character is very great, among the more seriously minded in every land an impression is abroad which makes one ask whether the end might not be at hand and whether we might not already have come to the fourth seal.

IX

THE MARTYRS UNDER THE ALTAR

And they cried with a loud voice, saying, How long,
O Lord, holy and true, dost thou not judge and avenge
our blood on them that dwell on the earth? Rev. 6, 10.

Especially the fifth seal is conclusive in behalf of the correct understanding of the seals. This seal has nothing to say about what in the course of history shall take place in the earth, but rehearses an event that takes place in heaven. No angels here appear upon the scene. The martyrs occupy the center of the stage; not those of a given period, but "the souls of them that were slain for the Word of God, and for the testimony which they held", in short, of all who in the course of centuries from Abel on, had suffered martyrdom. These martyrs who up till now had been at rest in heaven, seem suddenly to wake up, as it were, from their state of holy calm, and to raise a bitter cry. "And they cried with a loud voice saying, How long, O Lord, holy and true, dost thou not judge and avenge our blood on them that dwell on the earth?" Many, if not the most of them, had suffered martyrdom already many centuries before. If these martyrs had all these years awaited quietly the issue of the great feud between God and Satan, without calling on God for vengeance, and now suddenly do so with one accord in so beseeching a manner, something must have happened to account for this. So we ask: What made these martyrs thus suddenly call on God? The question is the more urgent, as something in their cry affects one strangely. These martyrs are in a state of absolute holiness. They had died unto all sin, and lived in heaven holy lives with their God and their Mediator. Wherefore then suddenly from the great choirs of holy martyrs so loud a cry which, superficially at least, does not impress one favorably?

What do these martyrs want? Forgiveness of those who were their enemies and persecuted them to the death? Was there something in their cry of what Jesus laid upon their heart, when He

77

said: "Bless them that curse you, and pray for them which de-
spitefully use you" (Matth. 5, 44)? Not at all. Their cry is
for the direct opposite. Their cry is for vengeance, as they can
not bear the further delay of judgment. It was tarrying too long.
They count on the wrath of God that is to come and must be
visited upon their cruel persecutors. They can scarcely endure
the suspense, which shows that they deem the moment to have
arrived when the relation of life would be changed, the end
ushered in, and the judgment of God come upon the enemies of
His sacred cause. All Scripture bears witness in unmistakable
terms to the time when tolerance and forbearance shall end, and
Christ shall no more be seen in the form of a servant in which
He dwelt on earth and suffered and died. When the time of the
end is near the moment too will come when Christ shall bring
in the last judgment; then there shall be no more room for forgiveness or reconciliation, but the Mediator shall execute judgment in the world of demons and in that of the lost children of
men. Of what this shall be, in the nature of the case believers
in the earth can form no idea, but the blessed in heaven who
there await the end of the world, understand its meaning. It is
no secret to them that in the time of the end the Mediator shall
destroy the power of Satan, and for all that have died in unbelief
shall usher in a future which He paints again and again in the
dark colors of the "weeping and gnashing of teeth".

And while all the redeemed in heaven await the moment of
this final decision, the martyrs do this the more eagerly. When,
because they bore witness for Christ, they were put to a violent
death, in their person the cause of Christ was assailed. Hence
the honor of Christ which in their death was trodden under foot
must be restored. And in the day of judgment this will be done.
This is what the martyrs have been anticipating, for they know
that this cannot take place until the final decision is at hand. And
seeing what now was taking place on earth these blessed martyrs
perceived that the time of the end had come. With an eye to
this they can not understand why the Mediator should not avenge
their blood now. So everything is clear, though it implies that
they saw the coming of the end, that to them it seemed as though
there could be no more delay, and that they felt this so keenly
that they could not imagine why the execution of the vengeance

of the Mediator upon His enemies should tarry. And as the expected retribution did not take place, they were sore troubled, and hence their united cry that their blood might be avenged as vindication of the honor of the Mediator which in their martyr death had been derided. So everything runs smoothly, and clearly proves that the fifth seal has nothing to do with what in the course of centuries takes place on earth, but solely refers to what shall come to pass when the time of the end draws near.

In entire accord with this is the answer they receive: "that they rest yet for a little season, until their fellowservants also and their brethren, that should be killed as they were, should be fulfilled." In connection also with what follows in the remaining chapters it is obvious that this saying refers to what will come to pass under the tyranny of the antichrist, and after the appearance of the great Witnesses. And since the Apocalypse as a whole admits of no other interpretation than that all this will only come to pass just before the parousia, so this call of these earlier martyrs for vengeance will immediately precede the last seal. This view is further confirmed by what in the matter of the "white robes" is done to the good of these martyrs. As v. 11 reads: "And white robes were given unto every one of them." In the nature of the case this is meant spiritually. These martyrs had not yet been raised from the dead and were still without their glorified bodies. They were disembodied spirits. A "white robe" is the garment of him who has achieved victory in the field of battle, the mantle of state of him who has triumphed. So it expressly reads that they were 'long white robes'. Of course this is meant symbolically, and cannot but mean that this robe of the victor is the pledge of the perfect triumph that awaits them. Robed as victors in long garments of white they can the easier await for a little season the coming vengeance of their Saviour, in which they too would have a part.

But this also sets aside the interpretation that makes the seals refer to what in the course of centuries awaits the world or the church of Christ. For if the fifth seal refers to what will immediately precede the parousia, it also proves that the four preceding seals must refer to the time of the end. The fifth seal of the martyrs is in the midst of the seven seals and does not conclude them. The fifth seal is not a portrayal of what takes place

on earth, but in heaven at the time of the end; and as it comes
between the four preceding and the two following, it shows that
all they prophesy belongs together, forms one whole and is bound
to one chronological order. The coming of the end would cause
a great commotion not alone upon the earth, but also in heaven;
and from this must be explained why what is to take place on
earth and what is to come to pass in heaven is here so clearly and
circumstantially put together as one whole. If then it can not be
denied that what here is said of the martyrs can only take place
immediately before the end, it follows that the opening of all the
seals can refer only to what is to be awaited with the approach
of the parousia and of the judgment. First then comes the triumphant Christ riding on the white horse, not with the sword,
but with the bow, as the final judgment will yet tarry for a little
season. After Christ and under His leadership, and thus as His
instrument follows the red horse whose rider carries the great
sword, 'to take peace from the earth.' The third horse is black
and brings distress in the earth. They are all instruments of
Christ that bring the final decision. But the prospect that the
final decision is at hand also stirs the blessed martyrs, who can
not but think that now the hour of vengeance is come. And the
only response to their cry is, that they "should rest yet for a little
season"; which is more fully elucidated in Rev. 8, 1, where it
is said with the seventh seal, that there was silence in heaven
about the space of half an hour·

The sixth seal carries us from heaven back to earth again,
where it immediately creates dismay and consternation and a
tearing asunder of all created life. What had preceded had merely been preparatory to what now would come to pass. There had
been wars and famines and distress of nations, but all this was
possible in ordinary times. The extraordinary element first
showed itself in the martyr's cry. Yet this was merely a cry.
But as the sixth seal is opened we see the ordinary state of things
come to an end, and together with every created thing the world,
as it were, is lifted out of its grooves. As in an earthquake
buildings totter and threaten to collapse, so it is here. Hence it
is misleading to put what takes place at the opening of the sixth
seal on a par with an ordinary earthquake. In a terrible earthquake, think of Messina, whole cities have truly been, as it were,

laid waste. Yet what here is prophesied is far worse. "The stars of heaven shall fall unto the earth, the heaven shall depart as a scroll when it is rolled together, and all mountains and islands shall be moved out of their places. No such phenomena can occur in what we call the ordinary course of life. They depict conditions such as can only be imagined when the end draws near and everything is wrenched apart.

In the face of such horrors man naturally loses all self-control and all courage and daring. Nothing in the order of human society remains in place. Kings hurriedly leave their palaces and hide themselves in caves. And not only kings, but great men, and the rich, and chief captains and mighty men and slaves as well as free men, all fly from palace and house, from city and village, and look for caves and dens in the mountains in which to hide. And even these when reached provide no places of safety, and as with one voice the fugitives cry: "Fall on us, O mountains, and ye rocks, hide us from the face of God and of the Lamb, for the great day of His wrath is come, and who can abide it!" (See vs. 16 and 17). Who can say that this presents a scene of ordinary human life, or at most of ordinary phenomena of nature. What this describes is a general upheaval of all things, a tearing apart of every relation in nature and in human society that maintains the connection of the whole. What here presents itself is the beginning of the breaking up of creation, even as was said in vs. 12 and 13, that the sun became black and the moon red like blood, and like as when the whole earth is shaken by a mighty wind.

Nor is this all. Unexpectedly the eye is directed to a scene in the seventh seal, where we see four angels, each holding one of the four winds in his hand; and together for the moment they hold these destructive agencies in leash, lest the destruction of the creaturely world should be too sudden. And to make the arrest of the general destruction more sure, a fifth angel appears having the seal of the living God in his hand, and he cried with a loud voice to the four angels that held the four winds of the earth, that they should not yet begin the work of destroying the earth, the sea and the trees. So for the sake of the believers that are still in the earth, there is a momentary pause in the general destruction of creaturely life. For the angel with the seal of God

cried to the other four that held the destructive winds in leash,
saying: "Hurt not the earth, neither the sea, nor the trees, till we
have sealed the servants of our God in their foreheads." And now
the company of believers that are still on the earth come in sight
in two groups. First come the 144,000 from among the children
of Israel (concerning which later), and after these St. John "beheld, and, lo, a great multitude, which no man could number, of
all nations, and kindreds, and people, and tongues." which had
already entered upon blessedness, and "stood before the throne,
clothed with white robes, and palms of victory in their hands."
So everything ended in a heavenly song of praise and in an
ecstacy of worship, in which the Presbyters take the lead, losing
itself in the glorious confirmation of still greater blessedness:
"The Lamb which is in the midst of the throne shall feed them,
and shall lead them unto living fountains of waters; and God
shall wipe away all tears from their eyes" (v. 17).

With this the holy Apocalypse has come to the *seventh* seal,
which in breadth of scope far exceeds the narrow range of the
preceding six. The seventh seal is by no means ended in verse
7 of chapter 8, so that when the first trumpet sounds everything
connected with the seven seals is disposed of. He who takes it
this way does not understand the coherence of the book of Revelation. The seventh seal begins with chapter 8, 1, and only ends
in chapter 22, 8. There is only *one book* there (See 5, 1.) That
one book contains everything that is to be revealed, but in seven
unequal parts. The first six parts of this sealed book are relatively small and hence were soon unfolded. But when it came to the
seventh seal it was different. After this seal had been opened
a large roll came in sight, which contains the complete portrayal and communication to the end of what at the time to St.
John, and through him for all time to come, was to be revealed
to Christendom and so also to us.

The first seal showed the appearance of Christ as judge for
the last judgment. The second, third and fourth seals show the
means by which He would execute the same, to wit: war, famine,
death and hell. The fifth seal shows the scene in heaven, in which
at the time of the end the martyrs play their part. With the sixth
seal comes the general upheaval and tearing asunder of all creaturely life. And with the seventh seal comes the disclosure of the

future, which would still precede the Consummation. But what now comes and accompanies the seven trumpets and the seven vials, is not additional to the seventh seal, but flows from it and is part of it. The one book contains it all. That book consisted of seven rolls which were sealed and put together in one volume. And thereto nothing could be added. Verse 1 of chapter 8 shows this so clearly as to exclude all doubt. As soon as according to verse one of chapter eight the seventh seal is opened, it is plainly stated that before St. John obtained a full insight into this large roll, there was a pause of half an hour. But as soon as he obtained this insight, the first sign in that seventh roll or seal was that of "the seven angels which stood before God; and to them were given seven trumpets." And immediately thereupon (v. 6.): "the seven angels which had the seven trumpets prepared themselves to sound."

X

THE SEVEN TRUMPETS*

*And I saw the seven angels which stood before God;
and to them were given seven trumpets.* Rev. 8, 2.

Without for the moment going more deeply into the mystery
of the Revelation of St. John, it will be well to consider the
three series of the seven seals, the seven trumpets and the seven
vials. We must have a coherent synopsis of these three series,
before we can examine the rich design that is woven into them.
So we begin with the trumpets. These too are seven in number.
So they fit perfectly in the mystical frame that is placed before
us. There is no reason why upon, and as outflow from, the
seven seals there could not follow six or eight trumpets; and upon
these six or eight trumpets ten or twelve vials; but the following
chapters clearly show that such would not have been possible.
Not only that in connection with both trumpets and vials in the
literal sense the number seven is indicated, but also in the summary both times the number seven is evidently not merely nom-
inal, but essential. Both times seven trumpets and seven vials are
severally called by name, and in such a way that the seven
trumpets proceed from the last or seventh seal and the seven vials
from the last trumpet. They form a series of three times seven
phenomena, which together form one whole. If this were all, the
unfolding of both the course and content of Revelation would be
gradual. It would not be difficult to follow the course of procedure, in case the last of the seven seals gave rise to the seven
trumpets and the last of the seven trumpets gave rise to the seven
vials. Hence it can be said without exaggeration that the first
eight chapters in their order of succession and coherence present
almost no difficulty either to the understanding or the memory.

---

*In the original "The Seven Trumpets" covers chapters X—XIII.

The difficulty for the memory and intricacies which make a synopsis almost impossible first presents itself in Rev. 8, 13, where we are startled by the cry of *woe, woe, woe,* a cry which in the 9th chapter seems to refer to three intervening events, which interrupt the regular course of the seven trumpets, force themselves between these trumpets, and introduce entirely independent events· As evenly as the course of events runs in the first eight chapters, so divergent from that fixed rule is what is announced after the fourth angel had sounded and, after the fifth angel had sounded, immediately begins.

Even this would not so greatly obstruct our insight into the coherence of the Apocalypse as a whole, if this departure from the fixed series limited itself to the recital of independent events, as in the case of the three woes. But this is not so. The three woes might momentarily be dismissed from mind, without having the whole representation thereby fall apart. But this does not apply to the "little book" in chapter 10, nor to the appearance of the two Witnesses in chapter 11.

For the sake of clarity and perspicuity of the whole, it will be well therefore, to deal with each of the three series in turn, before we attempt to visualize more nearly the whole body of the Apocalypse, as at length it presents itself. So from the seven seals we turn to the seven trumpets. We do this the more readily as the seven trumpets present themselves almost in the same way as the seven seals, that is to say, at first they follow each other in quick succession, and only the last trumpets, even as the last seals, are attended by peculiar developments in the course of things.

It is to be noted that the seventh seal has no content of its own. The content of the first six seals is each time fully described in proper order of succession, but not one word is said of a content or special perspective of the seventh seal. Without any preliminary statement it is told in Chapter 8, 1-2, that the seventh seal is opened, that seven angels appear on the scene, to whom seven trumpets were given. This impresses one as though now the seven seals are ended, and we come to an entirely different part of the Apocalypse. Everything makes it seem as though in the main we are through with the seals, and that now we come to an entirely new series in which seven angels appear, to each of whom a trumpet is given, and that now these seven angels in

regular order are to announce a judgment of God. But before
they begin their sounding, as a sort of introduction, another
scene is presented, which is dealt with more fully later on, but
deserves mention at this point. It is this. Before these seven
angels begin to sound their trumpets, the holy apostle John sees
an eighth angel, not on the earth, but in the sanctuary of the
throne room of God where he takes his place at the altar. In his
hand he holds a golden censer, which is frequently spoken of in
Scripture as the exponent of prayer. Such is the case here.
Much incense is put into this censer, which he is to offer "with
the prayers of the saints upon the golden altar which was before
the throne." As a result of this "the smoke of the incense, which
came with the prayers of the saints, ascended up before God out
of the angel's hand." And this is not all. The time of grace is
past. What now proceeds from the throne of God is a beginning
of the retributive justice that is to be visited upon sinful men and
fallen angels. And so we read in v. 5: "And the angel took the
censer, and filled it with fire of the altar, and cast it into the
earth." And as soon as this sacred censer was emptied, "there
were voices and thunderings, and lightnings, and an earthquake."

All this tends to make it very clear that the great action which
is now at hand, does not proceed from men, but from God. The
hour of His vengeance is come. Men have not accepted His
grace. Rather the holiness in His grace has been defiled and
scorned. It is as though the whole world has set itself against
it. The patience of God has been of long duration. There has
been no hasty cutting off of grace. Presently in the two Witnesses (Rev. 11, 3) there shall be a last invitation of grace.
But the time of the end is come. And now preparation for it is
made with haste. The new earth and the new heaven are at hand,
but judgment must come first. And to this end those seven angels,
and with them the angel having the golden censer, are sent forth.
Ever bear in mind in this connection that from the time when
the tabernacle was built in the wilderness, there has been a constant reference to the tabernacle which is in the heavens with God.
Moses was not at liberty to build the tabernacle after his own
plan. What in the tabernacle in the wilderness was to become the
place of worship, had to be a copy of the tabernacle which occupied a conspicuous place of honor in the throne room of God in

heaven. So the fact presses itself upon us, that the throne room of God in the heavens is no empty space, but that there the original of the sanctuary stands out in dazzling light. So there is an altar there, and a censer out of which dreadful elements are cast into the earth, so soon as God commands. In Exodus 25,9 we read: "According to all that I shew thee, after the pattern of the tabernacle, and the pattern of all the instruments thereof, even so shall ye make it"; and again in v. 40: "See to it, that thou make them after their pattern, which was shewed thee in the mount."

In Matth. 24, 31 Jesus prophesied that at the time of the end angels would go forth with trumpets. "And He shall send His angels with a great sound of a trumpet, and they shall gather together His elect from the four winds, from one end of heaven to the other." St. Paul refers to the sound of the trumpet in connection with the end, when in 1 Cor. 15, 52 he writes: "In a moment, in the twinkling of an eye, at the last trump: for the trumpet shall sound, and the dead shall be raised incorruptible." To the same effect we read in I Thess. 4, 16: "For Christ Himself shall descend from heaven with a shout, with the voice of the archangel, and with the trump of God: and the dead in Christ shall first." In Hosea (8, 1) the trumpet serves as a musical instrument, that would sound when at the time of the end the Lord would show His glorious Majesty; for so it reads: "Set the trumpet to thy mouth! He comes as an eagle against the house of the Lord!" In Israel the trumpet served two purposes. It was sounded when the people went into battle, and in sacred festivals to arouse the enthusiasm of the people. In keeping with this is the reference here to trumpets. A great commotion is here said to go out from the sanctuary above; but in addition to this the retributive vengeance of God's justice breaks forth into flame. The immediate effect of the sound of the trumpet shows itself therefore so disastrously upon life here below. Every thing that follows these trumpet blasts in the earth creates terror.

The first mention of the trumpet in connection with the holy occurs in Exod. 19, 16, at the giving of the law on Sinai. "And it came to pass on the third day in the morning, that there were thunders and lightnings, and the voice of the trumpet exceeding loud, so that all the people trembled." And v. 19 adds: "And when the voice of the trumpet sounded long, and waxed louder and louder, Moses spake, and God answered him by a voice." Again v. 18 of the next chapter reads, that the people not only saw the thunderings and the lightnings, but also heard the noise of the trumpet from heaven, whereupon "they removed, and stood afar off". So the trumpet was always associated with what takes place in heaven, even as in the Apocalypse here; and it is no less striking that its first application in priestly use was not on the occasion of a festival, but on the great day of Atonement, when likewise the retributive vengeance of God's justice was in question. So we read in Leviticus 25, 9: "Then shalt thou cause the trumpet of the jubilee to sound on the tenth day of the seventh month. In the day of Atonement shall ye make the trumpet sound throughout all your land." We need to enter no further into the use of the trumpet here. With an eye to the use of the trumpet in the Apocalypse it suffices to call attention to two Old Testament particulars. In the first place that the trumpet is not only sounded in the tabernacle or temple in the earth, but also in the throne room of God above; and again, that the trumpet is sounded especially when the just wrath of God is to be poured out in judgment.

So taken, we understand why in the Apocalypse, when the second series of signs begins, the trumpets are not sounded by soldiers or by priests, but by the angels from heaven. Judgment draws near. The day of grace is ended. The wrath of God announces itself and is attended by the trumpets, which are not to be sounded in the earth, but in the ear of God in the throne room of the heavens. Those trumpets give their signals for the war, whereby God will destroy the world of men that perversely continues in sin and refuses to repent. In His anger and under the pressure of His holy wrath God now commands His angels to proclaim war against His world of men. And to show that this outbreak of God's wrath can no longer be arrested or delayed, seven trumpets successively are sounded, and each sounding is carefully explained, so that John might understand their meaning, and that by his Apocalypse, if necessary, century upon century it might be proclaimed among the children of men.

From this follows at the same time that we must not imagine these several soundings of the trumpet to be centuries apart, but rather that these seven trumpet blasts closely follow one upon the other, and so unite in one mighty action that from heaven comes down to the dwellers upon earth. Obviously the first four trumpets announce closely related judgments, while the last three have more of a significance of their own, and the seventh trumpet rings in an entirely distinct part of God's judgment, and ends in the *vials* of God's wrath. That there is something akin to an artificial splitting up in this division, can not be denied. Yet the supposition that John is the author of this division, so as to bring out the whole in a more artificial order, rests upon pure self-delusion. In the creation there is a divine order which coheres in forms that are related with the sacred number seven. Man may work without order, but not God. In all His works is a precise order of succession. So it was in the seals, so it is here in the trumpets, and so, as will presently be seen, in the vials. This divinely methodical procedure accounts for the severity in the form. See it in the rainbow, yes see it in all the creation of God. So does the Almighty work without deviation. There was ever an element of truth in Pythagoras' philosophy of numbers.

As to the effect of the soundings of the seven trumpets we read in chapter 8, 7, that when the first of the seven angels had sounded, there was "hail and fire mingled with blood, and they were cast upon the earth", and this wrought such havoc in nature that "the third part of trees was burnt up, and all green grass was burnt up." This devastation that came with the first trumpet naturally recalls the plagues of Egypt. It even partly seems a repetition of what took place in Pharaoh's kingdom. A deeper study of the text however shows that while there is analogy, there is no similarity. For there is an element in this plague which is not in the plagues of Egypt. While the magicians were able to imitate the first plagues, when it came to the later plagues they were utterly unable to do what Moses and Aaron had done, and frankly confessed the same. But in the first trumpet-vision this is still more strongly expressed. The element in what St. John here saw, which was nothing short of the miraculous, was *the blood* that was mingled with fire and hail. If it said that the fire and hail were mingled with blood after they had been cast upon the earth, we might think that the fire of the lightning and hail killed people where it struck and caused pools of blood to form on the ground, which might account for the mingling of the fire and hail with blood. But the text does not say so. In v. 7 it is stated that the hail and fire were mingled with blood, and only then were cast upon the earth. Therefore these words are not understood when this blood is taken as lying on the ground, into which the fire and hail fell. No, the blood in question here was blood that God from heaven cast upon the earth, to bring out in lurid light His judgment upon human life. As when a mischievous lad, who has pulled feathers from a harmless dove, is shown, before he is punished, the beautiful feathers by way of reproach for his shameful deed, so in a wondrous way the Lord here mingles blood with what He gives man to see, in order, by showing him this blood, to hold his unsparing cruelty and injustice before his eyes. And so terrible is this first downpouring of fire and hail that, while not entirely, yet, for a third part nature is utterly destroyed and consumed. At the first trumpet blast all gardens, parks and fields are burned by the fire of the lightning. And this is but the beginning of woes, and as we shall see presently, the second trumpet brings a much greater evil upon the earth. For as we read in the 8th verse: "When the second angel sounded, as it were a great mountain burning with fire was cast into the sea, and the third part of the sea became blood."

XI

THE SECOND, THIRD AND FOURTH TRUMPETS

And he said unto me, Thou must prophesy again before many peoples, and nations, and tongues, and kings.
Rev. 10, 11.

As was observed above, the second trumpet also brings a calamity upon nature. It affects navigation and commerce, but only incidentally, as this was not the direct object of the plague. And while it presents an apparent similarity with one of the plagues of Egypt, this plague is on a much larger scale, and like the first trumpet impresses us as directly wrought by God from heaven. It brings the sixth seal to mind. What then took place was a violent upheaval in the ordinary state of things, so that all the kings and rulers and philosophers fled to hide themselves in dens and caves, with the despairing cry: "O mountains, fall on us, and hide us from the face of him that sitteth on the throne." The impression was general that judgment was at hand, as the cry implies: "The great day of his wrath is come; and who shall be able to stand?" Looking back on this it has been asked, whether what took place under the sixth seal was not much more terrible than what had taken place with the soundings of the first and second trumpets. And this question naturally arises when here we merely note the consternation of these terror-stricken people. But it will not do to view each of the first four trumpet calamities, if we may so call these plagues, by itself alone. Here too as in the case of the first seals it is wrong to imagine these first four trumpets as centuries apart. Rather what the first four trumpets announce follows in quick succession, and only with the fifth trumpet, where man appears active again, do these trumpets cover broader ground. The first four trumpets proceed after the analogy of the plagues of Egypt, but as no man takes part in it, like Moses in the Egyptian plagues, the succession must be taken to be even yet more rapid.

91

It is one sounding of four angels immediately after each other, and this the rather and the more, because in the nature of the case the Apocalypse does not say that all this has taken place or does take place, but merely prophesies that at the time of the end all this shall take place.

As said before, the special significance of what follows after the second angel has sounded, is its heavenly origin. So we read: "And the second angel sounded, and as it were a great mountain burning with fire was cast into the sea: and the third part of the sea became blood." As in the case of the first trumpet, so here a violent action from heaven creates commotion in nature and in human society. Yet always in such a way, that the emphasis falls on the disturbance in nature, only the effect of which causes distress in human life. Each of the four trumpets is directly concerned with nature, and there God's Almightiness works the great havoc. Of course what takes place after each trumpet blast is meant, as a judgment on man, to ruin all human life, but it does not begin with man. The world began to exist with the creation of the earth, and only then did man make his appearance. And in this order follows the destruction of all earthly existence. Each time the action begins with the earth and with what nature produces on the earth, and only then we learn what overtakes man.

Here again in the nature of the case "the third part" is not meant in the literal sense. It merely indicates that the state of things had not yet entirely become involved, but rather that while the greater part of the life of nature had still been spared, the invasion nevertheless had been so violent and dreadful as to destroy well-nigh the half. What chiefly attracts the attention is the wondrous object from heaven that is part of the plague. The miraculous element here is, that something from above is violently cast into the sea. The text reads that it had the appearance of a *great mountain,* which but indicates its prodigious size and enormous weight. It was no mountain taken from some mountainous chain here or there, but something that the Almighty had directly called into being and caused from the high firmament to be plunged into the sea. Again the blood-tint shows itself in this connection. The text reads: "and the third part of the sea became blood." A phenomenon of like nature occurred with the first trumpet. Then "there was fire and hail mingled with blood", but here much stronger still, as a third part of the almost immeasureable volume of waters that form the ocean is turned into the color of blood. This change was so radical that no fish could live in it and the third part of the creatures that were in the sea; and had life, died. Even this was not all. The change in the color of the water was accompanied by so violent a storm, that "the third part of the ships were destroyed."

It should especially be noted that the second and third trumpet-plagues by God's wrath were directed more against the water than against the land. The first trumpet brought destruction upon plants and grass. Forests, and plains on which cattle pastured, were entirely burned. The second trumpet works ruin in the immeasurable sea-level and therewith to the means of human communication. This could have been done by one of the forces of nature. We can not be impressed too deeply by the fact that also ordinary earthquakes work such destruction in the earth, as sometimes is appalling, and one can well imagine that such earthquakes might sometime assume such proportions as to fling the earth out of her orbit. It can also be said that in everyday life lightning can work much mischief. Even meteors at times can assume threatening proportions. He who in the mountains has seen meteors of an older date, can readily see the possibility of earthquakes, lightnings and meteors assuming such gigantic proportions as to work general destruction. For so far as the great convulsion that awaits our earth will thus limit itself to natural causes, it will all assume a much more dreadful form than we know anything of, but will be the same in kind, the signs of which we already now observe.

Here on the other hand we see in what took place after the second trumpet blast something that can not be explained from nature, but which comes from above to this earth. And it is noteworthy that now the third part of the sea-level is entirely destroyed, that this destruction is accompanied by a wondrous action from heaven, and that finally also here the blood, albeit merely in color, points to the death-threatening outpouring of God's wrath.

With the third trumpet the waters of the earth are attacked anew, yet this time not the waters of the sea, but inland waters. Although rivers only are mentioned, it plainly includes brooks, lakes and waterways. There is no reason why any sweet water should be excluded. By this third plague the dwellers upon the earth are compelled to drink these corrupted waters and so incur all sorts of diseases, even death itself. As a rule people do not drink river-water, so that even if the great rivers had been poisoned, and the sweet rain- and well-water had been kept pure, this third plague would not have been so dreadful. And even if river-water in times past was more commonly used for drinking purposes than now, in this instance it must be understood that all sweet waters were affected and man either perished from thirst, or by drinking foul water died. As it reads: the plague from above smote not the rivers only, but also "the fountains of waters" which may well include the sweet water of lakes and waterways.

The wonderful part of this third trumpet is, that what took place is explained as the action of a great star that fell from heaven. This shows anew that this plague also was not of earthly origin, but was sent from heaven. Grant, that there is something analogous here to the plagues of Egypt, yet it is clearly indicated that this plague was of an entirely different origin and character. It is emphatically stated that it came not from Beneath, but from Above, and was caused by a body of great size that fell from heaven to earth. Too much should not be made of this "great star". Also elsewhere in Scripture we constantly notice that the distinction between names by which natural phenomena were called, was then so much weaker than now. We speak of the Sermon on the Mount. Matthew 5, 1 plainly reads that Jesus, "seeing the multitudes, went up into a mountain." Yet this mountain is nothing but a hill, and a low hill at that. No mountain-discourse could intelligibly have been heard by a multitude. So in the case of this star, it might simply have been a meteor, and as meteors as a rule are small, though sometimes very large, likely at this time it meant a singularly large and wondrous one, so that there was no exaggeration in calling it "a great star". The miraculous element here is something entirely different. Not so much in the falling from heaven of a star of greater size than the earth, but in fact that the meteors burned like torches and covered and destroyed a third part of the rivers and fountains of waters.

"And the name of the star is called Wormwood," which name is attributed to the fact that the waters into which it fell became undrinkable. While this shows some analogy to what was done by Moses' rod in Egypt, more than analogy also this is not. With Moses it merely meant making a part of the river Nile undrinkable, while here it is said that the sweet waters of a third part of the earth were affected. By the side of all the sweet waters of Europe, the Nile fades into nothingness; and even these together with all the sweet waters of Asia, America and Africa do not form a third of the whole. So we can safely ignore every reference to what Moses brought to pass. Surely divine powers were at play in what took place in Egypt, yet not apart from human action, in which of itself they found their limitation. Here on the other hand are operations which no man could produce, but proceed directly from God. So here we can reckon with dimensions which leave, what Moses did, far in the rear.

This gigantic set of meteors was called Wormwood. Had this been a star that had struck the third part of the continents, either Asia or America must have been meant, but such a gigantic body must immediately have killed all the people of that part of the earth where it fell. It might then be thought probable that a moon of one of our planets or of some other star or a comet had collided with our earth; even then the dwellers in that part of the earth where the collision took place would immediately have perished. But from v. 11 we learn that the people whose land was struck by this star survived the shock, and only later were affected by the bitterness of the waters, so that "many died of the waters, because they were made bitter," and this shows convincingly that it could not have been a single meteor or moon or comet, but must have been a complex. Also the globelike form of our earth demands this view. No globelike form, such as that of our earth, could possibly have been covered for a third part by another globelike heavenly body. And this again shows that in the Apocalypse we deal with language and a mode of representation which can not be taken literally.

Now follows the fourth sounding and with it a wondrous action in the starry heavens. Thus in the four signs there is order of succession. First the cultivated fields and farmlands are attacked. Then the ocean becomes a scene of terror. In the third sign man is deprived of drinkable water. Yet in all this no action is destructive of the whole earth. In each instance the judgment of God affects but a third part of the whole. But with the fourth sign the destruction of the earth, seas and rivers is extended to the heavenly lights. So only all the circles of our physical universe are reached. We inhabit the earth, our great waters afford us international communication, we quench our thirst with sweet water from rivers and fountains, and life is furthermore sustained by rain and light from the skies. In addition to all this we are subject to the influences of atmosphere and starry firmament. From the atmosphere and the heavens overhead the divisions come of day and night and seasons, as well as all sorts of powers and diseases. Some conditions of weather and seasons dampen our spirits and depress us. So long therefore as our attention is directed to the produce of the ground, to ocean commerce, to drinking from rivers, fountains and lakes, but no account is taken of the air, atmosphere and starry heavens overhead, the representation is incomplete.

Of this fourth sign the Apocalypse records, that "the third part of the sun was smitten, and the third part of the moon, and the third part of the stars; so as the third part of them was darkened, and the day shone not for a third part of it, and the night likewise." This does not refer to a third part of the year, but to the whole year, so that for a third part of each day the sun shall be eclipsed, and for at least three hours in daytime it shall be as dark as night, and for an equal number of hours by night neither moon nor stars shall give light. Thus there shall be anxiety by day, and anxiety by night, and that depressing heaviness of heart of him who gropes his way in the dark. We make light of an eclipse of sun or moon, as it occurs but rarely and is soon over, but think of an eclipse of sun or moon, an absolute darkening of all the light of heaven recurring each day and each night and continuing several hours, and the mere thought of it is appalling. And such it shall be continually, when the fourth angel shall have sounded. And that even this will not be all, is indicated by the loud voice of an angel flying through the midst of heaven, saying, *Woe, woe, woe,* referring to what only *after* the sounding of these four trumpets is to come.

XII

THE FIFTH, SIXTH AND SEVENTH TRUMPETS

And in those days shall men seek death, and shall not find it; and shall desire to die, and death shall flee from them. Rev. 9, 6.

The fourth trumpet ends God's judgment so far as it concerned nature. Next in the order of procedure comes the destruction of human life, first under the fifth, then under the sixth trumpet, while the seventh or last trumpet marks the transition to the last series of plagues,—that is, to the vials or bowls, which will pour out the final destruction upon all the earth, and bring in the Consummation. The fifth trumpet brings the *"locusts* upon the earth: unto which was given power, as the scorpions of the earth have power." This effects us strangely, as to us neither of the two animals that are here mentioned has a clear metaphorical significance. We scarcely ever see them, so they mean nothing to us, and we almost never speak of them figuratively or metaphorically. Hence to understand the fifth trumpet we must familiarize ourselves with the manner of Oriental life in ancient Palestine. There we must inquire what locusts meant in popular speech, that we might grasp the sense of the fifth trumpet. In daily life and in all literature the names of animals have a symbolical use, as well as the names of flowers and plants. So we speak of the rose, the violet and the snowball. "Don't be so cocky" is used to soften too great piquancy. We call a person "Foxy" by which to indicate unfair use of advantage. The serpent stands for wily misuse of power. We say: "He is as blind as a bat" to indicate lack of sense. In short all sorts of animal names serve in figurative speech to give forceful expression to our estimate of persons and things. Faithful as a dog! is universally a well known metaphorical manner of speech; though we quite understand why this was never said in Scripture, as by reason of his uncleanness the dog was taboo in Israel. And this metaphorical use of animal names, by which to express our opinion of a person was also common in the East, and notably so in Israel. In catechetical and confirmation classes the attention of the pupil should be called to this. It would do much toward making our Western public more at home in the Scriptures. But as a rule this is sadly neglected, which for many people makes Old Testament prophecies as well as the Apocalypse difficult reading, and consequently unenjoyable. Especially with the Apocalypse this accounts for much grave misunderstanding, since it is prophetical and highly figurative. And yet this could scarcely be otherwise, since the last book of the Bible is a forecast of the closing period of life in the earth, and it would be difficult for this to be other than of a very mystical character.

The vision of the fifth trumpet in particular presents this difficulty, as it borrows its figurative language from two kinds of animals, the locust and the scorpion, which were plagues in Palestine. At times locusts came down upon the land in such swarms and worked such destruction that in a few days no leaf was left on bush or tree, no blade of grass on the ground; and naturally to the mind of the writer nothing resembled a sudden invasion of an enemy or raid by a hostile cavalry more nearly than a plague of locusts. A swarm of locusts means a vast military host. The locusts here are even reinforced by scorpions, since locusts injure vegetation but do man no harm; and the sting of scorpions is poisonous. To convey therefore a clear notion to the reader of the dangerous character of the military power which St. John here pictures by locusts, he expressly adds in v. 3: "and unto them was given power, as the scorpions of the earth have power." So the locusts share the poisonous and dangerous character of scorpions. A military power of colosaal numbers had to be indicated. But while scorpions are never very numerous, locusts, when there was a plague of them, came by millions at a time. Thus this twofold figure of speech foretold that the invading military power that was to come, would be as colossal and numerous as locusts and as dangerous as scorpions. So only was the picture complete, and readers were given an idea of the terrible military power which, when the antichrist appears, will arrogate dominion to itself over all the earth.

Old Testament writers spoke of locusts in the same way. Joel 2, 10-11 describes a plague of locusts as follows: "The earth quakes by reason of it, the heavens tremble; the sun and moon become dark because of it and the stars withdraw their shining, and the Lord utters His voice before His army, for His camp,— that is the army of locusts—is very great." The effect from of old of that terrible plague was that every branch was stripped bare, every leaf and flower was consumed, and almost nothing of vegetation remained save withered branches and twigs. In Jeremiah 46, 23 we read: "They—that is the hostile armies— are more than the grasshoppers, and are inummerable." So Nahum 3, 17 reads: "Thy crowned are as the locusts, and thy captains as the grasshoppers." More impressively still reads Amos 7. 1-2: "Thus hath the Lord God shewed unto me; and behold, He formed grasshoppers in the beginning of the shooting up of the latter growth; and it came to pass, that when they had made an end of eating the grass of the land, then said I: O Lord God, forgive, I beseech thee: by whom shall Jacob arise? for he is small." Hence they who lived in the East and were familiar with life in Palestine had no difficulty in understanding the image by which the Apocalypse, in chapter 9, pictures the military power. The reader knew at once that it meant the advance presently of a dreadfully numerous and most formidable military host.

How is the rise of this gigantic army introduced? Writes St. John: "I saw a star fall from heaven, and to him was given the key of the bottomless pit; and he opened the bottomless pit; and there arose a smoke out of the pit, as the smoke of a great furnace; and the sun and the air were darkened by reason of the smoke of the pit. And there came out of the smoke locusts upon the earth." Obviously a star in the literal sense can not handle a key. So that star can only mean that a spirit from heaven came down to the earth which had power to enter into contact with the demoniac underworld of Satan. That a human spirit can be imaged by a star is not surprising. From of old military princes have been decorated with the badge of an order which has almost always been in the form of a star. Again it is to be noted here that three places are indicated: (1) heaven, where God is enthroned and whence all action proceeds; (2) the earth, on which moves all human life; and (3) the abyss as the abode of Satan. The last-named is *the pit*. And the mighty spirit, which is imaged as a star, is given the key that unlocks the gate to the demoniac world, or as this is metaphorically expressed, " to open the bottomless pit."

No sooner is this done than smoke arises from that demoniac abyss, which means of course that demoniacal power comes up from beneath to establish Satan's dominion in human society at large, preparatory to the coming of antichrist. As immediate result, "out of smoke"—that is, under the unholy inspiration of antichrist, a great army gathers itself to gain dominion over the whole earth, and this gigantic military power is represented by *the locusts*. These locusts are not to prey upon nature, but are expressly commanded to hurt only that part of mankind "which have *not* the mark of God in their foreheads." This implies an almost universal falling away from the faith in the earth. There is still a Christian church so-called, but in reality it is no longer such. Relatively only a small part of mankind has remained faithful to Jesus Christ. To prevent confusion, God has even put a mark upon believers. It has pleased Him to put a seal upon the foreheads of His elect and faithful ones. And now it would seem as though this demoniac host were to be sent out against these believers who had thus been sealed by God. Yet such is not the case; and this is worth noting, as otherwise there is danger of wrongly interpreting this trumpet. It is expressly stated that these locusts,—that is, this unholy military power is to throw itself upon the apostates, who have forsaken God, and consequently have not the seal of God in their foreheads.

At the same time it should be observed that this military power is not to throw itself upon those apostates to kill but merely to torment them. So the demoniac anti-christian power, which by military organization will firmly establish itself in all the earth, must begin by subjecting to itself in the military sense all those that have fallen away from Christ. This coming military power has need above all things else of gigantic forces entirely subservient to itself. So the whole apostate world must be organized in a strictly military way; not by false hopes enticing apostates into military service, but by hard measures and cruel

threatenings compelling all that are of military age to enlist. This
military reign of terror will then pursue its course so demoniac-
ally, that the victims, as v. 6 reads, "shall seek death, and shall
desire to die" but it will be of no avail. Their life shall be unbearable; for under this military tyranny their torment will be
"as the torment of a scorpion, when he striketh a man" (v. 5).
They will be tormented by these powerful military overlords
until at length they have become serviceable tools of their brutal
and wicked violence. All lands in all the earth will then be under
this reign of terror. Unbelieving humanity shall no longer have
dominion in the earth, but the demoniacal power from the abyss,
or as it is here called "the bottomless pit" shall have supreme
control.

In verses 7 to 10 we have a full description of that military
power under the image here of locusts. Their shape, so it reads,
shall be like unto horses prepared unto battle. This shows that
the image of the locusts serves exclusively to indicate the vast
numbers that shall constitute this demoniacal military power, re-
sistance against which will be as little possible, as for the farmer
to protect his orchard, flower-garden or pasture-lands against
the approach of a horde of locusts. Having thus indicated the
vast numbers and irresistibleness of the advance of these de-
vastating hordes the writer pictures the violence of the character
which this military power shall display, after its discipline shall
be perfected. By reason of the strength and impetuousness of
their method of procedure that military power shall then seem
more like horses than like men. They shall appear like unto
horses prepared unto battle (v. 7). They will not look like
mercenary troops, shabby in clothing and armament, but they
will have magnificent helmets on their heads, "as it were crowns
like gold", and under these shining helmets their strong human
faces will clearly be visible. Their faces, says v. 7 will be
"as the faces of men." Only one thing will detract from the
vigorousness of their appearance; they will, as is common in
the army, give themselves to women, and then something Sy-
baritic will characterize them; something which St. John indicates
by saying that they will have their hair in fashion as though
they were women. This will make the contrast the more striking, for when they open their mouth they will show teeth "as

the teeth of lions." Also their armament will strike terror. That wherewith they will cover themselves will all seem like iron, both the breastplates and the shields. And the approach of their files shall be so dreadful as to make one think that he hears "the sound of chariots of many horses running to battle" (v. 9).

The last particular in the description of this vast military power is that "they had tails like unto scorpions; and there were stings in their tails," and hence had power to hurt men in every way. This particular again of course is borrowed from the animal world, but this was necessary to signify the atrocious cruelties which, when they attack, they inflict upon their victims. Again v. 11 clearly shows that the reference here is not to actual locusts, but to military *corps*. Proverbs 30, 27 aptly remarks: "The locusts have no king." In this they differ from the bees that have a royal head over them. But it does not hold good in this instance. A vast military host as is described here is not thinkable apart from a capable leader, and when the Apocalypse was written such a leader was only found in the person of a king. If then locusts have no king over them, here a king can not be left out; wherefore v. 11 reads: "And they had a king over them, which is the angel of the bottomless pit, whose name in the Hebrew tongue is Abaddon, but in the Greek tongue hath his name Apollyon."

Whether *Angelos* is correctly translated here by angel is doubtful. Satan was originally an angel, and the demons who with him fell away from God were angels also. But in Holy Scripture they are not usually designated by that name. Hence Kliefoth is correct, when he takes the word angelos here in its original significance as *messenger*. So this person of eminence was a messenger from hell, and is therefore called: "the angel of the bottomless pit." About his name also there can be no dispute. As v.11 reads: "His name was: *destroyer,* which is the meaning of the Hebrew word *Abaddon,* as well as of the Greek word *Apollyon.* So the use of this word solely indicates once more that, while the monstrous power which toward the end of days will set itself up as ruler of the whole earth will consist of men, they will be inspired by a spirit from the underworld, which emanates from Satan. These demons will not as yet destroy everything, but under the antichrist bear rule over all mankind. The agents of what shall come to pass shall indeed be men, but they shall act under the supremacy of a spirit from the bottomless pit, clothed with power by the antichrist.

XIII

THE SECOND AND THE THIRD WOE

One woe is past; and, behold, there come two woes more hereafter. Rev. 9, 12.

In Rev. 9, 12 we read that of the three woes that were announced in chapter 8, 13, the first is now past, and two more woes are to come. The second now begins with the sounding of the sixth angel. What the second woe will be, is described in Rev. 9, 13 to Rev. 11, 14. In the last named verse we read: "The second woe is past; and, behold, the third woe cometh quickly"; while in verse 15 the statement follows: "And the seventh angel sounded." The announcement of the seventh angel then eventuates in the vials, as we read in Rev. 15, 1: "And I saw another sign in heaven, great and marvellous, seven angels having the seven last plagues; for in them is filled up the wrath of God."

We now turn to what was sounded by the sixth angel, and we observe that this is of the same nature as the actions that followed the five preceding trumpets. Nothing is said of any human action, or of one from the underworld, but everything proceeds from God's Almighty hand. Here also God alone is active and the creature entirely passive. It is worth noting in this connection that as is stated in 9, 15: "Four angels were loosed, which were prepared for an hour, and a day, and a month, and a year". This could not have been more accurately told. The words in effect declare that, in all that is about to ensue, the action is not of men, and not of the antichrist, but the initiative is of God. All action here proceeds from God. This implies that the whole course of events that ends in the Consummation is in every particular the doing of God. It is God Who, when presently judgment is about to take place, acts upon the existing state of things with heavenly powers at His own appointed hour. Nothing that occurs in all this approach to the Consummation depends upon man; and in nothing has Satan the deciding choice. God the Lord, as Sovereign disposer of things, plans, prepares and directs

all things with an eye to His final purpose; and this is strikingly
emphasized by this reference to year, month, day and hour.
Nothing is left to chance or to the free play of the creature.
Every disposition is from Above, and though our computation
of time has no place in the eternal, this does not alter the fact
that the advent of the eternal Will into our temporal existence
must be observable on the dial of our clock. It is with this as
with our death. When we die we go out from time and enter
upon the timeless eternal; but this does not prevent the survivors
from being able to state accurately by the clock at what hour of
the day, month and year the deceased breathed his last.

How markedly everything here becomes more and more the
action of the Almighty is by nothing so clearly shown as by the
increasing activity of angels on every hand. With the preceding
trumpets angelic action was the exception, but with the sounding
of the sixth trumpet almost everything is done by angels. Though
we can form no idea of it, yet the number of angels is so incalculably great that whatever goes out from above is, almost without
exception, performed solely by the instrumentality of angels. He
who thinks at all realizes that angels do not solely exist to sing
praises and to worship. They are "ministering spirits," that is to
say, as stated in Hebr. 1, 14: "spirits sent forth to minister". It
is not too much to say that in fact all action of God upon the
creature is effected by means of the service of angels. Hence
that with the sixth sounding, when the divine actions from above
more and more unveil themselves, the reference to the angels
that fulfil God's pleasure is more and more frequent. So now it
appears from 9, 13 that, so soon as the trumpet sound is heard
for the sixth time, a voice is heard from the throne room of God,
even from the four horns of the golden altar which is before
God, saying to the sixth angel which had the trumpet: Loose the
four angels which are bound in the great river Euphrates. We
infer no ranks in the corps of angels from this, yet it shows
that one angel can be the superior of another angel. For the
angel which had the trumpet is given authority to command the
four other angels which were at their appointed posts at the river
Euphrates. The Euphrates naturally brings Babylon to mind,
and Babylon is, as in all Old Testament prophecies, and unto the
end of time, the symbolical name of the earthly power which has

established itself among men and set its face against God.

These four angels do not seem more evilly minded than the others. They had been commissioned to kill the third part of the dwellers upon earth, and hence had not done this on their own initiative. Whatever charge an angel of God executes, after the fall of Satan and his demons no good angel can ever be prone to sin. Every form of unholiness that could break out among angels had under Satan become demoniac; the other angels have ever since been absolutely holy. There is no sin in them. Thus when an angel is charged to destroy an army, spread a pestilence or cause suffering in any other way, in doing this he but executes God's will and in holiness is bound to his God. Such is the case here. The seven angels which were to sound the trumpets were commissioned to bring suffering upon the world of men, as likewise the other four angels were. They had been charged not only to inflict suffering and pain, but with the advancing judgment of God to inflict torment to the death, of the horrors of which we can form no conception. A third part of the present population of the world would number more than 500 million, and this vast number of human beings were in one instant to be deprived of life. And though the third part in this instance can not be taken literally, yet it fairly indicates the vast number of people that would be involved, and how dreadful the slaughter would be.

If now we would suppose that by pestilences and other fatal diseases the angels themselves were to slay this vast number of people, the next verse shows, on the contrary, that the destroying agency is to be cruel war. The 16th verse refers to the armies that would work this bloody havoc among the nations. These armies that are to go forth into all the earth is said to number "two hundred thousand." This number formerly would have been regarded as a wild flight of the imagination. Ten thousand times ten thousand makes 100 million, and double this runs up to two hundred million. All the men under arms in the late world war, not in Europe alone, but in Asia, China and Japan, as well as in America and Africa would hardly reach this number, though it would not fall far short of it. In the Netherlands one fourth of the population was in military service. In the belligerent countries it was one seventh, and divide the almost 1600 million of the earth by seven and we are in excess of the two hundred million. We take pains to make this plain, because statements like this and others in the book of Revelation are so readily looked upon as pure play of the imagination, while in fact the further we advance on the way to the end of things, the more surely statements in Revelation like this prove to be well founded.

Little can yet be said of the description in vs. 17-19 of these sanguinary armies. The portrayal of the scene which these innumerable armies will create is again orientally mystical and is only dimly plain to us in very general outlines which we can not particularize. All we can gather from it points to the brute force and terrible powers of these armies to work havoc and dismay, and it is most worthy of note that their deadly power consists mainly of "fire and smoke and brimstone." In times past this could scarcely be taken otherwise than purely figurative. But according to later reports of war fire, smoke and brimstone play a more and more leading part in modern warfare. No one ever thought in bygone days that it ever could take place in measures such as we now see· But as actual fact we now see sword and gun more and more given the discard, while belligerents on both sides are more and more intent upon overwhelming each other by fire, smoke and brimstone. This calls for serious consideration. The apocalyptic prophecies shall all be strictly fulfilled, and in connection with this bear in mind that the prophet had a clear vision of the things which would come to pass in after ages, and so could announce them with surprising accuracy in the very form in which they now are seen. This applies, as was shown above, to the countless millions of soldiers that are now in uniform, as well as to the implements of war at the disposal of these millions—notably fire, smoke and brimstone.

Without going further into the figurative language which describes the appearance and equipment of these armies, it should be noted that even the prodigious slaughter on the fields of battle did not turn those that escaped, to better thoughts. So we read in the 20th verse: "And the rest of the men that were killed by these plagues yet repented not of the works of their hands, that they should not worship devils, and idols of gold, and silver, and brass, and stone, and of wood: which neither can see, nor hear, nor walk: Neither repented they of their murders, nor of their

sorceries, nor of their fornications, nor of their thefts." This too
should be considered in the light of the great changes which since
the late great war have come upon all the world. This prophecy
too in bygone times was looked upon as of little moment to us, as
wars were then waged mainly in Europe, and in Europe worship
of idols was out of date. But there has come a change even in
this. We read in our daily papers that the great world action
is no longer confined to Europe alone, and that the heathen nations in other parts of the world are more and more to be reckoned with. In the World War Japanese and Indian soldiers and
officers took part on European fields of battle. From Africa came
bands of darker hue. That the problems that confront the world
are no longer exclusively to be handled by the nations that have
been baptized, no one will deny. Now that China and Hindustan
have entered the arena of the world's life, the prophecy of Rev.
9, 20-21 is almost literally being fulfilled. Heathendom comes
more and more to the front, and in an unprecedented way slaves
to idols are participants in the settlement of world problems.

This is deeply significant to him who accepts the authenticity of
the Apocalypse, because even one hundred years ago all this was
but cursorily read and no one thought all this could ever be fulfilled; and naturally unbelieving majorities now do not incline to
recognize in current events the fulfilment of apocalyptic prophecy.
Yet he who accepts that prophecy can not deny that in recent
years whole series of phenomena have presented themselves which
exactly square with what the Apocalypse foretells; and especially
since the world war positive indications are abroad that apocalyptic predictions, whose fulfilment almost no one expected, have
now surprisingly and almost literally materialized, and the question is whether the Consummation is not already close at hand.
As regards Paganism, this fulfilment of prophecy has not only
shown itself in the presence of heathen troops in the war of 1914,
but even more pronouncedly and subtly in the sympathetic attitude of the more highly cultured classes in Christian lands
toward the heathen sentiments of Plato, Aristotle and Buddha.
And this makes one ask whether this spread of heathen cults
among Christian nations does not clearly show that even now
the closing verses of Revelation 9 are lamentably yet strikingly

confirmed by what real life gives one more and more to see and hear.

We do not enter here into what is told in chapter 10 of the little book which, even as to Ezekiel, is handed to St. John, though we may have to refer to it later on. Previous to the third woe, however, in chapter 11, 14, the appearance of the two Witnesses, which is still a part of the sixth trumpet, is highly important. From Revelation 11, 3 we learn, that with the sounding of the sixth trumpet two witnesses shall appear in the earth, who for a thousand two hundred and sixty days,—that is, almost four years, shall proclaim an entirely special message. The appearance of these two witnesses is extremely important, for so much as they shall sound a last call of grace to the world. Not as though these witnesses will appear as ordinary evangelists, by their inspiring word to call those that are not yet absolutely reprobate to repentance. This is not the impression that is given by what is said of their ministry. Rather both these witnesses are imposing personalities which could not but occasion terror and dismay among the still sensitive multitudes. "Fire would proceed out of their mouth, and would devour their enemies," as we read in v. 5, " and if any man will hurt them, he must in this manner be killed." Instead of persuasively presenting the Gospel invitation, these witnesses dispense terrible reproof. "These have power to shut heaven," so reads v. 6, "that it rain not in the days of their prophecy: and have power over waters to turn them to blood, and to smite the earth with all plagues, as often as they will."

These witnesses remind us of Moses in Egypt rather than of Jesus in His Sermon on the mount. Yet it must not be overlooked that, even as Moses, they were able to bring to conversion those that had any susceptibility left; and in this sense it must be confessed that in these two witnesses the last call of grace is consummated. But it was of no avail. Antichristian action had gone too far, and soon the cruel representative of antichrist, in the form of the first beast, would overcome and kill the two witnesses. Instead of grief, this would create hellish joy among the nations. Even their dead bodies would not be given burial. As objects of mockery they were to lie in the street. Says v. 10; "They that dwell upon the earth shall rejoice over their death, and make merry, and shall send gifts one to another." This lasted but three and a half days, For then "new life from God entered into them, and they stood upon their feet; and great fear fell upon them which saw them." But they did not remain in the earth, for "they heard a great voice from heaven saying unto them, Come up hither. And they ascended up to heaven in a cloud." This made a deep impression. And we read that in that same hour there was a great earthquake, in which were slain of men seven thousand; but we also read that there was a remnant into whose souls the fear of God entered, and 'they' gave glory to the God of heaven (v. 13). And with this the second woe is past.

XIV

THE HEAVENLY VISION. (Revelation 14)*

*And I saw another angel fly in the midst of heaven,
having the everlasting gospel to preach unto them that
dwell on the earth, and to every nation, and kindred,
and tongue, and people.* Rev. 14, 6.

While from here to the end of chapter 12 the effect of the last
trumpets is more fully described, and the account of the seven
last plagues only begins with chapter 15, the 14th chapter stands
in between, which has frequently given rise to misunderstanding.
Even Kliefoth makes it seem as though the content of chapter
14 is an isolated phenomenon on a par with the seven seals, the
seven trumpets and presently with the seven vials, and thus,
as a fourth group of visions should be placed between the trumpets and the vials. So there would not be a series of *three,* but of
four great revelations, in which case the action of Christ and of
the six angels in chapter 14 would be like that of the seals, the
trumpets and the vials. Some go even yet further in this. For
after the outpouring of the vials, there still follows a final act
which ends the Apocalypse, and as in this closing act there also
appear seven angels, it is inferred that there actually are not
three, nor even *four,* but *five* series of visions. Notably Kliefoth
reckons with five series of major importance : (1) the seven seals,
(2) the seven trumpets, (3) the seven angels of chapter 14, (4)
the seven vials, and (5) the seven angels which bring the Apocalypse to a close. This calls for a careful examination of chapter
14 to see what it really portends. We should clearly understand
whether the angels in chapter 14 form an independent whole, like
the seals, the trumpets and the vials, or whether they stand apart
from these series, and merely refer to the ordinary, normal actions in this earthly life for which the Lord our God so often has
employed His angelic host. The difference here is great. God's

---

*In the original "The Heavenly Vision" covers chapters XIV-XVIII.

action upon His world by angels is an entirely common and universal phenomenon. In distinction from this the seals, the trumpets and the vials are one coherent prophecy. Hence the question is whether the actions of the angels in chapter 14, and afterwards those at the close of the Apocalypse bear the same peculiar character as those of the seals, the trumpets or the vials, or do they stand apart by themselves as ordinary, normal actions such as God has so often been pleased to work by His angels.

Many commentators, including Kliefoth, have been misled by the number seven. As there are seven seals, seven trumpets and seven vials, and as both before as well as after the vials there are seven intervenient and subsequent phenomena, it has been inferred that also the latter phenomena form series that are on a par with, and of like significance as, the seals, the trumpets and the vials. But this will not do. Impartial and unprejudiced examination of the rich content of chapter 14 shows that nothing is said of seven such angels that constitute a solidary group. Chapter 14 records in the first place an appearance of Christ, and after that, not *seven* but *six* actions that are performed by angels. To evade this difficulty, it is said that the Son of God has at times appeared in the form of an angel, as for instance to Abraham. But this is not entirely correct, as the Son of God appeared to Abraham in human form. One can say that angels too have appeared in human form, which we gladly admit; but from this it does not follow that the Son of God first assumed an angel form, and then as an angel appeared in human form. So this can be laid aside as of little significance. In chapter 14 there is an appearance of Christ, but not a word is said of Christ appearing in the form of an angel. What there we read leaves no room for this idea.

Read carefully what vs. 1-5 in chapter 14 have to say of this appearance of Christ. "I saw, so the apostle writes, and, lo, a Lamb stood on the mount Sion, and with Him an hundred forty and four thousand, having His Father's name written in their foreheads." That this refers to Sion in heaven and not to the temple in Jerusalem, goes without saying. The whole representation carries us up into heaven and gives us a place in the glory of the redeemed. Of the tabernacle the Scriptures tell us that it was built after the model of it in heaven. The forms of taber-

nacle and temple are temporal and pass away, what remains and
so bears an ever enduring character is the Sion above, the sanctuary about God's throne· So when according to the text the
Lamb stood on the mount Sion, it means that in heaven the Lamb
of God is triumphantly exalted. Also that there the Lamb is
surrounded by the hundred forty and four thousand of the redeemed, having the Father's name written in their foreheads. In
the second verse St. John expressly adds that he heard a voice
from heaven, the voice of harpers harping on their harps, but of
such volume of heavenly fulness that to him it seemed "as the
voice of many waters, and as the voice of a great thunder." And
where did they sing? According to v. 3 those heavenly hosts
were not singing on the earth but "in heaven before God's
throne." which is further confirmed by the saying that they sing
"before the four beasts, and the elders," all of whom are in
heaven before the throne of God. And finally it is said that "no
man could learn that song but the hundred and forty and four
thousand, which were redeemed from the earth" (v. 3).

Thus there is no intimation here of what shall affect the life
of the church *on earth.* We are permitted here a look into the
superearthly, into the heavenly life, and the 144,000 here are
spoken of as Christians who had ended their earthly course, had
stood their ground in the midst of bitter persecutions, and as
martyrs had entered upon eternity. "These" we read in v. 4,
"were redeemed from among men, being the first fruits unto God
and to the Lamb. And in their mouth was found no guile: for
they are without fault before the throne of God." All this admits
of no doubt whatsoever. Nothing is here said or prophesied of
what shall presently *take place* in the great struggle *on earth*
between faith and unbelief. The great struggle between the world
and the church of Christ is of agelong standing. By thousands,
and tens of thousands believers have run their earthly race and
have entered upon glory, and while at the hand of this vision we
are spectators of heavenly scenes, we hear the song of praise that
is sung unto the Lamb, not here on earth, but above, and in holy
harmony the praises of the Lamb are sung by the four beasts, the
four and twenty Presbyters and the 144,000 that are already
blessed. So, here, nothing is said of angels, and nothing is said
that savors of a prophecy concerning things that are to transpire

on this earth. What we here read affords us a look into the life of the redeemed above, whose heavenly blessedness amidst holy heavenly scenes is vividly portrayed, and we hear the harmonies of the jubilant song of the redeemed before the throne of God sounding forth the praises of the Lamb. The most careful reading of these five verses brings no intimation to our mind of an appearance of angels. The scene they describe has nothing in common with it, and stands by itself alone. The attempt to turn this inset of chapter 14 as by magic into an appearance of angels must therefore be set aside, and it is a matter or regret that even Kliefoth subscribed to this incorrect view and did not hesitate to assign Revelation 14, as a similar series of prophecies, a place between the trumpets and the vials.

And yet this view must be discarded. Vs. 1-5 do not introduce angels, but the Son of God, and do not deal with things to come, but what in heaven is already materialized. The rest of chapter 14 introduces not seven, but six angels, in which there is nothing uncommon or abnormal. Angels have always been the middle-links, if we may say so, which establish the coherence between our life on earth and the over-ruling providence of God. This is not always apparent, neither is it always indicated, but in this instance it was necessary, because the trumpets were now ended and with the vials the last period begins. Now all action went out from God. Every impulse and operation is from Above. And this is always indicated in Scripture, as in this instance, by pointing to the mediating operation of the angelic host.

This does not say that at other times the angelic host is inactive. It may rather be assumed that angelic activity is continuous, though not displayed before the human eye and only in special cases is observable by man. The angelic host is so enormously great in numbers as to make it unreasonable to assume that they are active only at those times when so stated in Holy Scripture. So we must assume that the angels are always at work, though only in special cases we are made aware of it. Note what is said of Satan regarding this. He too was an angel whose action on the world has been constant from the hour of the fall. Our own heart bears witness to the seductive suction that goes out from Satan to annoy and pursue us almost daily. Were this not so, Jesus in the Our Father would not have put as daily prayer the supplication in our lips: "Deliver us from Evil". No one can presume that in this prayer which He gave us for daily use our Lord would have introduced this petition so emphatically, if it only covered the case at special times and on highly exceptional occasions. There is no petition, for instance, in the Our Father, for healing of sickness and disease. So we conclude that the menace of fallen angels is one of the dangers to which we are exposed every day of our life, and against which we are hence in daily need of God's protecting care. And if this shows that fallen angels every day seek to be in contact with us, it follows that holy angels who are charged to watch over and protect us must likewise do the same *every day,* yes *every moment.*

Jesus never loses sight of the relation between the world of angels and the world of our earthly life. Think of the petition: "Thy will be done on earth as it is in heaven." In the Our Father our *daily* life reflects itself, not what only occasionally occurs in our life. We pray for our *daily* bread, and for provision in every need that occurs each day in our life upon earth. So it must be understood that our contact with the world of angels, of evil and of good, is a matter of *daily* occurrence. Of course this contact with the higher world differs, in that it is either common or uncommon. Though every day some evil angel knocks at the door of our heart to tempt us, some days we are little aware of this demoniac influence, while other days temptation violently assails us. But as we are open to demoniac influence, we are likewise open to the protecting influence of holy angels. Also this protection can one day be very striking and another day scarcely be perceived. Both Satan's attack on Jesus and the angel-watch in Gethsemane were exceptional, though Satan's attack was more violent.

This being so, it goes without saying, that the more the Consummation draws near, and with it the final conflict between God and Satan, the more these demoniac attacks increase in malignant intensity. Naturally therefore in Rev. 14, with the transition of the trumpet to the vials, both the action of evil angels and the counteraction of good angels are in greater evidence. It would have been unnatural if, in that hour of greatest danger, the holy angels had not done their utmost to avert the power of Evil. It is no surprise therefore that in Rev. 14 the holy angels are presented as ceaselessly on the watch for God's honor and the salvation of His elect, and that here, more than elsewhere, these *holy* angels appear in the fore, and are pointed out as with the finger. They are not there by chance, and it is not enough to show that they labor in behalf of salvation; it must also be shown that their constant effort is to carry God's plan into execution and with it to protect believers, and also to make God's wrath against the unholy break out more visibly. Hence it is nothing strange that here the action of the angels to carry out God's counsel into effect is introduced, not as an aside, but as a necessary and impressive occurrence. Angels have this peculiarity that they can function in the execution of divine commands invisibly and imperceptibly, as well as, when the case requires, visibly and perceptibly. As instances of the latter recall the heavenly choirs in the fields of Ephrata, later in the temptation of Christ in the wilderness, and later still in Gethsemane. So it was entirely natural that, when after the trumpets, the vials were to appear, the action of the angels should be out in the open and show itself in objective reality. Thereby indeed the great process of the Consummation advanced a considerable step forward, and it scarcely could be otherwise than that here should be repeated on a larger scale what had presented itself in connection with the temptation in the wilderness and other occasions, that is to say, in the execution of their sacred functions angels were bound to come out from the invisible into the visible.

All this however, and this is the point, has nothing to do with the succession of the seals, the trumpets and the vials. This appearance of the action of the angels is entirely ordinary, though as a rule we are not aware of it and only at times this action comes within the sphere of our human observation. But that which announces itself as prophecy in the three series of seals, trumpets and vials, bears an altogether independent prophetical character. Note in this connection that what is called apocalypse, in reality is prophecy. Apocalypse is the removal of the cover that conceals the mystery, and merely intends to give prophecy, but prophecy of a given character, even such that it sketches for us in clear outline the last days of the Consummation. This has nothing to do with the ordinary actions of the angels upon our life. Such a prophecy or apocalypse affords us a deeper look into the approaching future, and gives tne fixed order of succession in which the coming events will follow upon one another. Hence the fixed course of the approaching things, which begins with the *seals,* in which God's counsel discloses itself. These are followed by the *trumpets,* which announce the great war that in judgment is waged against the sinful world. And as everything totters and collapses, and the vials put an end to the existing state of things, and whatever set itself up in opposition to God is destroyed, the process has run its course, and nothing more can come save the passing away of what is and the triumphant manifestation of the *new earth* under the *new heaven.* Withal the activity of angels steadily goes on, of good angels and demons, and Rev. 14 depicts this constant activity of the angelic host with irresistible insistency.

Hence it is of utmost importance that it be well understood that what chapter 14 describes does not take place on earth, but in heaven above. In the first place we learn what the Lamb of God is doing, and that He takes part, in anticipation, as it were, in what is to take place on the earth. And not only He, for the angelic choirs also are deeply concerned with it all. They are vitally interested in what is to take place in the earth. The great conflict that is about to take place on earth is determined upon by a decree from Above, and the angels of God who are to play a part in it, in anticipation already live in what is to eventuate. They know what they will be permitted to do in it and what they will be privileged to accomplish. And before it takes place they are keenly alive to it all. They do not need to wait until as with eyes they shall see what is about to happen, for they see and feel already now in anticipation what is to come. And so is made plain to them, in a series of visions, what once shall be the historic ending of life here below. The first is that the Gospel shall not limit itself to the small circle that in St. John's days had received the glad tidings, but presently goes forth to all dwellers upon earth, to every kindred and nation (v.6); which glorious prophecy goes hand in hand (v. 7) with the admonition to forsake vanity and give God the honor of all things. Over against this glorious call comes in the second place (see v. 8) the sight of fallen Babylon, which does not mean the ancient Babel but the whole unholy world power, The third angel (see v. 9) shows that the issue of what is saved, and what with the fall of Babel is lost, depends upon the beast that shall present itself in the antichrist. The decision of this shall announce itself. Every thing that makes choice of the beast of the antichrist, passes away for ever. And over against this v. 12 speaks of the patience of the saints, that keep the commandments of God and the faith of Jesus. Hence the order issued to St. John already now to write: "Blessed are the dead which die in the Lord from hence- forth: Yea, saith the Spirit, that they may rest from their labors; and their works do follow them" (v. 13).

In this vision Christ now appears a second time. A cloud sails in the heavens upon which sits one like unto the Son of man; not now as the suffering Lamb, but as the crowned King who triumphs and therefore holds the sharp sickle in his hand, which shall bring to nought and destroy what can not remain, "for the time is come to reap, as the harvest of the earth is ripe" (v. 15). Presently the angels also take a sickle and reap as Christ reaped. So the grapes of the vine of the earth are cast into the great winepress of God's wrath, and human blood is seen flowing out of the winepress even unto the horses' bridles and to a distance of sixteen hundred furlongs. This is an awful picture of what shall be the destruction of the apostate world, when it shall no longer be susceptible to conversion. All this is seen in anticipation by the angelic host above, as the advance reflection of what shall eventuate in the hour of the Consummation. It it not yet come. It still tarries. But in the sphere of the seals it is seen in advance and is shown to St. John in symbolic vision.

XV

THE SEVEN VIALS. (Revelation 14)

*And the seventh angel poured out his vial into the air;
and there came a great voice out of the temple of
heaven, from the throne, saying, It is done. Rev. 16, 17.*

We now come to the seven vials, with the outpouring of which
the end of the historic course of earthly life is reached. After
the vials other things will come to pass, but these will no longer
form a part of earthly history. When the seventh angel has
poured out the last vial, as we read in Rev. 16, 17, there came
a great voice out of the temple of heaven, and thus from the
throne-room of God's majesty, saying: *It is done,* which means
that the historic course has reached its end and that the Consummation is at hand. The word vial here affects one strangely because it is not generally used, or even known, as the name of a
drinking vessel. Druggists are more familiar with it, as in their
business a vial is a sort of bowl. The word comes to us from
the French. The French version of the Bible uses the word
coupe, but in English the word used is vial, which is derived
from the Greek, and according to Rabe seems etymologically
related with *pinein,* to drink. As the English vial and the French
viole or *fiole* are of similar origin, it seems that the word has
come to us from the French, and so has become current among
us. The Germans, including Kliefoth, prefer the word bowl, as
in Latin the word is *phiala.* So there is no need of changing the
word *vial* in our English version into *bowl.* This might do if it
were said that these vials were to serve as drinking cups. But
this is not so. These seven vials are vessels filled with the wrath
of God, which are now to be poured out by seven angels. So the
word *bowl* in the sense of a drinking cup would not be in place.
Though we admit that the word vial affects one strangely, yet
it is best to retain it. It means a vessel which is somewhat more
wide than deep, and contains the wrath of God, and from it,
seven times, came forth the wrath of God, as the seven angels

120

successively poured out the content of it on the earth, the sea, the fountains and in the air.

Note again how, even as the seals and the trumpets, these vials occur in fulness of number. In all three series the rythmic number seven appears. This must be emphasized, because this is not so with the angels in the 14th chapter, nor with those at the close of Revelation. There each time the number is six, with Christ as the seventh unit. As these are visions seen in heaven Christ appears as the Lamb, and again as the King of kings, surrounded by His angels which do Him service. But with the vials the angels appear as an independent group, and their number seven is left intact to indicate that in the historic course that is here described, they hold an independent position. It must be admitted that the visions in chapter 14, in which Christ is seen together with six angels, are related to the angels with the vials, yet each is independent of the other. First in chapter 14, the heavenly prelude, so to speak, is shown, and only afterward, what was here merely prelude becomes reality. In the heavenly prelude everything passes pageant-like before the eyes of the angels as presently it is to become real, but only in chapter 16 does the reality, as on earth it was to show itself in the firmament, appear in the open, and so the latest period of history, as in the seven vials has been appointed of God, discloses itself.

In dealing with the seven vials we do not need to go back again to the visions in chapter 14, for they present nothing but what, immediately after, chapters 15 and 16 present in regular course. The only difference is that the visions in chapter 14 are the prospects, as in anticipation they are enjoyed by the world of angels above. There is naturally a radical difference between what the angels, as it were, see in advance, and what conform to this is presently to eventuate in the earth or in the firmament. The angels are conversant with what takes places on earth. It is no news to them, as in the world above what is and is to come in the earth is not vainly surmised, but as in image clearly seen.

Hence there is nothing enigmatical or inexplicable in the fact that, in the sanctified visualization, Christ and His angels have lived in advance through all that is to be materialized in the era of the vials. Hence that in chapter 14 we are told, as already present in the mind and imagination of the heavenly spirits, what appears in chapters 15 and 16 as only afterwards to have been realized on earth. The only question now is, why this which was lived through in heaven as in holy ecstacy before it is materialized on earth, is shown with the vials, while with the trumpets, to which the same applies, nothing is said of this. Let us therefore first of all, put the question why, with respect to the same course of events, we here have first set forth the highly imaginative life of heaven and after that the real life on earth.

In answering this question we must rest assured that, as with the vials, so with the seals and trumpets the angelic hosts are vitally concerned with what is to take place on earth. Let us not lose from sight the explanation in 1 Cor. 13, 12. There we are told that in the stirring events of the world's life we do not see God's counsel in reality, but as in a glass darkly, so that everything makes not a dim, but rather a dark impression upon us. Yet, so the Scripture goes on to say, it will not be thus in the life above. For there we shall see face to face. Here we know in part, on the other side of the grave, in the life that is eternal, we shall know even as also we are known. If this applies to us after death, for so much as we have died in the faith, it applies also to the angels, in short to all of the heavenly life. Darkness and obscurity, that here weigh upon our insight and perception, will pass away and our knowledge will be all-sided and clear.

This must be strongly emphasized. The general impression is that, while earthly life is active and full of all sorts of interests, life in heaven is one of solemn stillness which is broken only now and then by an anthem sung by the angelic choirs. But this is incorrect. Christ, the angels and the redeemed lead not only after the Consummation, but already now, an active life that is rich and full of all sorts of absorbing interests. The Son of God not only functions constantly as both High Priest and King, but also lives in unbroken fellowship with angels and with saints. Of course we find it extremely difficult to form any idea of the social state in heaven; but this is certain, that in the Father's house there is commerce which Christ maintains with His angels and the companies of the Redeemed, and this furnishes the key to the otherwise so inexplicable 14th chapter of the Apocalypse. Only the strangeness in this chapter accounts for the questionable explanations of it that abound. In the Dutch Bible take the marginal reading on the sixth verse, where the reference is said to be not to real angels, but to believers of high eminence in the earth, who thus are spoken of as angels. So it reads: "These angels we understand to be the faithful witnesses of Christ and preachers of the Gospel at the time when anti-Christendom is at its height, who openly warn the world against it." The arbitrariness of this explanation is obvious. The appearance of an angel is recorded six times, and every time it is an angel who knows the secrets of the future and proclaims them. And all this is taken as pure form of expression and understood as the appearance of human witnesses in the earth. In Rev. 1, 20 the pastors of the seven churches are spoken of as angels, as it reads: "The seven stars are the angels of the seven churches," but this is explained by the double meaning of the Greek word: *Angelos*. Angelos means *messenger* as well as *angel*. Hence this interpretation can not satisfy. The scene enacted here is not in the earth, but in heaven, and these six spirits here appear in their nature as angels of God.

We only reach a reasonable interpretation of chapter 14, when what it presents is understood of the commerce of Christ with His angels in the house of the Father. And Christ and His angels are in constant fellowship with the church in the earth. They are not mere spectators of what takes place on earth, but from heaven they direct the life of God's church on earth. Thus Christ and His angels are continually concerned with the life of His militant church. They do not merely look upon but act upon it. They are keenly alive to future happenings in the earth and they further their coming. Having this in mind we come to an understanding of this 14th chapter. It carries us up into heaven and gives us to see the life of holy intimacy that there is lived by Jesus and His angels and the companies of the redeemed. Hence there are no seven angels here, but Christ appears, and, as in consultation and cooperation with Him, one angel after another acts, and mirrors to us as it were, what is to come. The chapter transports us into the holy company above. In that company Christ is the Headperson and Leader. Therefore vs. 1-5 first point to Him, center all attention upon Him, and deal solely with Him. Only after that are the angels introduced. Now this one, then the other. Successively one after the other speaks. And thus the topic of conversation in this holy company is the course of events that presently will come to pass in the earth. As in a public meeting now one and then another speaks, while the matter in hand is discussed under the inspiring leadership of the chairman, so it is here. The Lamb of God, as the High Priest, begins the program, which provides the angels opportunity in advance to live through, as it were, what is to take place and to explain each his own part therein. It is no news to them, for they know and see what is to come. And now one angel after the other speaks his mind in respect to this; and for this reason it reads each time: "I saw another angel . . " "Another angel came out of the temple." "Another angel came out from the altar." What actually happens in heaven is here circumstantially told. Angel after angel, each in turn expresses in words what is depicted to him in his holy imagination of things to come in the earth.

So we must set aside the misleading representation, which all too many form of life in heaven, in distinction from our life on earth. It is not true that whereas life on earth teems with interests of all sorts, life in heaven is dull, and its monotony is broken only now and then by an angelic song. On the contrary it is our earthly life that is depressed and circumscribed, while the holy, glorious life of Christ and His angels and the Redeemed in heaven far exceeds in richness of interests and freedom of action our drab life here on earth. And here a glimpse is afforded us of that rich, holy life of heaven; and only with this in mind can justice be done to chapter 14. It follows that this occupation of Christ and His angels with what is to come is not confined to this instance alone, but incessantly goes on; the difference being merely that with the seals and trumpets, St. John was not told of it. Only in respect to the incidents of chapter 14 was this done, and it is not difficult to understand why it was not done before. The seals did not bring in the end. They were followed by the trumpets, and upon these presently the vials were to follow. So the transition from one to the other was obvious and needed no explanation.

But here the mutual relation presents itself in an entirely different way. After the seals came the trumpets, which in turn were taken up and carried further by the vials; but after the vials there was nothing more to come. The last word of the vial-angels would be; "It is done." But though in our language this expression can not reproduce with equal force the finality of the Greek word: *Gegone,* nevertheless it states the fact that now the course of events has come to the Consummation and that in this mighty process there was nothing more to follow. But this could not be foreseen and therefore had clearly to be declared. St. John must not be led to expect that after the vials a fourth group of events was to come. No impression was to be conveyed that the series of historic events would uninterruptedly go on. We know enough of the danger of such an interpretation from what, especially in our days, again and again renews itself as future expectation. How few people labor under the presentiment that the end of things is begun and the Consummation is at hand! The majority of those who express their feeling regarding the future of this world's life, have nothing to say of what Christ and His apostles have positively foretold. It is indeed commonly held that, while mundane affairs will assume new shapes, they will steadily go on. The Consummation is not wanted, and heavenly things are taboo. Preferably nothing is said of a new earth under a new heaven. It is granted that such has been foretold by Old Testament prophets and by Christ Himself, and after Him by His apostles; but this concession is all it means, and no further heed of it is taken. Note how even in these days of general unrest the world over, Christian writers scarcely so much as suggest the coming Consummation. Naturally the man of affairs in public life is not interested in anything that portends the coming of the end; but for this reason chapter 14 puts a special emphasis upon that end of things.

Everything here concentrates itself in this one word: *Gegone,* that is to say, "It is done." This emphatically tells the church of Christ that earthly life will not ceaselessly go on; that some day it shall end; that every experience of life, of sorrow and of joy, is but a preparation for the end; and when the vials are poured out life here on earth will cease. To make this evident, yes to bring it out in bold relief, here and here alone we have the record of the expectation of the end as in anticipation it is visualized in heaven. It was plainly to be understood that after the vials there would be no fourth lengthening of life in the earth. That impression was to be averted, and all expectation cut off that earthly life would extend itself and again in modified form go on. No matter how long life's burdens had been carried, it would not go on forever. Toleration of unholiness of life could only be justified by the final ending of the conflict between holiness and sin in the utter destruction of the demoniac and the triumph of the holy which nothing can avert. So it had always been preached in Israel; so it had been foretold by Christ; and so it had been confirmed by the Apostolate. There was to be no vestige of doubt about it. Hence it was absolutely necessary to ring in, as it were, the coming of the vials by a positive asseveration that now the end had come and the Consummation had begun.

Hence it will not do with Kliefoth to put this angelic testimony in chapter 14 on a par with the seals, the trumpets and the vials, as though *four* revelations were given one after the other. The content of this chapter is entirely peculiar by itself, has an entirely independent object in view, and by affording us an insight into the life above solely tends to confirm the positive certainty of the coming Consummation.

XVI

THE CONTENT OF REVELATION FOURTEEN

And I looked, and, lo, a Lamb stood on the mount Sion,
and with Him an hundred forty and four thousand,
having His Father's name written in their foreheads.
Rev. 14, 1.

As we proceed upon a fuller examination of chapter 14, let it
be noted that this chapter forms one coherent whole. It has
been tried to separate the appearance of the Lamb in vs. 1-5 from
what follows; but this will not do. The words in v. 6: "And I
saw another angel," refers to what went before, as these words
by themselves alone are unintelligible. When it reads: And I
saw another angel, there must have been angels in what went
before, who took part in the vision. This is almost selfevident
since St. John saw the Lamb standing on the mount Sion, provided this is understood of the heavenly Sion and not of the
Sion in Jerusalem. If Christ is dealt with here as after His
Ascension He dwells in the heavenly Sion, it goes without saying that there He is surrounded by angel guards. This is con-
tested by the commentators who maintain that the Sion here is
the earthly Sion, but to us this seems indefensible. Christ is
here spoken of as the Lamb, but when for His final triumph He
comes down to earth, He comes not as the Lamb, but as the
triumphant King. But there is more that here excludes the
earthly Sion, and compels us to apply what here is said to the
heavenly Sion. He who has travelled in Palestine, and has
seen the mount Sion at Jerusalem, as the writer has, knows that
this little mountain can not be said to accommodate 144,000 believers. Yet so we read in v.1: "And I looked, and, lo, a Lamb
stood on the mount Sion, and with Him an hundred forty and
four thousand, having His father's name written in their foreheads." This could be said of the heavenly Sion but is not applicable to the Sinaitic hill across from the mount of Olives.
Also what immediately follows points to the heavenly Sion. St.

John hears a voice of praise from afar, and expressly states that he heard this voice *from heaven,* and that it was so great and impressive as to have the sound of many waters and as of a great multitude, which as it drew nearer sounded as the voice of harpers harping with their harps. This heavenly song did not turn itself toward the earthly Sion, but toward the throne of God.

This appears from v. 3, which reads that these singers sang their song as "a new song before the throne, and before the four beasts, and the elders," which in the nature of the case can only refer to the heavenly Sion. There, according to Rev. 14, is where the four beasts and the twenty four Presbyters were, and not at Jerusalem. The same is implied by the additional statement that "no man could learn that heavenly song but the hundred and forty and four thousand, which were redeemed from the earth" which can only mean that they had already arrived in the heavenly Sion. All this is selfevident so soon as it is recalled and noted in this connection, that the earthly tabernacle and temple were but weak imitations of the glory of the Sion and the temple above. Already Moses taught this, and all Scripture confirms the impression that life in the heavenly sanctuary around God's throne is not formless and drab, as in that heavenly Sion there is an effulgence of glory compared with which all the earthly wealth of Jerusalem's sanctuary fades, as it were, away into nought. If these 144,000 "were redeemed from the earth" and have part in the song of the blessed, they are no longer in the earth but have entered upon the glory of heaven. This is confirmed by what immediately follows. As we read in v. 4: these 144,000 "were not defiled with women, for they are virgins, and they follow the Lamb whithersoever He goeth. These were redeemed from among men, being the first fruits unto God and to the Lamb." There would be no sense in this if these believers were still in the earth. For while in their earthly state they might be said to be single, it could not mean that they would remain so. Hence it is only when we take these 144,000 as martyrs who have fought their last fight and have triumphantly entered upon eternity, that these readings have any sense. Also the closing words in v. 5 can not refer to mount Sion at Jerusalem. They read: "And in their mouth was found no guile: for they are without fault before the throne of God." This can not be said of people that are still in the earth, as in this dispensation sin cleaves unto the greatest of saints, and no one on this side of the grave is sinless. That these 144,000 are without fault before the throne of God but shows, that the reference here is to believers that have left earth far behind, and now before God's throne as blessed children of God are indeed "without fault."

Of course the angels were witnesses of this heavenly scene, in which the Lamb of God, surrounded by the redeemed, as it were, calls in the end. In the heavenly Sion the Lamb can not be thought of apart from His angels. Even the throne of God is no lonesome place of honor where no creature has a place, and where silence reigns supreme. As often as a glimpse is afforded us into the higher life we see the Majesty of God closed in, as it were, on every side by Seraphs, Cherubs and other angels, together with the companies of the redeemed. Having this in mind there is nothing strange about the words in v. 6: "And I saw another angel." In v. 2 we do not read that it was the blessed martyrs alone that sang a new song and played on harps, but that these 144,000 alone *could learn* that song. This indicates that it was not the redeemed, but other heavenly beings that sang this new song and played it on their harps, and that the 144,000 learned it of them, and then sang it after them. So the Seraphim and Cherubim and the angelic choirs began the triumph song, and after them the blessed took up the glad refrain. It is not fair to say, therefore, that vs. 1-5 have nothing to do with angels, for if not by name and surname, they deal with them in fact. There is no need of imagining here the presence of the angelic host, as it is implied in "the voice of harpers harping with their harps." Afterwards that song of praise was also sung by the redeemed, but it was first sung by other creatures of whom the blessed learned it, and "these others" can only have been the angels before God's throne.

If then in v. 6 we read: "And I saw another angel fly in the midst of heaven, having the everlasting gospel," the connection between this and what went before is very close. First we are told of the angelic choirs that sang the new song, and then that another angel showed himself. First the angels were taken en

masse, as they are before God's throne, and together raise their
jubilant song, and after that it is indicated that certain members
of this angelic choir have certain special things to do, and of
these angels six appear in turn. We repeat this number six, for
"another angel" appears only in verses 6, 8, 9, 15, 17 and 18, and
every attempt to make seven out of these six has miscarried. They
are six in number and no more, and that some commentator has
mistaken Christ for an angel is an exegetical blunder which we
have refuted above. What on the other hand has been too little
emphasized is that vs. 1-5 certainly do not speak of any one angel
in particular, but of the angelic host at large, in whose midst
are the four beasts and the four and twenty elders. So verses 1-5
do speak of angels, even with emphasis. Only, they deal with the
angelic host at large, while v. 6 very definitely introduces "another" angel who has a particular task to perform, and this goes
on to the end of the chapter.

That all this will come to pass only when the Consummation is
at hand, does not alter the fact that in the heavenly regions it
has already been lived through in advance. Everything that is to
come is already actual fact in the mind, in the representation and
imagination of Christ, of His angels and of His redeemed. Even
in our childhood days we know something of what living through
a thing in advance means. When a child has been invited to a
party, if he is at all of a vivid imagination, in happy anticipation
he enjoys beforehand all the pleasures and delights of the coming event. In later years this anticipatory enjoyment of things
grows considerably less, yet even with a wedding anniversary
both bride and groom enjoy in advance the coming pleasure.
Especially with young children the pleasure of looking forward
to a coming holiday is most pronounced, and not infrequently
gives rise to the complaint that the reality did not come up to the
anticipation. Imagination ran too high and expectation looked
for too much, than that reality could come up to it, and hence the
disappointment. But there can be no such disappointment here.
The coming joy of the blessed and of the angels does not only
correspond in part, but fully and entirely to what they have antici-
pated. Hence that in anticipation they already live in it. And only
so could the glory and the blessedness which Christ and His re-

deemed and His angels already now enjoy, be truly depicted by way of foretaste of what presently is to come.

The antithesis between our perceptions here on earth and life in anticipation of future events as it is enjoyed in heaven, very strongly expresses itself in this. If no prophecy had come to us regarding it, we might have a faint surmise but no certain knowledge of things to come. Now in some measure this foreknowledge is in hand. He who is versed in Scripture has a definite outlook upon things to come, which already now affords him comfort. We owe this anticipatory delight to the grace of God. Yet it offers but a very divided reality. Not alone that from these exalted thoughts we are diverted again and again by the cares of our so much lower earthly life, but when we try to understand something of the blessedness to come, which will also be our portion, it is all too strange to assume a fixed form for us. So there is nothing, about which opinions among believers differ so widely, as to what awaits us after death, and what the Consummation will bring to pass. Most people are content with merely a vague outlook upon future things, and they who take a more serious interest in these matters so rarely arrive at unanimity of feeling. One can almost say that at no point do representations differ so widely as where the question arises as to what the Consummation will bring. This often makes our insight into things to come so nebulous, and almost makes one shrink from entering more deeply into the study of it. But in the holy fellowship of Christ and His angels and the redeemed in the better life above, all this uncertainty of representation falls away. In the heavenly sanctuary the whole future stands outlined before the sacred perceptive faculty in clear perspicuity. There is no lack there of anticipatory representation by which the celestial inhabitants live already now with perfect accuracy in the things which the Consummation will bring to pass. It is only now and then that we direct our thoughts to the things that are to come, but in the sphere above the things that are to come are uninterruptedly and unceasingly alive in the representation. For no single moment does the Consummation cease to play a part in the lives of the saints above. Even if our knowledge of what in the life of heaven engages the mind and the thought and penetrates the inner perception is not entirely adequate, this much is certain, that the holy companies above, so to speak, never can cease from anticipating life in the Consummation.

That only in the chapter in hand an inspiring impression of this is given, tends to prepare us for the fact that presently the vials will end the process which the seals began. This does not mean that now the angels are told beforehand the prophecies about the seven vials that are presently to follow. In the world above one can not be engaged exclusively with one part of the great whole that will come to pass in the Consummation. In the higher world from which all action proceeds, one ever feels intensely interested in the sum-total of things to come. Hence these six angels here do not merely tell what is to be looked tor at the last moment, but speak out of the fulness of their own busy life. Their sacred task is to make ready what is to come, to introduce it, and to make it come to pass successively in all its parts. Hence chapter 14 is no literal communication of what presently, with the vials in chapter 15 and 16, is to follow. The program, if we may so call it, which the six angels present in chapter 14 is entirely different from what presently will follow in the prophecy of the vials. Chapter 14 presents the whole system of everything that from the world on high shall reveal itself in the earth, and by which whatever in God's providence has been determined with respect to the end of things shall be carried into effect. The vials give only the third or final scene: while on the other hand Christ and His angels and His redeemed in the holy company above are constantly engaged in preparing and making ready what in the end must come. The further analysis of what the six angels in this chapter announce, or communicate, will show that they reproduce almost the whole eschatological prophecy of Christ, in Matthew 24-25, while of course chapters 15 and 16 deal exclusively with the last part of it.

So this is not a simple repetition of things which the following visions will communicate in a more or less modified form. Chapters 15 and 16 constitute a wholly independent part of the Consummation, as it will eventuate in the earth, equally as independent and complete in itself, as were the seals and the trumpets. Only it comes *afterward* and forms the last act. The vials will end the whole process and at length everything will be summarized in the short saying: "It is done," that is to say, everything is now come to an end, the distance of the whole way is now covered. This third and concluding act is followed by no fourth or fifth. Here on the other hand comes the sure and indubitable indication from the angel world above, of which blessed world Christ is the center, that now everything is coming to an end, and what great events will introduce the same and bring it to pass. Thus the content of chapter 14 is entirely different from that of chapters 15 and 16. The latter merely describe the distinctive features of the final conflict, while the former depicts what in the unseen world around God's throne holds all of life in constant tension and is the subject of all thought.

The only difference is that in so far as also in the world above with the closer approach of the end the events of the past withdraw into the background, the spirits become more intent upon the things that now draw near. If the chapter in hand had been given after the seals and before the trumpets, the attention would not have been centered so fully, as now, upon what will prove to be the concluding act. Obviously when two periods out of three are ended, attention will more specifically turn to that last period. So here let us distinguish well. In the great process there are two kinds of actions. On one hand actions that unremittingly go on in all three periods, such as the preaching of the Gospel among all nations and peoples. Alongside of this there are events which in one period assume a different character from what they do in the other, as for instance the coming of the antichrist, which will strike the keynote of fiercest antagonism against the Holy and His people. As to the third and last period, that of the vials, obviously the first sort of action goes on as it did in both previous periods, but as regards the events that are still to come, in the third or last period there will be no repetition of what had come to an issue in either of the former two. Hence what the angelic world felt and experienced in advance at the approach of periods one and two, assumes an entirely different character at the approach of period three. And so when these six angels appear two things are dealt with: first that which from the beginning had unremittingly gone on, like the preaching of the Gospel among all nations, as was noted above, and secondly the new things that are now to come. So we see verses 6-20 of chapter 14 divided as into two parts. Part one, which treats of what is applicable to all three periods, and part two which deals with the new events to come which at length will conclude the process. Of necessity this second part required more fulness of detail.

In connection with this, Christ appears not only in the beginning of this chapter, but also in the middle part of it, and in entirely different forms. He appears in vs. 1-5 as the suffering Messiah, Who by His suffering redeems and saves His people, "I looked, and, lo, the Lamb stood on the mount Sion." Over against this in the 14th verse not the Lamb, but the crowned King of the Kingdom of God is the Rescuer, from Whom proceeds the power of salvation, but at the same time also the power of judgment. The first part of this chapter reveals nothing of the splendor of the Son of God, but solely the saving power which the Lamb of God is able to revive. They that here occupy the place of highest honor are the redeemed as first-fruits unto God and unto the Lamb, and the result of the salvation is, that they follow the Lamb whithersoever He goeth. But as in verse 14 the glory of Christ and the triumph over His enemies is celebrated, nothing is said of the Lamb; the cross, as it were, is gone; the marks of the suffering Messiah have given place to the crown of gold, indicative of the Kingly majesty of the Conqueror. And crowned with a golden crown, the Son of God holds a sharp sickle in His hand with which to destroy His adversary and to achieve the radical change of the whole universe. Thus according to the representation, as judge of the whole earth Christ comes down upon the clouds, and as we read in v. 15: to Him that sat on the cloud is spoken the word of majesty by an angel of God: "Thrust in thy sickle, and reap: for the harvest of the earth is ripe."

The subdivisions of this important chapter will be dealt with more fully later on, but now we offer the following resume. Chapter 14 is (1) the record of a vision that was shown to St. John, which he was to hand on to the church of Christ, to inform her that the time of the end is at hand and that the vials were to disclose the last apocalypse. The apocalypses were to be three in number — the seals, the trumpets and the vials which were to complete the process; (2) this vision does not take us to

the Sion at Jerusalem, but to the Sion above, where an insight
is given—not in what life on earth will further present but—
in what in the sanctuary above is the image of things to come as
it presents itself to Christ, to His angels and to His redeemed;
(3) this vision could have been given to St. John after the seals
and after the trumpets, but that there was no occasion for it then,
because at that juncture the end could not yet come, while here it
is entirely in place, because now the last part of the eschatological
process began, and St. John, as well as presently the church,
should understand that the vials would mark the end of earthly
history, and the new order of things would immediately ensue,
and by the execution of the judgment "the new earth under the
new heaven" would reveal itself; (4) the content of chapter 14
forms one whole, and does not divide itself into three, but into
two parts. To say that chapter 14, 1-5 belongs to what went before, and the vision in hand only begins with v. 6, is not correct.
The reverse is the case. The vision here consists of two parts
in both of which Christ directs the course of events; (5) in part
one Christ appears as the Lamb of God because the work of
redemption still goes on, and in part two Christ appears as King
and Conqueror, and as the Judge of the whole earth; and (6)
this look into the hidden world of heaven is no supplement of the
other visions, but means exclusively to show St. John and his
readers that the time of the end is come, and to make it plain
that the process that was going on had to unfold itself in its
three parts, and with the vials would conclude the eschatological
history.

XVII

THE FIRST, SECOND AND THIRD ANGELS
IN CHAPTER 14

*Here is the patience of the saints: here are they that
keep the commandments of God, and the faith of Jesus.*
Rev. 14, 12.

Now we come back to Revelation 14 to see what the message
of the six angels means.

The first of these six "other angels" in this heavenly vision
is seen flying "in the midst of heaven, having the everlasting
gospel to preach unto them that dwell on the earth, and to every
nation, and kindred, and tongue, and people, saying with a loud
voice, Fear God, and give glory to him; for the hour of his judgment is come: and worship him that made heaven, and earth, and
the sea, and the fountains of waters." Evidently this angel is
still in heaven from whence, as it were, he looks down upon the
earth. In looking down upon the earth from a great height one
is not so much impressed by the land as by the water. For there
is much more sea on our earth than land, and anyone looking
from the moon or from some planet through a telescope down
to our earth, would naturally be most impressed by these inter-
minable sheets of water. He who from the top of the highest
mountain in the earth would look out through the farthest reaching telescope would observe something in the distance of the
ocean, but would still be impressed that land was the main thing
on the earth and the water accidental. Yet he who from the
heights of heaven tries to see the whole earth at once, is first impressed by the immeasurable water surfaces, in which watery
depths the inhabitable earth, merely as a large part of the great
whole, seems to lie anchored.

By itself there was no occasion to call attention to the ocean
first. Of course there were ships abroad then but, compared
with the numbers that now traverse the seas, they were so few,
that by the side of the millions of people that dwelt on the land

the number of sailors counted for little. Yet from what the first angel said, we are rather impressed that what sailed and moved upon the waters was the main thing. Millions of people live on land, but the reference to them is extremely short, in fact consists but of one word. The text reads: "Worship him that made heaven, and earth," and this is all. It does not enlarge the idea of the earth by referring to its cities and towns, its villages and table-lands. It merely says *the earth,* without the addition of anything more, though what inhabited the earth was given the first consideration. But when the angel speaks of the waters he at once describes them fully, not merely as seas, but also as fountains of waters. What need would there have been of this, if indeed the speaker had stood upon the earth, and had merely looked abroad upon the inhabitants of the world. But seen from heaven the earth presented itself as here described, the firmament on high, then the land, and then in particular the immeasurable Ocean which, with the waters of lakes and rivers, breaks the surface of the earth. This is the more worthy of note as in the preceding verse the angel points to the whole population in the world divided into nations, kindreds and peoples, and distinguished by the languages they speak. Looked upon from on high the earth presents the image of vast waters, by the side of which the land in turn is washed through by the waters of rivers and lakes. But the spiritual knowledge which the angels have of the world of men here refers to the organic coherence of our human race with its rich distinctions in nations and kindreds and peoples, not only physically by color and form, but also spiritually segregated more still, than merely distinguished, by differences in language.

When one asks what engages the attention of the angel as he looks down upon our world, the answer is: *The Gospel.* For of him we read that he holds in his hand, as it were, the everlasting Gospel, not to keep it to himself, but to preach *unto them that dwell on the earth,* and this mass of people is not taken as a group of onelings and as individuals living by themselves, but as one organically coherent whole that on the part of God has been divided into nations and kindreds and peoples, even in this way, that the wealth of their allsided intellectual and spiritual life expresses itself in their several languages.

Thus this also shows itself as seen from heaven. On earth a look covers so little that we never see more than a small fraction of any people. So we almost never obtain a lasting impression of humanity as a whole. An occasional conference on a large scale will bring many thousands together, but even this can not convey an adequate impression of the many nations and peoples in the earth. But looking down from heaven the angels see our human race as a whole, which enables them to distinguish the many variations, together with the unity that organically binds them together. Hence the main thing here is, that they see the Divine idea of our human race vividly before them. For that Divine idea of our human race is not formed from its present state of deterioration, bastardization and division by sin, but from what originally God purposed it to be, and by creation adapted it to the realization of that purpose. The angels from on High do not see similar units and onelings, but traces and remnants of original solidarity, such as still characterizes our human race, in which, if we may say so, they were ideally present in the hour of creation. There were then but two human persons and presently with Cain and Abel four, but these four persons possessed all the data which, with proper development, would later gradually have shown themselves. In the variations, that solidarity has gradually become invisible to our eye. But not to the eye of the angels. From on Hgh they still see the traits and traces and lines of this original solidarity in our world of men which are still discernible to the practiced eye.

The angels still cherish this ideal conception of our human race, and so make much of the ties that organically still bind humanity together in kindreds, nations and peoples, as they present the diversified life which, well differentiated, distinguishably arises in their languages. This does not imply that all human languages arose from the original ordinance of creation. By the confusion that resulted from sin, language has not suffered less than anything else the loss of original purity, making all speech disingenuous. But also here it is not all pure arbitrariness and inglorious confusion. All differences in language originate from a fundamental variation, which from the creaton has characterized the speech of man. As we think of the language that is spoken in heaven, and of what the language shall be on the new earth under the new heaven, we need not conclude that one language will then be the sole means of speech. Variations, even rich variations are imaginable, without the loss of mutually understanding what is said. And so we can understand that in their fellowship above the angels, speaking of our world of men, picture to themselves the rich organic development that will characterize it on the new earth under the new heaven, both as organically one and yet as richly variated.

The saying of the first angel implies also that at the time of the end the Gospel shall have been preached to all nations, as well as that meantime Christ and His angels continually labor for the extension of the Gospel in all the earth. Not only do human agencies engage in the great work of missions, but Christ and His satellites continually act upon this missionary movement, and co-operate to achieve the high end which here they picture to themselves. Naturally in connection with this it will not do for one moment to represent world wide missions as really the result of the effort of the churches. The churches must co-operate, and no Christian is exempt from responsibility in this cause. And yet we are but instruments in Christ's employ, and the great work of adding souls to the numbers of the saved is always the result of the constant action of Christ and His angels, and of the missionaries as instruments, that goes out into all parts of the world. So there is nothing strange, but something absolutely indispensable in it, that this work of missions which applies its influence to the organic coherence of mankind should be the subject dealt with in heaven above by Christ and His servants. And so v. 6 reads that one of the angels had the Gospel, even the everlasting Gospel to preach, which naturally does not mean that he had a written Gospel in his hand, but only that the glad Tiding, which must call all peoples and all nations unto life, goes out, as it were, from heaven, to be preached here below, and thus at length to reach the whole world.

If herewith the task of the first angel is accomplished, in v. 8 we come to the message which the second angel brings. "And there followed another angel, saying, Babylon is fallen, is fallen, that great city, because she made all nations drink the wine of her fornication." One realizes the contrast between the messages of the first and second angels. The first angel spoke of what would bring the church of Christ to her richest revelation. He spoke of the Gospel which from Christ goes out to all nations in the earth, and of the organism of mankind which, thanks to this Gospel, would revive again in its original coherence in kindreds, nations and peoples. He brought to light what would bring the salvation of God's elect to pass., But with the second angel the vision turns away from the elect and the people that is to be saved, and deals with those that shall perish. "Babylon is fallen, is fallen, that great city," and such "because she made all nations drink of the wine of the wrath of her fornication."

And what are we to understand by this great Babylon?

Surely not the ancient city of Babylon that once dominated the whole region of the Tigris and Euphrates. What here is said of Babylon forms a vision that was shown to the holy apostle John on Patmos, when the new dispensation had begun and ancient Babylon and its world power had passed away. It had been destroyed by the Persians, and after the Persians Alexander with the Greeks had kept house there. That power once so great had utterly come to nought. Think of Antiochus Epiphanes. Then centuries afterward Roman rulers had come and had subjected all the tribes of the Kingdom of Alexander to themselves. The Romans had also taken possession of the holy land and their satrap had reared on Golgotha the Cross for Israel's Messiah, and in the year 70 their general had taken Jerusalem and well-nigh utterly destroyed it. Thus when a quarter of a century later St. John is told that Babylon is fallen, it can not hark back to the capture of Babylon by Cyrus five centuries before. So a literal interpretation will not do, and Babylon must be taken in the figurative sense, as that World Power which at all times has been inimical to the Kingdom of God, to Christ and to His church. Hence it is not strange that this World Power that is opposed to God is spoken of by the name of Babylon. It has not pleased God to create our human race in Europe, neither in Africa, but in the center of the great-Asiatic continent, in the very region where later the great Babylonian Empire took its rise. There may have been pitiful and distressing apostasy from God in other parts of the world, but this does alter the fact that both the creation of our human race, and the apostasy from God by sin, had taken place in central Asia, and that consequently the formation of peoples or nations was there begun. What Scripture records of the building of Babel's tower floods the meaning of this with clear light. The rulers which founded the first ordered institution of state in Mesopotamia were aware from the first of the danger that threatened their power, in case the masses turned away from them and scattered to East and West, to North and South in the wide world that was open to them. This urge to migrate to all parts of the earth was part of the divine plan. This inclination and tendency was bound to arise, but naturally it would decrease the population around Babylon and other, perchance dangerous, popular centers would be established elsewhere. So the course of events was foreseen. So it was bound to take place according to God's counsel. And so it actually has taken place in history.

This, however the State authorities in Babel tried to oppose. The steadily growing population was not permitted to spread itself abroad, all had to remain subject to the power of Babylon's Government, which would gradually obtain thereby domination over the whole world. Yet this was not the plan of the Lord, which was the free, rich development of mankind in all the earth, in all sorts of peoples and nations to make their way through the ages; while Babels' plan was to oppose and arrest this free development. If necessary by force of arms, everything had to remain together in closest union. The king of Babylon was to be master of all mankind, and not God's plan, but his, must prevail. And God has frustrated this plan. The tower of Babel, which was to serve this unholy plan came to nought. The power that frustrated the building of that tower came from heaven, and the spread of the nations and kindreds over all the earth began. And so Holy Scripture shows how this destruction of Babel's tower and this spread of the nations has dominated all the further life of mankind. This was not a spiritual action in itself, but rather one that took place by reason of national politics, and yet it was temporarily spiritual also, in so far as that life of the state that had wandered off from God, sought to establish a false religious power in the room of the true religion, and so idolatry and the demoralization that goes with it had been bound to give rise to a world that stood diametrically over against the holy.

To lay the foundation of a predominating vital principal, on which to found a world-plan that directly antagonized the counsel

of God, was plainly no local event that would affect but one
people, but a world event that would affect all nations for all time.
It would make itself felt, and work its way through, long after
Babylon had ceased to count, and other rulers had taken its role
in hand. But whatever subversive proportions presented themselves in connection with this, it always showed the ancient Babylonian trait, and it can still be said that it all sprang from Babel's
original intents and purposes. And this accounts for the otherwise strangely affecting fact, that Scripture always introduces this
world power that is inimical to God, by the name of Babylon or
Babel, even as the city, the great city Babylon. Nothing remains
of Babel but its ruins, but it is still called Babylon, because Babel's
restlessness marks the starting point of the world's development.
Here it began, and from here it has propagated itself to all the
great Powers of the world. And however much it spread and
divided itself and modified its form, it all sprang from the one
ancient selfsame root, ever bore in every way similar fruit, and
dominates now, as really as in the days of Babylon and Rome,
the whole course of human life. Hence, it is not said that the
strongholds of the great city Babylon would withstand all divine
supremacy. Cyrus's capture of Babel had shown the contrary. No,
the reference to Babylon as that *great city* has a different meaning. It indicates the radical difference between the influence upon
human life in the country and life in the city, which more often
than not concentrates itself in the thickly populated
parts of the world. New York dominates life in America, and in
Europe unquestionably London, Paris, Berlin and Vienna are the
four great capital cities from which the spirit of the nations
emanates. So it was from of old. In St. Paul's days the dominating influence emanated from Imperial Rome, reason why he was
so bent upon preaching the Gospel there. And thus it can and
must be granted that in the early days of the world power Babel
exercised the great moulding influence upon human life. In Babylon the great evil was begun. The unholy principles which gave
birth to the demoniac have from there been carried out into all
the world. So it is entirely natural that Babylon as the great
metropolis should for all time be the historic name of a demoniacal world life, that both in its beginning and in its course of
progress, as well as in its peculiar typification, wages war against

Almighty God. From of old the vigorous life of the great metropolitan centers of the world was the source from which falling
away from God and consequent demoralization springs. Where-
ever this now shows itself is, in principle, all one with what
sprang up in Babylon. And so Babylon, and notably Babylon as
the great city, is the immortal name that designates the demoniacal revolt of the sinful world against its God.

That after-effect of ancient Babylon is by no means yet arrested. It may rather be said that this spirit of ancient Babylon
seems to break out in the revolutionary circles of our times in a
way that was scarcely deemed possible before. The student of
ancient Babylonish history knows that here at least some religious
need still made itself felt. Abraham the patriarch came from the
land of Babel to Palestine. Again, the wise men of the East at
Bethlehem's crib bore witness to a religious need which had ever
been manifest in Babylon. Even in Nebuchadnezzar and Belshaz-
zar we see how in those ancient times something of the Paradise
tradition still lingered to good effect. But this would not keep on.
This appreciable religious element would steadily count for less,
until the antithesis between the heavenly of the High God and
the world-idea of the unholy world power would reach its climax.
And this the second angel announces. He gives us an insight into
what is well known in heaven, namely, that at the time of the
end this dreadful Babylonian power shall utterly be destroyed,
so that Babylon's cry of despair shall sound throughout all heaven
and re-echo in the earth. So we learn how already now in
heaven Christ and His angels see the future dawn, when Babel
and the spirit of Babel will be done for for ever. The word "fornication" is here used together with "the wine of wrath" to indicate that the sinful world power has ever been intent upon in-
fatuating the human spirit as in a state of intoxication; to make
one feel how this state of unholy excitement turns the sacred
character of tender passion into voluptuous wantonness; and how
age upon age God's wrath is turned against this unholy demoralization of life. So here also in v. 8 every word is given its full
due, and each word is significant, always provided that this
chapter be not made to refer to our earthly social state, but is
duly recognized as the subject matter that is dealt with above in
the intimate fellowship between Christ and His saints.

Of the third angel we learn that he gives his message "with a loud voice." This is not said of the first angel who preaches the Gospel, but of him who appears in v. 7 when "the hour of judgment" is come. Calling it ' a loud voice' implies that it is an expression of *the wrath* of Christ and His angels above, over against the sinful life of the world. From heaven it was always love seeking to save what could be saved, and this voice was always gentle and winning. But when it comes to the sin of the world, and the wrath of God against that sin, the gentle voice turns into one that thunders and becomes even a loud *cry* (v. 18). Almost the only attraction of the Gospel in general is the tender love of God, as the world has no use for the interpreters of God's wrath. It has often been a matter of surprise that when in the Psalms the singer calls down the wrath of God, he has not been rebuked. Read Psalm 73. But not so in the heavenly council above. When Christ above with His angels and saints anticipate what is to come, there is always a twofold drawing of the heart that operates with equal force along perfectly parallel lines. There is wondrous tenderness far surpassing all human love, and equally definitely and strongly holy wrath against every creature that comes short of the glory of God, and we hear the keynote of the saying: "Thou destroyest all them that go a whoring from thee" (Ps. 73, 27).

What this third angel says with a loud voice, refers to the misery that is worked by Satan and the great beast in the earth. "If any man worship the beast and his image, and receive his mark in his forehead, or in his hand, the same shall drink of the wine of the wrath of God, which is poured out without mixture into the cup of His indignation; and he shall be tormented with fire and brimstone in the presence of the holy angels, and in the presence of the Lamb. And the smoke of their torment ascendeth up forever and ever: and they have no rest day nor night, who worship the beast and his image, and whosoever receiveth the mark of his name." So with the third angel we pass from Babylon of the days of the first rise of world power to the time of the end. Age upon age the outlook had been hopeful upon some change for the better in the sinful life of the world, only to meet with disappointment in the fact that there is no diminution of evil, and that it is vain to expect it. That rather the demoniacal evil that more and more rules the world, steadily increases, expresses itself in a more and more pronounced form, and continually increases might, and that where at length the antichrist unveils himself, man, instead of becoming more spiritually minded rather bestializes himself, does not seek after God, but after the beast, in that beastiality does what idolatry did when it imitated God, and makes an image of the beast, even as Israel at Sinai made an image of Jehovah in the form of a golden calf, and now asks for a mark of appurtenance to the beast and his image, even as circumcision in Israel was the sign of appurtenance to the congregation of God. Neither can the referenc to the beast and his image surprise us. Where Satan as antichrist usurps the place of God, he too must have an image of himself, and where in idolatry man puts himself in the place of God, here in place of the image of the highest, is the image of the beast in all its hideousness, and circumcision is superseded by the mark in the forehead or in the hand. So these figurative expressions are quite plain. So also is "the wine of the wrath of God." Why is the wrath of God spoken of as wine? Drunkenness leads to sin and to doing mischief to one's neighbor. Crime records show how much murder has been committed under the overstimulation of wine. When under the power of the passion that wine arouses man assumes the right of doing away with what annoys him, it is plain when here by way of antithesis it is said of God, that that wrath against idolatry and the antichrist arouses a passion in Him, that makes Him turn unsparingly upon every demonical, uncompromising and cruel outbreak. It is even said that this wine of God's wrath is poured out *without mixture,* to indicate that forbearance has had its day, and that eternal misery awaits the man who defiantly and without repentance sets his face against the holy majesty of the Lord.

V. 12 adds: "Here is the patience of the saints: here are they that keep the commandments of God, and the faith of Jesus." In conclusion it means that the predominant antithesis is being consummated. That antithesis is the Triune God and His Majesty in heaven above, and over against this in the depth of perdition the antichrist, by whom Satan makes his final effort to put an end to the glory of God.

And between these predominating powers of God and Satan
stands the redeemed host which is to proclaim whose the triumph
is to be, God's or Satan's. They are said to be saints, even in the
twofold sense which must carefully be noted, namely that they
keep the commandments of God and live by the faith of Jesus.
This is as it were, the combination of Old and New Testaments,
in the Old Testament all effort being bent upon the keeping of
the commandments of God and in the New Testament all energy
being centered upon the faith of Jesus. Yet, if originally this
gave rise to conflict, so that the legal standpoint had to be abandoned, in the holy company here this conflict is ended, and now
in the keeping of God's commandments through the faith in
Jesus, salvation is sought and found.

Therefore v. 13 reads: "Blessed are the dead which die in the
Lord from henceforth," which means that thus far there had
always yet been a difference between the blessedness that is
already now enjoyed in the Father's house and the perfect bliss
that shall characterize life on the new earth under the new heaven.
But now that the end of the Consummation is at hand, even this
difference falls away. Believers on Jesus who are to die in the
final conflict previous to the Consummation, shall at once enter
upon the perfect glory and enjoy to the full everything that the
final outcome has in store for them. The faithful, who suffer
martyrdom in this last period, rest during the times that are still
to follow, in the enjoyment of their spiritual labor, and their
works do follow them.

In this glorious vision St. John sees the image of the final
outcome, such as Christ and His angels and saints are meantime
preparing and bringing closer to us. There are three effects of
what Christ and His angels are doing: (1) Christ unremittingly
holds out the offer of the Gospel to all peoples and nations, lest
so much as one of the elect should be kept in ignorance thereof
and the call of pardoning grace should not all along be sounded
in the earth until the very latest moment, and no joy should
abound in heaven over the glorious fact that there always will
yet be sinners that repent, even to the very last; (2) the proclamation by another angel that Babylon is fallen, which means that
Christ and His saints already now in anticipation live in the
glory that shall characterize life when once everything that sprang

from Babel shall have been destroyed, no more to be a blot on God's creation, and (3) there is a third angel who in the heavenly life above has an eye upon the holy flock of the Lord, in the last conflict supports the elect, leads them on to victory and in the end calls and brings them to eternal blessedness.

XVIII

THE PAROUSIA. (Revelation 14)

And the winepress was trodden without the city, and blood came out of the winepress, even unto the horse bridles, by the space of a thousand and six hundred furlongs. Revelation 14, 20.

So we come to the description of the parousia in v. 14: "And I looked, and behold a white cloud, and upon the cloud sat one like unto the Son of man, having on His head a golden crown, and in His hand a sharp sickle." Naturally this too is not to be taken literally, as though Christ already now came down to earth. We still have to count with visions, yet in this sense, that Christ and His angels will not reckon with the parousia as a far distant future event and in anticipation live in the same, but immediately after His Ascension began to reckon with it· Christ was in no need of a revelation or prediction of anything that was to come. The whole future course of things, the ingathering of the elect, the conflict between believers and unbelievers, and the coming of the final issue stood clearly imaged before the consciousness of Christ. So it would come and so it would be, not as a display of power outside of Him, the effect of which He was merely to observe, but rather that He Himself would materialize it all and bring it to the birth. As an architect has prepared the plan and all the specfications of the palace which he is to build before the ground is broken and the first stone is laid, and thus in advance has a clear vision of what is to come, so Christ has not wondered what might come to pass, but from the first has seen as before His very eyes, clearly and plainly, the whole plan of redemption and the ultimate aim, and has ever been busy with making every requisite for the realization of this plan turn from purpose into reality. The unity in the thought of this grand and comprehensive plan of redemption has ever since the Ascension engaged the mind and the imagination of Christ and His angels, and will so engage it until the end of time.

With this Divine plan before His eyes Christ has, as it were, in anticipation, lived in His parousia and has seen in advance everything that is to come to pass. This must the more firmly be held in mind, because the apocalyptic predictions of Christ in Matth. 24 and elsewhere always make the same impression. What is to come stands ever clearly before the eyes of Christ, and therefore what is to come, always presents itself in the apocalypse as immediately taking place. This too is immediately connected with the "Come, Lord Jesus, yes, come quickly!" Thus when to St. John, and through him to us, an insight was permitted in all this, everything in this vision was bound to present itself as though it were actually already taking place. With us there is always yet a considerable difference between what now is and what is to come, and what we observe shows merely in part what is coming. Naturally such is not the case with Christ. He knew already so well what is to come and what He is to bring to the birth, as to know the persons that are to take part in it; and though it is still a future event, He sees it so clearly now, that presently the reality itself can not make it clearer to Him, but rather shadow it.

When therefore St. John is given a wondrous glimpse into the life of heaven he observes, of course in a visionary manner, how Christ and His angels live in the things that are to take place at the parousia and in what the parousia itself shall be. This is strongly evident in what is here said of the cloud. That cloud is entirely accidental, and nothing would prevent us to think that Christ might return to earth on a day of a clear sky. To Christ on the other hand all this is so certain, even down to particulars, that He knows that that white cloud will be the first to attract attention to the fact of His coming. Also the sitting on that cloud strongly reflects the impression which believers in the earth will then receive of His coming. Yet the depiction of that white cloud could not have been omitted. For next to that white cloud we now read that as the sign of His glory, He shall appear with a golden crown on His head and with a sharp sickle in His hand. Even this, as the sickle most clearly shows, is all figurative language. The sickle is an implement in use with the culture of trees and of the ground, but not on the scaffolding of a building or on the field of battle where human life is cut off. So the word sickle shows that the thought here is figuratively expressed. And if such is the case with the word sickle, the same naturally applies to the white cloud and the golden crown. Little is told us of what on the new earth will characterize even the human appearance. Will it be man in the paradise form, or clothed and crowned with adornments? Hence our utter ignorance of what shall mark the appearance of Christ. It is merely indicated that it shall be an appearance of wondrous, glorious beauty. Hence the glistening whiteness of the garment, the brightness of the golden crown, and the terrible sharpness of the sickle which is purposely imaged as sharp.

Thus it shall once come to pass, thus Christ is at work now in preparing this issue, and thus from the glorious consciousness of Christ and His angels it is given St. John to see in vision. Nor is this all. Christ in heaven does not only clearly see in advance all that is to take place, but He is ever occupied with it. All things will thus be consummated by Christ Himself. Only one question remains. The divine ordinance does not go out from Christ, but from the Father. If the harmony between the parousia and the counsel of God is to remain unbroken, it must become clearly evident, as a special point, that what Christ and His angels will do, is not only in harmony with God's counsel, but is the direct outflow of it. And to make this clearly evident the text in v. 15 reads, that out of the temple, which is with God, now again another angel comes forth crying with a loud voice to him that sat on the cloud: "Thrust in thy sickle, and reap: for the time is come for thee to reap; for the harvest of the earth is ripe." Only then the judgment follows, as indicated in v. 16: "And he that sat on the cloud thrust in his sickle on the earth; and the earth was reaped." Some expositors have thought this very strange. How, it was asked, can an angel order Christ what to do, or tell what He intends to do. But this seeming strangeness entirely disappears when one notes the distinction between the enactment of God's eternal counsel and the fulfilment of that counsel by Christ. The Son, so to speak, recives His charge from the Father and executes the same. And such is the case here. Christ brings out the last judgment, but He does not do this of Himself.

He but carries out the counsel of God. And therefore an angel now comes to Christ, who as in God's name tells Him, that the moment for the cutting off of the lost is come. The case here is the same as when Christ told His disciples, before He suffered, that no one knows the hour, not even the Son, but only the Father Who is in heaven. Naturally the angel who brings this message comes out of the temple. In that temple thrones the Majesty of the Triune God and from that temple the issue goes forth.

There is nothing hazy about the image of the sickle. Mankind is here presented in the image of vegetation. We are not sure whether only one kind of vegetation is indicated, and if so, the vine. What is here said can well be applied to two things: The common harvest in the wheatfield and the choice harvest of the vine. In that case the harvest of the wheatfield would stand for what comes upon humanity at large, and the wine harvest for what would come upon the leaders of the peoples who have estranged the world from God, and with the lost are now consigned to eternal doom. The naming of the sickle pleads for this understanding of the harvest in a twofold sense. When grapes are to be taken from the vines the sickle is not in mind. Grapes are picked or cut with a knife, while the sickle is used with what is reaped in the field. So the text does not merely read: Thrust in thy sickle, but: Thrust in thy sickle, *and reap,* which expression is not used when it comes to the harvest of the vine. And such the less, as in v. 16 follows: "and the earth was *reaped.*" It seems therefore preferable in vs. 15 and 16 to think of the general judgment that comes upon all of the human race.

The last but one or fourth angel according to v. 17 now begins the judgment: "And another angel came out of the temple which is in heaven, he also having a sharp sickle." This shows that the last judgment involves a spiritual work of immeasurable extent. The last judgment means not merely that Christ from the judgment seat shall pronounce judicial sentence as though this were the end of it, but rather that judgment shall come not merely upon humanity at large, but also upon nations and peoples severally, and much stronger still, upon every person individually. More than once, therefore, the Scripture speaks of *books* that contain the record of every man's life and demeanor, saying, that in the day of judgment these books will be opened and the writing in these books will determine the particular lot that awaits each individual. So nothing is said of a general address or of a judgment in one all-including form. God's judgment comes personally in every individual conscience, and through the conscience to every man's personal life. And therefore, the angels are always represented as instituting an investigation, to determine the final lot of every man. In keeping with this not only Christ, but His angels as well have a sharp sickle in their hand and together institute the investigation. That one angel only is mentioned here makes no difference. The whole angelic host here appears as included in that one angel. And as Scripture elsewhere speaks of ten thousand times ten thousand angels, the representation of the last judgment becomes so much more vivid when we accept as fact, that together with His angels Christ institutes this personal investigation, and, thanks to this co-operation, very shortly brings it to a close. Also the time when all this will transpire depends upon God's counsel. It depended upon when the harvest of the earth *would be ripe*. That ripeness does not refer to the spiritual ripeness of faith, but to the issue which at last will show what has become of our human race. There is first a time of waiting for the issue, when conversion is still possible and thereby a change in the condition of things is thinkable. But when once all the seeking means of grace are exhausted, and all conversion and return to God is cut off, there is no more reason why grace should tarry, wait, and postpone the issue. Then humanity is ripe, that is to say perfectly ripe for the judgment which it brought upon itself.

For the demoniac tempter of lost mankind this judgment is made the more grievous by what we read in vs. 18-20. There another angel appears, which can also mean a group of angels. That only one is mentioned solely tends to bring out the special character of the task which this last angelic group has to perform. So we read: "And another angel came out from the altar, which had power over fire." This altar too is taken as the one that serves as the altar of burnt-offering in the temple of God in heaven. Thus nothing is said of an earthly temple or of an alter of stone or metal. Also here in vision is, as it were, imaged and depicted what once will come to pass, when something of the holy environment around the throne of God will come down to us from above. "Power over fire" here means, that the offering was burned on the altar, and thus became a prey of the fire, which fire here is taken in the general sense as the element that burns, destroys, consumes and brings to nought. And now it comes to the grapes in distinction from the wheat harvest. The wheat harvest is no longer counted with, if at least our idea of the expression "thrust in thy sickle, and reap" is correct. In any case the turn now comes to the grapes and the vine, upon which the sentence is passed that they must be burned with fire.

The image of grapes here affects us strangely, because the grape is a superior fruit and is highly prized. But such is not the meaning of the image here. Neither should this bring drunkenness by wine to mind. That the vine is mentioned is simply because grapes are so highly esteemed as fruit of a very choice kind, and here refers to the leaders of the people who had excelled in power and in honor, and thereby had misled the nations. Nothing is said of this vine and of these grapes by way of appreciation; rather they are spoken of as poisonous weeds which the sooner the better must be cut off and burned. In a highly authoritative manner the angel in v. 18 is told: "Thrust in thy sharp sickle, and gather the clusters of the vine of the earth; for her grapes are fully ripe." In countries where wine is made, newly picked grapes are immediately cast into the wine-press that presses out the wine and separates it from the skins and seeds. In this sense v. 19 reads: "And the angel thrust in his sickle into the earth, and gathered the vine of the earth, and cast it into the great wine-press of the wrath of God." If the grape is the finest sort of fruit, the reference in this figurative language is to those who in the world of men are counted as the highest, and the saying that what as their spirit comes out of them is cast into the winepress of God's wrath, states in a dreadful way that the noblest on earth had turned into its opposite, that the finest had become the meanest, and nothing was in store for what the world called highest save to be cast into the depth of malediction and ruin. So we realize that the image of the grapes, which at first affected us so strangely, in the end so forcibly expresses what would take place. All the world's past had aimed so high to reach without God, yes in opposition to God, noblest results in culture and science and practical resourcefulness. At length it had wandered off in this so onesidedly that antichrist could succeed, yes, had succeeded, in acquiring power over all the earth. At this pass it was actually deemed that the highest had been attained, and that of all vegetation and fruit of the ground the vine had become the noble grape. But in the end it appears that all this has only been delusion and self-blinding, with the inevitable result that everything has turned into its opposite, and the life-sap of it all is poured into the winepress of God's wrath to be destroyed and to be forever doomed.

In closing comes v. 20: "And the winepress was trodden without the city, and blood came out of the winepress, until the stream of human blood was so great that it reached to the bridles of the horses, not at one point where it had reached the highest, but over a surface that covered a thousand and six furlongs." For a correct understanding, everything here depends upon what is meant by that city. Evidently that city itself is not the main thing, for we read that the winepress was not trodden *in, but outside of that city.* Already this shows that the oft advanced notion that this meant to represent the city of Rome is plainly an error. Even if one takes it to be the Imperial city of Rome, it would not answer the question why not that city itself, but what it contained should bring the issue. It might be taken as referring to Jerusalem, and the ancient Hinnom with its horrors, but even then, as will appear, the ancient Jerusalem will not do, but must here be taken in the figurative sense, so that what here is indicated extends across the whole earth and to all peoples.

Of course the outlook upon what precedes the Consummation differs according as one views it from the earth, and looks up to heaven whence it comes, or whether like Christ from heaven he looks down upon the earth. And so it is with what we read in chapter 14 of the winepress of God's wrath, of the blood up to the bridles of the horses, and of the sea of blood of 1600 furlongs in compass. Seen from the earth this will prove to be the last dreadful scene of mortal combat with the antichrist, who monopolizes

the whole world of which he wants to rob the Christ. This conflict will not be confined to one field of battle, to one continent
or to one people, but this deadly conflict shall spread over the
whole world, extend to every people and nation, and shall engage
all mankind of every tribe and tongue as in bond against the
Almighty. It will be the last mortal combat under antichrist and
will involve the wondrous moving action of Gog and Magog in
the East. Seen from the earth the beast also had to be reckoned
with, as well as the image, the antichrist and Gog. But this last
earthly scene of the world's life is described in chapter 14 as seen
by the angels from above, and then of course rebellious human
life as a whole did not present itself in its several parts, but in
its connected unity. Neither peoples nor nations are seen, but
our one human race as a whole. So the whole compass of human
life is here taken together, and naturally this makes one think
of God's Majesty as represented on earth in the holy city, against
which all the turmoil of Satan directs itself. Under the dispensation of the Old Covenant it took the form that Jerusalem was the
center, that that holy city itself was the issue at stake, wherefore
the final battle was fought under Jerusalem's walls. So the vision
in hand borrows its characteristic features from these former
conditions and relationships. All the higher life of faith as at
length it will show itself in the martyrs, is depicted in the image
of the ancient Sion. Everything that presents itself the world
over in a divided and scattered state is subsumed in this one historic image, which was bound everywhere to represent the ancient
antithesis between Jerusalem and Babylon, and so in the historic
features of this original antithesis brings the final antithesis to
light.

So here we have a twofold figure of speech. First that of the
vine, as explained above, and the grapes of the vine, and the
winepress into which the grapes are cast, and this figurative
speech goes on to the end. And now follows the second figure
of speech, that Jerusalem is besieged, to express what presents
itself in all the world as the after-effect of the holy, and that the
battle under the walls of Jerusalem is like the battle that at
last will be waged in all the world. Of this we read: "And the
winepress was trodden without the city, and blood came out of
the winepress, even unto the horse bridles, by the space of a

thousand and six hundred furlongs." So here the image recedes and gives place to the intended reality. *Wine* is taken as symbol, partly because of its blood-like color, and partly because it so often demoralizes and poisons life on earth. Thus where at first wine and the winepress were dealt with, here the thing which wine represents, that is, human blood, is treated. In the last conflict the shedding of blood would actually be relentless. The antichrist would spare nothing. He would raise vast armies and, as military forces that nothing could daunt, give them free rein against the people of the earth. No military power of whatever people would be able to withstand this anti-Christian military might. The battles, previous to the final issue, would be terrible. In these desperate conflicts human blood would flow like rivers, and to depict this tremendous outpouring of human blood in the striking features of an imposing image, the text refers to it as a sea of blood of one meter and more high and covering a surface of a thousand and six hundred furlongs.

Sixteen hundred furlongs is a stretch from 34 to 48 square miles. Others take it as a round sweep whose radius measures 1600 furlongs. In either case it points to a bloodshed on an unprecedented scale, in which no human life is spared. And as this bloodshed will take place in all the earth, it is here depicted as in one place of such dimensions as to require a ten hours journey to encompass it, be it in circumference or a radius of that length. Naturally this is not the image of things as shall be seen from any point on earth, but as from an infinite distance it will present itself to those that are in heaven. In this connection we are not to imagine that heaven here is taken as reaching no higher than the clouds above the earth. On the contrary it is indicated that distinction must be made between two particulars, namely: the infinite distance between God's heaven above and our firmament, and the much shorter distance between the clouds and our earth. To give any adequate idea of that immeasurable distance between the heaven of God's throne and our earth, what on earth extends in length and breadth to all points of the compass must needs be depicted as presenting one scene in one spot. Just what one sees in looking down from the top of a mountain. A score of villages with their houses spread far apart seems, when seen from the top of a high mountain, like an insginificant little

group.   And so it is with the text in hand.   Where the vision
transported St. John into the sanctuary above, where Christ and
His angels are enthroned, the extended table-lands of earth upon
which many nations had built their homes must needs appear as
a human life compacted within narrow bounds. It is only that
life in the precincts of the holy city, therefore, that is mentioned
here, and the whole world is subsumed as residing in that beautiful domain. And to indicate that this is mere figurative language, and that from that infinite distance things so presented
themselves, but that on earth they would assume infinitely broader
dimensions, so vast a quantity of blood is spoken of, as in a lake
or sea stands over three feet high, and extends 40 miles in length,
whether in circumference or radius.

The very mention of a stream of blood one meter in height
shows that this can not be taken literally. In case of murder,
homicide or war the victims' blood does not pile up but sinks
into the ground, or runs off sideways. If a few hundreds fell in
one field of battle, a small pool of blood might form itself, but
it would not last. It at once would soak into the ground or run
away in rills, and by no stretch of the imagination could a soldier
picture to himself a sea of blood one meter high and 40 miles
long. Such a representation is only possible when what covers
vast stretches of country on the earth, is taken as seen from an
almost infinite height, so that there presents itself at its narrowest
what in reality dropwise over so broad a domain soaks into the
ground. What is here said of the horse bridles refers of course
to the world power that, equipped for war, presents itself in a
mighty cavalry to spread terror and dismay whereby to insure
victory, while in fact this same cavalry is forced to surrender,
and can not even seek refuge in flight, because the blood-stream
rises so unbelievably high as to render escape impossible. What
now remains is merely the symbolic-technical question as to what
we must think of the 1600 furlongs. Taken literally these 1600
furlongs for the field of battle as such are not too much. This
used to be thought so, but he who is at all familiar with the immeasurable fields of battle on the West and East fronts of Europe
now, realizes that their proportions are far more gigantic, and
that he who would measure them with the 1600 furlongs as a
standard would not reach the end of the line. This however should

not mislead us· It can not mean that once there shall be a sea of
human blood of such unheard-of dimensions. No field of battle
is measured in that way, nor can it be done, and the mistake of
those who in their exposition took such to be the case, was merely
that they did not bear in mind the symbolic character which in
the Apocalypse almost all numbers and all times assumed.

This has fully been elucidated in the case of the number *seven*,
but the symbolic character does not confine itself to this. It extends to the numbers twelve, seventy, hundred and thousand, always after the standard that a thousand years with the Lord are
as one day and one day as a thousand years; something which
the Chiliasts could never understand. Thus the number 1600 in
v. 20 must be taken symbolically, even as the number 666 in the
last verse of chapter 13. All these numbers have always given
rise to most serious misunderstandings simply because people
have tried to analyze these products of Eastern imagination with
the precision of our Western mode of thought. But it can not
be done. The Eastern way of representation as we see it with
the Babylonians and Israel is most symbolic, and thus also in
the symbolism of numbers artificial, and only he who can accus-
custom himself to this, can fully appreciate what the Apocalypse
offers by way of numbers. Undoubtedly this frequently renders
the text unintelligible, and makes it difficult to grasp the meaning. From the first therefore, Western exegetes have been tempted to make the most of unthinkable explanations. But fortun-
ately there have been those, even in the West, who have taken
pains to accustom themselves to the Eastern manner of representation. Especially Professor Kliefoth in his study *Die Zahlen
Symbolik der Heilige Schrift* (see Theol. Tidschrift 1862 p. 424
v. v.) has happily come to understand the significance of the use
of numbers in the East. Also the very important work of Dr.
K. Chr. W. T. Bahr, *Symbolik des Mosaischen Kultus,* Heidelberg 1839, is worthy of special notice, and the study still goes
on. But in any case he who ignores symbolism invites failure,
and it is a matter of congratulation that Prof. Kliefoth here too
has given an analysis of this symbolically used number. On page
148 of the third volume of his Exegesis of the Apocalypse he
writes: "Here also we can only take the number 1600 symbolically." A twofold possibility presents itself here. Hoffmann and

Ebrard maintain that 1600 is the multiplication of 40 x 40. In that case the length of that pool of blood would merely indicate the dreadfulness of the punishment that awaits the godless. Even as 40 years marked the distress that came upon Israel in the wilderness. So this punitive number 40, multiplied by itself would indicate a much more grievous visitation of wrath that would come upon the antichrist and his satellites. Against this it can be said that while the number 40 is used in this sense the Scripture gives no example of a 40 x 40 by which naturally the intensity as it were would be infinitely heightened. But we do not say that this is impossible. Especially when in this connection eternal punishment is indicated, there is even something that favors it.

Yet Kliefoth has offered another explanation of this mystical number, namely, that it springs from 4 x 4 x 100; which also brings 1600. As may be granted 100 is the exponent of 10 and 4 x 4 or 16 the exponent of 4. In that case 4 stands for the expanse of the surface to the four points of the compass. If one wants a more minute indication of the significance of the four points of the compass he comes to the 4x4, even as with the winds we not only count with East and West, North and South, but often more accurately with North-West and South-East and South-West and North-West. Thus to indicate the four points of the compass more accurately there is nothing uncommon in the 4x4, but rather something that also in the West is often applied. If in this way the number 16 refers to the surface, it is equally rational to suppose that the 100, taken as 10x10, is the exponent of the number that points to history in the economic sense. In that case it mainly intends to indicate the eternal character which the final issue in judgment would bear for those who to the very last have set their face against God. Their case would for ever more be hopeless; a distress and an eternal future misery which in every direction and for all times would consummate in doom.

And in the Apocalypse this was the point of first importance. The vision that came to the holy apostle in chapter 14 afforded him a glimpse of the heavenly vision by which Christ and His angels live in anticipation of what is to come. It was of highest importance here to make him understand that after the seals the trumpets would follow, and after the trumpets the vials, but that after the vials there was nothing more to be expected, so that presently the final issue would ensue, which would determine every one's eternal destiny, of individuals not only but equally much of peoples and nations, yes finally of the whole world. Necessarily therefore the potentiation of the 10 and the potentiation of the 4, and the relation of both, expresses itself here most strongly. So taken it is out of the question that chapter 14 merely offers a weakened and shortened indication of what the following chapters would elucidate more fully. Every attempt of this sort has led to what also in the marginal notes of the Dutch version is so greatly to be regretted, namely, the entirely wrong application of all these visions to great historical events. This application was bound to invite purely arbitrary interpretations. And he who in our marginal notes on chapter 14 carefully traces the entirely arbitrary applications that have been put forth at random, as it were, must conclude that none of these earlier explanations have furnished any proof for the correctness of what was asserted and represented. It was just put that way. It was claimed that the interpretation that was given bore resemblance to the historic event at least to some extent. And of course almost every expositor in turn had his own idea. But they never were, nor did they ever become, agreed. The pity of it is, that the glorious consolation of the end which chapter 14 offers,—provided we take it as the rich world of thought regarding things to come which ever since Christ's Ascension has engaged His mind and that of His angels—has remained alien to the former generations. Only when these applications to the past were abandoned, and the representation was solely applied to the Consummation, were we led away from all this abuse of Scripture, and brought to clear and soul enchanting insights.

XIX

THE SEVEN VIALS*

And they sing the song of Moses the servant of God, and the song of the Lamb, saying, Great and marvellous are thy works, Lord God Almighty; just and true are thy ways, thou King of saints. Rev. 15, 3.

With the plague of the vials or bowls, let us clearly understand that this third act, even more truly than the previous acts of the Seals and of the Trumpets, is played in heaven, so to speak, and from thence comes down toward the earth. This is not understood when, as is frequently done, heaven is taken to be formless and purely spiritual. Read attentively Paul's description in 2 Cor. 12, where he tells of how he was "caught up to the third heaven, and to Paradise, and there heard unspeakable words, which it is not lawful for a man to utter." To this mysterious narrative he twice adds the words that he could not tell whether it was in the body, or out of the body. But though he was unable to explain it, he knew that for one moment he had tasted life in the world above, and that in that heavenly country he had enjoyed not only a glimpse of the spiritual and the unobservable, but in that vision had also seen all sorts of things that presented themselves to him in sound and form, and thus almost assumed a material appearance. So here we face the mysterious fact that in heaven there are non-earthly things which nevertheless present themselves in sound and form. With this agrees what was told Moses in the mount, that the tabernacle in the wilderness was merely a copy of the real tabernacle or temple in heaven before God's throne. And in perfect keeping with this we are now told —not that these seven angels which had the vials came down to earth and there assumed human forms, and then were given the vials, but on the contrary—that the sending out of the vials took place in heaven and that from thence these seven angels looked

---

*In the original "The Seven Vials" covers chapters XIX-XXII.

down to the earth and moved towards it. Our dreams can here
give us a partial elucidation. In dreams we see things at times in
all their forms so really that on awaking we deem that it actually
took place just as we saw it. Sometimes that impression is so
strong that it takes some moments to free our mind from the
spell of it. Moreover from the nature of the case this is connected
with this other fact, that according to the Scriptures angels have
appeared on earth in human form, so that the impression was
that as men they talked with men. We can not solve this mystery.
We can not enter into the being and into the mind of an angel so
as to learn what goes on in him. Yet evidently both angel and
man can enter into the consciousness of a reasonable being, which,
while it has much in common with us, yet entirely differs from
us. As our visible world around us naturally accommodates itself to our consciousness, the same must be the case with the
angels, yet then there must be such a parallel similarity between
their world and ours, as to render observation from one sphere
into the other possible. Here it even goes so far, that what is
seen above is not a reflection of what is reality here, but rather
what we see around us here, reflects what is real about God's
throne. There is a difference between these visions not only in
form, but also in degree. For chapter 15 begins with the observation that what is now to come is not meant merely as a sign,
but as an exceptionally *great and marvellous sign,* and therefore
demand special notice, for St. John informs us, first that the
plagues that are now to come shall be the last, and also that the
wrath of God as revealed in the Seals and Trumpets and here
in the Vials, shall now be *consummated.* So we read in v· 1 of
chapter 15: "And I saw another sign, great and marvellous, not on earth, but in heaven, namely seven angels having
the seven *last* plagues; for in them is God's wrath consummated."
The emphasis on what now follows is the more striking, since
in what preceded attention was twice directed to phenomena that
were similar to those that are now to come to pass. Yet, and this
is the point, there was a considerable difference in degree between
what was seen in the two former evolutions and what comes now;
even such that what happened before seemed merely a foreshadowing of the real judgment, which now in a more aggressive

manner was to come. There is now no further preparation, no more transition. The end is come, and the emphasis falls upon the entrance of the Consummation.

The mention of the *sea of glass* also affects one at first somewhat strangely. It occurs already in Rev. 4, 6: "And before the throne of God there was a sea of glass like unto crystal." Here it is more fully treated. We learn that there was such a phenomenon as a sea of glass, not in the actual, but in a metaphorical and figurative sense. It was not a sea of glass, only from the distance it looked like one. We too are familiar with figurative speech. We are apt to say that at a great gathering there was *a sea of faces,* and quite in this sense the "sea of glass" here indicates that before God's throne there was a very great multitude of people. V. 2 immediately adds that this sea of glass was formed by those who had gotten the victory over the beast, and over his image, and over his mark, and over the number of his name, and that they stood on the sea of glass, having the harps of God, and singing the song of Moses and the Lamb. As this sea of glass is not seen in the earth, but in heaven before God's throne, it follows that these believers had no more part in the earthly conflict, but as martyrs had succumbed, and were now in heaven before God's throne, and together present a scene that reminds one of a sea of crystal or glass. Together they form the holy group of believers which in the bitter conflict with the antichrist and his image had not been overcome, and as victors have been admitted to the innermost circle around the throne of God, and there constitute a solidaric group of holy victors. The very word conqueror, or victor deserves emphasis. We are expressly told that they had gained a fourfold victory. They had been assailed by a fourfold temptation, and in each of them they had triumphed.

The final victory of these blessed ones was, that they had refused to kneel before the beast,—that is, the antichrist, and before his image. However grievous had been the tyranny of antichrist, they had courageously resisted, though they knew that it was a matter of life and death. And when the first refusal had proved a success, and they had maintained their stand, with equal fortitude they had resisted the further demands of antichrist.

They had refused to let him put his mark on their hand, and had heroically denied him the right of putting his mysterious number on them. The trial had been severe in having all this forced upon them, yet they had not yielded, though they were dragged to the scaffold, and there underwent death. They had died the martyr death, but now in the blessedness of heaven they played harps before the throne, glorifying their God and His Christ.

They were no small group but rather a very great multitude, and this brings to mind again the number 144,000, which in the 12 x 12 x 1000 mystically indicates a very great host. So if it merely said: "a sea of people" the expression would be entirely perspicuous. But the strange part is the additional particular, that it was a sea of *glass* or *crystal*. Yet also this is plain. The sea as looked upon from above can convey a twofold impression. It can be a dark, somber mass of water, or it can be clear and transparent. When there is a storm and distant thunder, everything is turbid and swarthy, while under clear skies and bright sunshine and with almost no wind the sea bears a restful aspect, and to some extent is even transparent, so that in shallow places one can almost see the bottom. Take this at its best, when nothing ruffles the surface and in the light wave-beat everything is clearly reflected, and the image of a "sea of people" is carried up still higher. It then means that this sea of people is a holy multitude which is as transparent as crystal and glass. This makes the meaning plain of that sea of glass that undulates around God's throne. It is the almost innumerable host of the redeemed, now more accurately imaged as a sea of people, in which nothing suggests anything that is tainted, darkened and imperspicuous, such as characterized the great multitudes on earth, but is entirely clear, limpid and transparent, so as to appear like crystal and glass. But still something more is added which introduces another element, for it expressly states that this sea of men was "purified as by fire." So it is not mere transparency alone that characterizes this sea of people, but also an inner glow which presents the brightness of fire. This points to what presents itself in sunlight. Bright sunshine makes things clear and transparent, and at the same time creates heat and soon creates a glow. This glow can become so intense as to burn, as it were, and to suggest fire. And this is what we see here. That martyr host is not only a sea of human faces with a splendour like unto crystal, but that splendour gives out heat, and what at first merely glistened now glows and radiates heat; which naturally means that the soul of these martyrs is aglow with holy indignation against all those things in the earth that overthrow the honor of God, and offer worship to the antichrist.

And in ecstacy of rapture that holy multitude of martyrs around God's throne sings and plays on harps. This naturally expresses deep and holy joy which is now their portion. Bear in mind how at first this multitude loudly and bitterly complained that the final judgment still tarried. In Rev. 6,10 they cry: "How long, O Lord, holy and true, dost thou not judge and avenge our blood on them that dwell on the earth!" To them it was said that "they should rest yet for a little season, until their fellowservants also and their brethren, that should be killed as they had been, should be fulfilled." This implied that the time for the final judgment had not yet come. And while it was still deferred, the martyrs in heaven were to pray and to wait. But now that the vials are at hand, things become different. There is no further need of tarrying or waiting. What has long been looked for is at the door. The last period is begun. The end is here. And with an eye to this there is no further word of complaint, but the martyrs with harps in hand raise the song of triumphant jubilation. Note that they sing to the accompaniment of *the harps of God*. They no longer play on earthly musical instruments which are the inventions of men, but they play on the harps of God which naturally means, that now it all becomes a God-inspired song of worship and of praise from which the latest trace of human perplexity and discordancy has been removed, and whose theme is the holiness of God.

But this necessarily brings with it that in this heavenly harpsong the note of saving grace is no more sounded, but the holiness of God voices itself in both its aspects of leading true believers to victory and of giving vent to God's wrath against all workers of iniquity and lovers of unholiness. So the heavenly psalm begins: "Great and marvelous are thy works, Lord God Almighty; just and true are thy ways, thou King of saints." Here God's holiness and Almightiness have all the emphasis; no longer

His atoning grace. This has reached its limit, and as the Consummation draws near God makes His appearance as the "King of saints," which very combination states so accurately the point in hand. In the period of enticing Reconciliation the great love of the Father in heaven went out after the child that had strayed from the path of rectitude and was lost. But that dispensation of grace has had its day. God no longer appears as Father, but as King, even as the King of saints, Who thus is no longer concerned about the lost. The operation of grace is ended. And hence that in the harp-song above the Almightiness of God, the justice of God and the Reality of God are glorified, so that He might shine forth in all the splendour of His Royal Majesty. V. 3 explains this as the perfect combination of the two seemingly mutually excluding elements, the one that brings Moses, the other that brings Christ to mind. So. v. 3 reads: "And they,—that is, the martyrs of the church,—sing the song of Moses the servant of God, and the song of the Lamb" which united song of Moses and the Lamb ends in this strophe: "Who shall not fear thee, O Lord, and glorify thy name? for thou only art holy; for all nations shall come and worship before thee; for thy judgments are made manifest." So there is no more mention of grace or of reconciliation. Almightiness, Holiness, Justice here govern the whole situation, and even the grace of the Lamb is ended in the Justice of God. The Lamb of God did not come into the world to detract aught from the holiness and justice of God, but that He might make that Majesty of God in the end shine forth the more gloriously. Seeking grace has been wonderful and fascinating in the extreme, but it could not be all. In the end everything unholy would in the most scornful manner turn against the holy, and then also the holiness of God would break out in final judgment, and everything that persisted in revolt against the Holy would come to nought.

That Moses is mentioned here, yes that the song of Moses as the servant of God is specially emphasized is, because in the Messianic dispensation the law,—that is, the justice (Recht) of the Holy God was paramount to all things else. So in the last judgment the Mosaic legal standpoint would necessarily become again the measuring-line for the Holy. Israel's dispensation could not effect the realization of the thrice holy, and to that extent the

Messianic dispensation ended in bitter disappointment. But now that Christ had come by a perfect reconciliation to lift up the Israel of God from that deep fall, and now that the "It is finished" had been spoken from the Cross of Golgotha, the holiness of Moses' dispensation of law came, as it were, from behind the Cross to the fore again, and in the end it would appear that all those who in the dispensation of grace had rejected Christ, would perish under the severity of that sacred dispensation that had been given in Moses. So when the end came, the martyrs in heaven saw these three things: First the Mosaic dispensation of law as the disclosure of the perfect holiness in the King of kings; then the dispensation of grace in the Lamb of God; and lastly, with the ending of the dispensation of grace, the final period which would again emphasize the transcendence of the justice (Recht) of God's holiness, but now, as it were, to bring in the judgment.

Here too it should be noted that we are told again, albeit in soberer form, what so strongly arrested our attention in Rev. 14, 6, namely, that in the end the distinction between nations and peoples will not be lost. In Rev. 14:6 we read that the Gospel would be preached to all nations and kindreds and tongues and peoples, and here in v. 4 we learn that "all nations shall come and worship before thee, O God," because "thy judgments are made manifest." This shows the folly of the saying that the division of mankind into nations and peoples, all speaking different languages, is but the pitiful effect of sin, which in the Consummation will disappear, that then it will all be one humanity without race distinctions and one language will be spoken by all; that all variations will then drop out and things will be drab and uniform. That this contradicts what we are told of the building of the tower of Babel, needs scarcely a reminder. The attempt then was to stay together as one people. There was to be no variation. As people of one sort, all were to dwell together. But their plan miscarried, and with a strong hand God achieved the differentiation of our human race. Yet this has not prevented the notion from being cherished again and again , that what was so sharply censured in Babylon's attempt, will yet be the ideal in eternity. But this finds no support in the Revelation of St. John, on the contrary rather it points every time again to the fact that the distinctions will be maintained in the future life, and even the differences of language will not disappear. This of course does not mean that all languages that are spoken now will also then in like distinction be perpetuated. We suffer under the corruption of language, and there is a confusion of speech and a disruption of language and a medley of tongues which is purely the effect of the derangement of our human life. Thus the intention is not that this shall go on for ever. But what Rev. 14 and 15 indicate, implies that according to its original aptitude human language is destined to expand in rich differentiation, and this deserves our closest attention.

Yet this remarkable phenomenon is differently indicated in Rev. 14 from what it is in Rev. 15. In Rev. 14 we have a glimpse of the world of prophecy as it waits to be fulfilled, and occupies the world of thought in Christ and His redeemed. But when what is alive in that rich world of thought is presently fulfilled, things are different. In that preceding world of thought everything is united, as is the case with a poet upon whose mental horizon looms the coming poem, or as an architect becomes conscious of the plan for the palace he is to build. In that plan and in the rise of that creative thought, things at first are confused, yet they are as clouds of light that make him perceive their image. But when it comes to execution everything takes on fixed forms, clearly outlined appearances, and one fact follows historically upon the other, that thus history might be consummated. So the case is not that Rev. 14 and Rev. 15 show us the same thing twice. What is seen in Rev. 14 looms up from the rich world of thought that engages the mind of Christ and His angels and his redeemed, and what follows in Rev. 15 is the chronological eventuation, the actual happening of what from the world of thought in Christ presses toward the reality·

XX

THE TABERNACLE AND THE TEMPLE

And the temple was filled with smoke from the glory
of God, and from His power; and no man was able to
enter into the temple, till the seven plagues of the seven
angels were fulfilled. Rev. 15, 8.

Now begins God's mighty work of bringing in the Consummation. What took place before was but a part of what is to come, and at first only one third part. The final catastrophy might have come suddenly, and as with one peal of thunder have worked wholesale destruction, so that of itself a new heaven and a new earth would have sprung from it, but God's majesty did not appoint it so. The end was not to come suddenly and at once, but gradually. It announced itself step by step, and only when the universe has twice been shaken, does the third and last shaking of heaven and earth bring in God's judgment in full. Yet even this last period would be marked by a succession. The end would not come by the outpouring of one vial, but by vial-outpourings in seven stages, which would then be followed by the new order of things. Note here how these vials are handed out to the seven angels by one of the four beasts. So we read in v. 7: "And one of the four beasts gave unto the seven angels seven golden vials." But the important thing that took place just before this was, as it stated in v. 5, that "the temple of the tabernacle of the testimony in heaven was opened." This carries us up to the throne of God and makes us see the surroundings thereof, and what there took place. That throne of God is not represented as a hollow affair losing itself in the unseen, but rather as exhibiting a world of heavenly wonders and, if we may so express ourselves, a vast Divine economy. What St. John here sees is no reflection of anything that is found in the earth, but rather the original, in its own manner of existence, of which only the reflection is seen in the earth. The original that is dealt with here is Above, and what in the course of time would show itself

169

in the earth was merely to be understood as an *image,* even a transient and changing image of what is real around God's throne in heaven.

As now we turn to the vial-angels it is interesting to note how they came by these vials. Going back to the Seals we remember that the book of the seven seals was in the hand of Him that sat upon the throne,—that is, of God Himself, and that it was said that no one could loose the seven seals, till at length Christ was authorized to do so. No creature therefore played any part in it. The Seals are attached to the book which is in God's hand and presently is opened by God's Son. Absence therefore of all human agency. The Lamb opens the seven seals. Already with the Trumpets the mode of procedure differs. We read in chapter 8, 2 that St. John saw the seven angels which stood before God; and to them were given seven trumpets. Thus here creaturely help is rendered, to materialize God's counsel. The seven trumpets are to be sounded by the seven angels that stand before God's throne. But here the mode of procedure changes. Here the creature appears not only as God's instrument, but even this instrument is not handled by God Himself. Between God and the angels with the vials the four beasts act as intermediaries. So v. 7 reads: "And one of the four beasts gave unto the seven angels seven golden vials full of the wrath of God, who liveth for ever and ever." So with the seals Christ Himself performs the act without creaturely aid. With the trumpets the creature takes part, yet the angels are given the trumpets directly by God Himself. But with the vials the removal of Divine action goes still further. Here the creature will not only pour out the vials, but also hand the same for this purpose to the angels.

Finally we observe that these seven vials or bowls are of solid gold. This is indicative of God's Majesty. Earthen ware is used in the homes of the poor, and metal household goods are of tin or iron or at most copper. But in the mansions of the rich, china is of the finest sort, and the royal board is graced by nothing less than choicest porcelains and table-ware of silver and gold. This difference is observed here. The vials by which Almighty God carries out His decree must not be coarse or common, but their choice quality must commend them for Divine use. It is not surprising therefore, that when God Himself prepares these vials, and the seven angels merely handle them, they should bear the hall-mark of the palace from whence they are carried out, and be of the noblest metal, which is gold. Bowls might readily be of porcelain or earthenware, but in this instance it had all to be of metal, and then of course of the noblest sort, for these vials or bowls must be the exponents of God's destroying wrath. Therefore is added in v. 7 : "Vials full of the wrath of God, who liveth for ever and ever."

Quite in keeping with this we read in v. 6, that the seven angels that were to pour out the seven vials appear clothed in holy splendour. They were "clothed in pure and white linen, and having their breasts girded with golden girdles." The uniform of highest distinction in the East is *white*. No so in the West. There at court the distinguishing uniform is mostly blue or red cashmere or broadcloth. In the East the white robe has the pref- erence. It is linen, and hence thin and light of weight. So when Scripture depicts social life in heaven as clothed in pure white linen, it indicates heavenly holiness and purity, while the majestic character of the luxurious courtdress expresses the glory of the spotlessness in the heavenly appearance. That the angels that are to go out with the vials are said to be clothed not only in *pure* linen, but in *shining* linen, refers not only to their holy and sin- less character, but also to the exalted dignity wherewith the angels in the heavenly palace are invested. The golden girdle at the breast likewise indicates the princely character of the court. It is all a picture of pure and lovely harmony. There is no super- fluity about it and no mystery. To receive the golden vials at the hand of one of the four beasts, these angels must be arrayed in their heavenly uniform,—that is in the heavenly palace uniform, that even in their dress they might exhibit the high dignity of the Majesty of God.

And now the place from whence they come. Vs. 5 and 6 say of this: "And after that I looked, and, behold, the temple of the tabernacle of the testimony in heaven was opened, and the seven angels came out of the temple." Of course no fore-court is here mentioned. At Jerusalem there had to be a fore-court because from thence the lure and call also went out to the heathen world to come to the worship of Jehovah. He who responded to this call, without having fully yet surrendered himself, stood afar off, and even the people of Israel remained in the fore-court. Only the priests went into the holy place, and the high priest alone into the holy of holies. As here, however, the temple is in question, the hour of decision is come, and now every one must know for himself where he belongs. Thus he who deems that his place is still in the fore-court is excluded. This is no time for hesitation or doubt. He who belongs to Christ must take his stand as priest, with the right of access to the holy place. Before Christ came in the flesh the fore-court was the meeting place for all people including strangers. After Christ's redemptive work was done, all believers are trained as priests. So when the hour of the final issue had come, naturally the fore-court was no longer needed, as now there were but two classes of people, those who by persistent unbelief were cut off from all fellowship with the temple, and the redeemed who clothed in priestly garments could dwell in the holy place of the temple. This is expressed by the saying that in heaven there is a temple, and that in that temple there is a tabernacle. This temple might be open or closed. Only in v. 5 we learn that the temple was opened, giving the redeemed and the angels of God the chance of looking into it. But thus it could not remain. Now that seeking and forbearing grace is ended, and the judgment of God's wrath brings in the final issue, the temple must be closed. This is indicated by the smoke from the glory of God's wrath, ever increasing in volume, till at length the whole temple was filled with it, rendering all access impossible. So reads v. 8: "And the temple was filled with smoke from the glory of God, and from His power; and no man was able to enter into the temple till the seven plagues of the seven angels were fulfilled."

This classing of temple and tabernacle together has a special meaning. Three kinds of revelations introduce the end: seals, trumpets and vials, but what is here prophesied of the temple does not occur with the seals, and not with the trumpets. It occurs with the vials, and so we ask, why only here this Divine use of the temple in heaven is mentioned. This temple did not originate at the time of the vials. It was there before. And while

nothing is said of it in either of the two preceding series
of events, here it appears as of almost first importance, and verse
by verse deepens the impression of the grave significance that is
attached to it. One feels that we are on the eve of a wholly new
period, which borrows its special significance from the fact that
it is to be the last. After the seals came the trumpets, the trumpets
were to be followed by the vials, but nothing was to come after
the vials. This makes so striking a difference, because under the
seals and trumpets grace was ever yet operative. There will
always yet be souls that go astray, but which at the last moment
turn to Christ; but the vials will put an end to this. Grace will
then have run its course, and Christ who as the Lamb of God
achieved Reconciliation, will then appear in His Majesty as Judge.
So there is an absolute change also in the Kingdom of God. In
Paradise already there was the lure of grace. Grace had at all
times operated as a saving power. He, the All-Merciful, has
through all these ages with irresistible power exercised compassion, and that day of salvation is now come to an end. It has
served its purpose and is now closed off. And the glory of God's
honor and justice re-appears unweakened and untempered to
hasten the end.

With an eye to this a striking change takes place in the temple,
or more particularly in the tabernacle above. Originally the
tabernacle and temple were the place where the sinner, by bringing an offering for his guilt, obtained reconciliation and forgiveness. For the individual person this was done in the holy place,
but for the whole people in the holy of holies. This implied that
believers were still ignorant of the perfect reconciliation that once
would be made on Golgotha. But the dispensation was ended.
Reconciliation in Christ had been achieved. By faith that perfect
reconciliation could be accepted. So true believers had now themselves become priests in the sanctuary, and tasted the sweetness of
the fruit of grace. But even this could not always last. Time
would come, when grace would be ended, and no offering brought
to the altar, or vicarous sacrifice of Christ, would longer avail.
Then the elect would be blessed and receive admission to the
Father's house of the many mansions, and they that had no part,
nor any delight, therein, would forfeit their claim to grace, and

in separation from God be prey to eternal doom. The point is, that grace is effective for a time; from the fall in Paradise till the last judgment, and this last judgment had now come.

In this connection an entire change takes place in the tabernacle or, if you will, in the temple above. The offering could now no longer either be applied or be effective, and the Law of the Ten Commandments in the holy of holies was to resume full power. He who conforms to the claim of that law had become reconciled and sanctified, drank the cup of eternal peace; and the great multitude that was led by antichrist into persistent rebellion against the Almighty perishes for ever, hence for them there is no more room in either tabernacle or temple. So v. 8 reads: "And the temple was filled with the smoke from the glory of God, and from His power, and no man was able to enter into the temple, till the seven plagues of the seven angels were fulfilled." The benefit of the atonement was now removed from the temple. When the last of the elect had safely been gathered in, reconciliation by the offering of Christ ceased to operate, and no one of the guilty multitude that confessed the antichrist could any longer reap benefit therefrom. Perfect holiness and justice now took reins in hand again with unweakened power. The justice of God brilliantly illumined the temple in all its parts. So long therefore as the seven plagues were not ended no one could enter therein. Everything now waited for the seven plagues to come. This alone would bring to pass the "It is done" of Rev. 16, 17. At the same time this implies that the outlook upon the availability of saving grace after death is absolutely irreconcilable with the here given explanation of the end.

XXI

THE FIRST THREE VIALS

And I heard a great voice out of the temple saying to the seven angels, Go your ways, and pour out the vials of the wrath of God upon the earth. Rev. 16, 1.

With the outpouring of the seven vials come the last seven events that will end the *historic* process. Again the number seven arrests the attention. This shows anew that in the historic process, as under God's direction it goes on in the earth, there is a holy rhythm. There are not just certain series of events, whether six or ten, but also what God achieves in the Consummation is bound to the sacred number seven. The outpouring of the seven vials will bring seven plagues upon mankind. Here also the initiative goes out from heaven. "And I heard a great voice out of the temple saying to the seven angels, Go your ways, and pour out the vials of the wrath of God upon the earth." So they are not happenings here on earth, or conflicts between governments and the rich, that will occasion what now comes, but the direct counsel and ordinance of God will bring to pass the things that will make the end. Here too the temple as appeared above is not the sanctuary of Jerusalem or of any other place on earth, but the temple near God's throne, as had already been intimated to Moses. Now that temple in heaven is closed. The change that there took place has been considered in the foregoing chapter. But the hour of decision is come, and the last seven historic events bring about the final issue. This does not say that there will be no more chance even in that last period for souls to be saved. To the very end regeneration and conversion will be possible, and only when in v. 17 it is finally said "It is done" will further ingathering be excluded. Only, this third and closing period of the vials is only partly taken up with the work of salvation. For so much as there is salvation there, it is accidental. The characteristic and main object of this last period is, that history comes to an end, that everything perishes, and gives way to the final

175

state of things. This is why v. 1 declares so positively that the
vials or bowls are solely filled with *the wrath of God*.

The seven vials, like the seven seals and the seven trumpets,
are divided into two groups, but with this difference, that here
the division is not 4 + 3, but 3 + 4. For the rest the division is
like that of the seven seals and the seven trumpets. Here too the
whole divides itself into two groups, the first of which
sets forth the particulars of the several events, and the
second brings out the coherence with the eternal. Almost
without one moment's intermission we are told that the first angel
pours out his vial on the earth, which brings an unbearable
epidemic upon mankind. The second angel pours out his vial on
the sea, which turns it into an unmeasurable pool of blood. And
the third angel poisons all rivers, lakes and fountains, and this
brings a deadly epidemic upon people in all parts of the earth,
and every sea and river and lake is turned as it were into blood.
Blood here is the token of death. The flow of blood from a
wound means the approach of death. So together these first three
vials mean, that mankind is near its end. A deadly epidemic attacks all human life, and water everywhere is turned into blood
and all life comes to nought. So ends the action of the first three
vials, and this is followed by the second period of the last four.
We learn this from the fact that the outpourings of the first three
vials follow each other immediately, without any intermezzo of
heavenly testimony while already between the outpourings of
vials three and four the facts are interrupted by explanation and
elucidation.

The testimony that now follows is borne as we read in v. 5 by
the angel of the waters, who had turned the fountains and rivers
into blood. "Thou art righteous, O Lord" says he, and to remove all doubt he adds: "which art, and wast, and shalt be";
and this righteousness of God consists in the fact that now all
chance of reconciliation is put aside and the last judgment is
carried into effect. So the words: "Thou art righteous, O Lord,
because thou hast judged thus" should be understood. In Gospel
times the impression might have been abroad that justice had
suffered violence at the hand of mercy. He who understands the
Cross and realizes that so far from being abolished or set aside

God's justice is perfectly fulfilled and maintained in the *Lama Sabachthani*, is differently impressed, though it scarcely need be said that the Ethicals, in particular, have darkened the glory of the Cross by their denial, that the Cross restores God's Justice to its rightful place. Thus according to their view mercy had triumphed over justice, and it was the chief glory of God that He had set the solemn claim of justice at nought, and, that apart from justice grace had been given free rein was the inspiration of worship. But in v. 5 of the chapter in hand this is contradicted and refuted. Justice (Recht) is the fixed order of things in God's providence and essentiality. As it is the human way of doing, that the police and judges at court good-naturedly let things take their own course without punitive interference, and teachers at school and commandants in the army or father and mother in the home weakly yield to anything that comes along, with never a thought of a stern measure to do justice to what is right, so it is deemed to be the case with God. In all things yielding, letting things go, tolerating and indulging, always hiding behind the shield of love, is then reckoned to be the very noblest behaviour of God. As a result of this, weakly letting things pass, condoning all things after the manner of tender-hearted mothers and indulgent fathers would have become the image of what was implied in the grace of God.

This unmotivated representation is here refuted. One faced the problem of strictly harmonizing two seeming mutually excluding acts of God. On one hand no *greater grace* was to be conceivable than the grace of our God. The highest exhibition imaginable of love, grace and mercy was to carry the day and bring things to an issue. But the profound mystery is, how the exhibition of such grace and mercy can go hand in hand with the absolutely holy maintenance of the justice (Recht) of God. There could be neither suggestion nor intimation of the surmise, that for the sake of sparing us and out of deference to our feelings, God the Lord could ever abandon His fundamental justice, and by weak indulgence deal capriciously with the question of right. On the contrary rather it had to be shown in the most convincing manner, how these two contradictions can be brought into harmonious relation, when on one hand nothing is detracted

on the part of God from the fundamental claim of justice, and
yét on the other hand grace and forgiveness can be applied even in
the case of most heinous transgressions. So the combination and
the interlacing of these two absolutely mutually excluding data
constitute the Gospel. To us the harmonization of these two,
that is to say, of justice with grace, and of grace with justice,
is absolutely unthinkable. The reconciliation of these two opposite data transcends all our power of thought. In the Divine
mystery alone could a solution of this be found. And that solution has only proved possible by the fact, that in Christ, as Himself God, in His forsakenness of God on the Cross, when the
Lama Sabachthani forced itself from His soul to His lips, the
fusion, the reconciliation and the making one of the two mutually
excluding ideas of justice and grace became possible. Here grace
falls short in nothing, and in nothing the justice of God. Both
now come to their full unfolding. Yet this is unthinkable, yes
impossible, so long as one refuses to confess his salvation in the
blood of Christ. Whatever Christ's example, Christ's preaching
and Christ's action upon our soul may achieve, so long as the
mystery of salvation is not acknowledged in the *Lama Sabachthani,* there can be no salvation.

From this follows, that the reconciliation and violation of
God's justice by the blood of Christ is merely transient and temporal, and must end in an absolute application of God's justice
for ever· There was no reconciliation before the fall, it was
only effected after the fall, and remains in force until the last
judgment.. After the last judgment there will be no more reconciliation, for then everything is brought back under the dominion
of the full and spiritual law of right, which is the outcome of
God's justice. There is eternal blessedness for the children of
God, and eternal wrath of God upon those who have persisted
in apostasy and rebellion. So the fruit of grace abides, but Reconciliation has lost its application. It belongs to a by-gone period,
and as before the fall, so now, God's wrath is turned in a punitive
way against everything in man that opposed God's justice and fell
short of His righteous claim.

This is emphasized in the words of the "angel of the waters"
in vs. 5 and 6: "Thou art righteous, O Lord," which means:

Thou art the God of justice, who will not relinquish the right,"
and therefore adds: "Which art, and wast, and shalt be," which
means: Who at no time in the past has suffered, nor in the present, nor ever in the future will suffer thy righteous demands
and thy justice to be lost in grace. So that when the day of grace
is past, law (Recht) and Divine justice will for ever vanquish
what violates His righteous claims, and unweakened and in-
violate the Divine Being will be glorious again in both His
aspects of peace toward the Elect and the Angels, and of wrath
toward those that have persisted in their sin. This the angel of
the waters testifies to St. John, as he triumphantly exclaims:
"Thou, Lord, dost not relinquish the right, which art, and wast,
and shalt be, because thou hast judged thus, and as they have
shed the blood of saints and prophets so Thou hast given them
blood to drink, for they are worthy." This of course sums up
all the people's sins in the one sin of their implacable cruelty, for
so far as they opposed God's holy revelation. This was the climax of all sin, since it made a mockery of all grace, and therefore it is here so emphatically put in the fore.

Sin had ruled all human life by its attack upon the saintliness
of individual persons, and in the end this sin had become the
cumulative sin of the nations, and in its worst and most dreadful form had shown itself in its unsparing opposition against
God's seeking grace. That grace had most clearly come to light
in what God by His prophets had preached and offered to mankind; and as not only heathen nations, but even Israel had again
and again laid violent hands upon the prophets, and instead of
giving them a reverent hearing had not hesitated to oppose, perse-
cute and finally put them to death, in all this the acme of self-
delusion and the uttermost reach of the enmity of the heart
against God had celebrated its triumph. Here again it is a question of blood. Hence there is nothing more foolish than the attempt, which has so often been tried in opposition to the
Gospel, of putting aside what is called that intolerable blood
atonement, and of putting nothing in its place save moral devlop-
ment. It is a matter of life, and life is in *the blood*. It borders
on the gullible when one tries to suppress in the Gospel every
reference to the blood. With respect to our salvation blood is

always again in the foreground, not by way of comparison, but
in its deepest conception. In the blood is the life; when blood
flows away life itself passes out; and only when blood regains its
vital power does life revive again. If by His Incarnation Christ
has saved us unto life, then with Him also the power unto life
must reside in the human blood. And so when He instituted His
Holy Supper Christ naturally pointed with all solemnity, in the
use of wine, to His blood as the vital principle for all His people.
Christ did not recoil at the severity that was implied in the blood
atonement. For nineteen centuries now He always maintains the
blood atonement of His Holy Supper. Not covertly in part, but
clearly and positively Christ has not merely intimated the blood
atonement, but purposely given it the foremost place, and every
time that believers in all parts of the world gather around the
sacred board of the Holy Supper of our Lord His blood is
spoken of, His blood is imaged in the wine, and in counting
with that blood our holiest emotions are aroused. So v. 6 of
the chapter in hand points to blood as the essential element and
exponent of life, when it says that not only the nations, but also
Israel has shed the blood of the prophets, and that therefore a
judgment and punishment *of blood* must come upon them.

And this is not all. According to v. 7 another voice is heard
in the temple of God in heaven, even a voice out of the altar.
"And I heard another angel out of the altar say: "Even so, Lord
God Almighty, true and rigteous are thy judgments." Note that
this cry goes out from the altar. The altar serves to receive the
victim, and to consume the offering by fire. As soon as the offering upon the altar was consumed, sin disappeared, sin came to
nought, and sin ceased its destructive operation upon the sinner.
On the altar sin went under and saved life came in sight. But
naturally this also only took place in the middle period between
the fall and the last judgment. There was no offering before
the fall, neither will there be any after the last judgment. This
reaches its conclusion in the sanctuary above. While grace lasts
and the final issue in judgment is not yet executed, on the basis of
the sacrifice of Christ, grace is still effective. But when at length
the sacred moment of the final decision is come, the sacrifice no

more renews itself, is no more brought to the altar, and without the sacrifice the altar will for ever bear witness to what God the Lord has done in the sacrifice of Christ for the triumph of His holy justice (Recht).

Therefore the special reference here is to God's *Almightiness.* "Yea Lord, thou *Almighty* God, thy judgments are true." This does not effect pleasantly him who does not believe in retribution. For then it is asked, what has the Almightiness of God to do with this matter in hand. The grace of God and His mercy may properly be spoken of here and even His holy justice, but why is the reference here to God's *Almightiness?* Yet this, as it were, answers itself, when you bring to mind the two kinds of parents spoken of above. Parents who let things pass, who are weak in the presence of their children, always go out of the children's way, and consequently can do nothing for their children morally, to lift them up to the levels of the higher life. This weakness likewise attributes to God, that He shows mercy because of complacency and leniency, while it fails of the frank recognition that redemption by the Cross is only understood when full justice is done to the Lama Sabachthani. Therefore it is so emphatically stated that God's mercy must not be taken as an indication of weakness, since on the contrary His grace, provided it is taken as inseparably connected with His law (Recht), shows the unimpeachableness of God's predominating Almightiness. In no particular is God's power and His almightiness, also in the world of morals, to be looked upon as assailed and weakened by grace. If one tittle or jot were lacking of the honor of His essentiality and the absolute truth of His sacred Right, God would not be God.

Significantly therefore the Lord Jesus begins the Our Father with the prayer: *Hallowed be thy name,* which does not refer to an external, formal, liturgical sanctification, but means to say: Let the plan for all creatures proceed from Thy being as it is in Thyself, so that as God thou wilt never accommodate thyself to us, but that Thy being, and, conform to Thy being, Thy name may ever unchangeably set the rule and establish it irrevocably, whereby in the end all creaturely being and life shall be governed. Never let Thy being adapt or accommodate itself to our need or to our impotence, but let Thy being, and thereby also Thy Name

ever unchangeably maintain itself in the face of every offence which the creature would commit against it. In the Our Father Jesus puts this prayer first, and every subsequent petition must proceed from, and remain connected with it. And in keeping with this the angel in the Apocalypse prays: Even so, Lord, Thou *Almighty* God, that is to say, Thou God, Who by Thy being dost govern and maintain all things, Thou dost send out judgments that are both true and righteous. This means that they proceed from the being of God, and sternly and fully maintain the claims of the being of God. Thus it is always again the protest on the part of the being of God against the false representation, as though the grace of God ever were weak leniency and condonation. God's being detracts nothing from the mercy, nor does the mercy detract so much as one iota from the full claim of the being of God. And though there is now a period of grace between the fall and the last judgment, in the Consummation grace ends and God's law (Recht) triumphs.

XXII

THE LAST FOUR VIALS

And men were scorched with great heat, and blas-
phemed the name of God, which hath power over these
plagues: and they repented not to give him glory.
Rev. 16, 8.

The fourth plague brings a change in our solar system. Just
what it is, is not told. It seems that in the main it will be a
change or, if you will, and aggravation of what sometimes already in part occurs in common life. The action of the sun upon
the earth is ever of two kinds. In winter there is cold and frost,
and at times summer heat is very oppressive. There is also a
difference between the cooler and more moderate climate of the
North and the sometimes scorching heat of the more Southern
and Eastern climates. Even now heat is so intense at times in the
Cordillera de los Andes, as to be a menace to him who is not used
to it. In American mountains the mercury registers at times
125° F. And the fourth plague prophesies that this unbearable
heat will be still more intense not in one part of the South only,
but in all parts of the earth that are inhabited by apostate nations.
So it seems that then the atmosphere will undergo an ominous
change, which will be of the nature of a change in the relative
positions of the earth and sun. In fact all of earthly life depends
upon this relation between our earth and the sun. When the action of the sun upon our earth weakens all natural life dies. At
the poles this is the case now. Were the relation between our
earth and the sun everywhere reduced to that between the poles,
a general death of nature would ensue. And so when the relation between our earth and the sun becomes what it now is in the
Cordilleras de los Andes, and this again intensified, there will be
such heat on the earth as to scorch and destroy all life as by
fire. And with an eye to the plague in the latter sense v. 8 says:
And the fourth angel poured out his vial upon the sun; and
power was given unto him to scorch men with fire." So what

was ominous at times before, here presents itself in aggravated form, and not only this, but the suffering which this still greater heat shall occasion will be world-wide and among all peoples. The sun which now is a blessing to all mankind shall in that last hour be a scorching and, at length, a deadly power.

This is seen by the results of this modification in the relation between sun and earth· "And men were scorched with great heat," as we read in v. 9, "and blasphemed the name of God, which hath power over these plagues: and they repented not to give Him glory." In the measure in which we feel such heat on a hot summer day, it creates discomfort and ill-humour in social life at large. When it become almost unbearable, complaints and cries of distress are heard on every side. Labor suffers by it. In New York at times people are prostrated by the heat. Now let the mercury climb to figures before unknown, and we can readily imagine the heat to become so stifling, that at length all normal life succumbs. Then it will seem as though one were attacked by glowing fire, as described in v. 8, till people feel as though they were actually burned alive. People all over the earth will then recognize this plague as a judgment of God, that is come upon them because of their sinful and demoniacal life, and this will affect them in two ways: either they will convert themselves unto God or in hellish anger they will turn on the Holy One. In the words of v. 9: They will blaspheme the name of God, and will not repent to give Him glory. If anything might have worked a change in the disposition of mind and heart, this plague of the awful heat should have done so, but this plague also fails of an effect, and therefore the text states so emphatically that what might have worked a salvation would only end in the aggravation of misconduct and blaspheming of God's holy name.

The contention that these seven plagues should not be divided into a series of three and four, but into a series of four and three, does not commend itself to us. It clearly appears from the text that the first three plagues bear a different character from the last four, and that in the representation the last four are differently clothed. The first three plagues bring disasters upon the life of nature. First a dreadful epidemic overtakes the peoples, and they are stricken as never before by any outbreak of pests, cholera or what not. The second plague kills everything that is alive in the sea. The third plague poisons the waters in rivers, lakes and fountains. But with the fourth plague something entirely different begins. This affects the position of our earth in the solar system, and thus the radical conflict between God and man reaches its climax. So here the blaspheming of God's name begins, which cuts off the last outlook upon grace, and the untempered and destructive wrath of God puts everything on fire. So the four coherent plagues that belong together begin their destructive work, as the outpouring of the fourth vial makes all peoples blaspheme the name of God; and the outpouring of the fifth vial marks the beginning of the mortal combat between God and antichrist, while the sixth vial starts the great battle with Gog and Magog, and the seventh vial brings in the final breach, so that now everything is for ever ended, and from Above the cry is heard: "It is done!", and a new order of things ensues. With the epidemic of sores and with the dying of all life in rivers and fountains, human, historic life on earth still goes on, but not with the fourth vial. There is now a total change in temperature, the antichrist makes his onslaught upon Christ, the battle of nations becomes deadly, and the seventh vial brings the final end, and with it the new order of things.

This entirely modified character of the last four plagues is not least strongly evident in the fifth plague. Of this we read in vs. 10 and 11 that "the fifth angel poured out his vial upon the seat of the beast," or throne of the antichrist, with the result that "the kingdom of the beast shall be darkened." In consequence of this, unbelieving mankind will angrily turn against everything that is holy; dreadful woes and pains will take hold of the life of the peoples, and because of these woes the nations shall gnaw their tongues for pain. Rather than turning them to repentance the terrible pain will incite the nations to blaspheme God, and the ruling nations will rise up in outspoken and unconcealed wrath againts the Holy One. This is for no small part aggravated by the continuance also under the fifth vial of the grievous epidemic. As we read in v. 11, men blasphemed God not only because of their *pains,* but also because of their *sores.* Evidently the antichristian powers had labored under the delusion that the battle was already theirs. Believers had been banished and had died or had been put to death. The world power seemed to have brought everything into final subjection to itself. All life on earth had become demoniac, and no longer Almighty God but antichrist was worshipped and glorified. But the fifth vial brings a radical change. The world power gives way and the power of God triumphs. The defeat is final and as God triumphs the demoniac world power crumbles and perishes.

The complete ruin of the existing state of things is indicated in the outpouring of the sixth vial by the total change that takes place in the great river Euphrates. We read in v. 12 that: "the sixth angel poured out his vial upon the great river Euphrates; and the water thereof was dried up, that the way of the kings of the east might be prepared." This reference to the Euprates does not mean that this will take place in the land of ancient Nineveh and Babylon. In fact the place of this final conflict is not named. Babylon and Euphrates are but symbolical historic names and are no indicators of given regions or places. They only state the important fact that the great opposition of the world against God began with what in by-gone times in Babylon and Nineveh had resisted Israel. The mighty Babylon with an idolatry of its own led the van in power of State, in development of art and of its own resources as well as of religion, and overshadowed by this great Empire was the small, almost puny Israel with no other shield for cover than its unique religious calling. By the side of the puissant Babylon and Nineveh, Israel seemed to be of no account, and yet in the end, as already now we see, Babylon and Nineveh were to come to nought, while Israel was to continue life in two ways: First as the Israel of God in the church of Christ, and again in the ever yet self-propagating race of the Jews.

But although ancient Babylon and Nineveh have come to nought, the fatal worldly power that sprang up in these great cities has at all times perpetuated itself in the life of the nations. The same spirit that once inspired Babylon still lives on unweakened in the worldly life of the great powers, and still dominates the life of the world. Names may have been changed, other nations may have appropriated Babylon's sinful lusts, but in every age and under every metamorphosis aspirations and aims have remained the same. Even a country like Japan is intent upon nought else, than upon what gave the key-note and ruled the thoughts in Babylon and on the Euphrates. Thus if in connection with v. 12 the ancient Euphrates needs no recalling, this does not alter the fact that what operates, inspires and dominates the life of the nations and in the hour of the Consummation will dominate the same, is the selfsame spirit that once ruled Nebuchadnezzar, and from Babylon has communicated itself to entirely different but like-minded and like-inspired nations, and will do the same until the end of time. What nations in the hour of the Consummation will be in the lead and will strive to force the issue, no one knows; only they will be those that have been inspired by the spirit of ancient Babylon, and through the long series of nations that have appropriated the hierarchy of the world unto themselves, have nursed the worldly inclinations of ancient Babylon; these in the end will celebrate their triumph in the kingdom of antichrist, and after *his* triumph, in his defeat, come to their own ruin. Having this in mind we understand what is meant by the three frogs in vs. 13 and 14. "And I saw three unclean spirits like frogs come out of the mouth of the dragon, and out of the mouth of the beast, and out of the mouth of the false prophet, for they are the spirits of devils, working miracles, which go forth unto the kings of the earth and of the whole world, to gather them to the battle of that great day of God Almighty." This too shows the more truly that we need not hark back to ancient Babylon and to the Euphrates in the local sense, but that Babylon here merely indicates the spirit of the world as already in ancient Babylon it set itself in array against Almighty God, and from Babylon has perpetuated itself in the successive world empires, and will do so till the end, with no other motive and with no other intent than to set up the world power as predominant over against God, and at length to force a final conflict that will show whether God and His Almightiness or Satan and his demoniac antichristian endeavor will achieve the final victory.

Dragon, beast and false prophet indicate the three great world powers of philosophy, politics and pseudo-religion. At the standpoint of the antichrist every spirit goes out from Satan, all power goes out from the antichrist, and all worship concentrates itself in the religion of the false prophet. So these three belong together. The one does not exist without the other two. Thus it is perfectly plain that these three are here taken together because fundamentally they are one. Even the image of the three frogs that is applied to them is not at all mysterious. Frogs are small creatures that hop about in water and in mud, and their croak emits one sound which is tuned to one key-note only. Their croaking is deadly monotonous and leads to nothing higher. And such is the case in hand. The three powers of philosophy, politics and pseudo-religion are inseparable, and are cither holy or demoniac. When they are holy everything is inspired by the Holy Spirit, gives birth to Christian government and glorifies itself in Christian public worship. But when action springs from the demoniac, Satan is the inspiring spirit, political power turns itself against Christ, and religion reduces itself to pagan chit-chat. This trio ever belongs together. If it is the divine trio, there is the higher, holy·life of the angelic song. But when the demoniac trio strikes the key-note there is nothing save the croaking of the frogs. This is the antithesis in vs. 13 and 14. Especially v. 14 confirms it. Here we are told that the ruling spirit will be the spirit of the devil, that political power will be in the hands of earthly kings who perhaps unconsciously serve Satan, and that the peoples, or as it literally reads "the whole world" shall gather to do battle, that is, in the final conflict against Almighty God. Signs of this appear already now. This state of affairs is not yet, but is on the way. Presently "the great day of God Almighty" dawns when things will actually be as here they are prophesied·

In connection with this there follows the announcement of Christ that His coming is at hand. "Behold" v. 15, "I come as a thief. Blessed is he that watcheth, and keepeth his garments, lest he walk naked, and they see his shame." Admit that Christ does not say this, but that here St. John repeats what Christ said to him in Rev. 3, 3, the prophecy is the same and shows anew how surprising the parousia will be. What is said of the garments wherewith one should be clothed, refers likewise to the suddenness of the Lord's return. They who are confident and un-afraid lay their garments aside upon retiring. In olden times it was customary to disrobe entirely and naked go to sleep. But when the Lord returns there will be no more time to rest, for His knock on the door may be heard at any moment, so not to undress is suggested, and fully clothed to await what comes. If one had retired and the parousia suddenly came, he would be unprepared and thoughtless and unfaithful, and just this must be prevented.

And now in conclusion the seventh sound is heard from Above, and the seventh vial does not announce the end, but makes it im-mediately occur, even in the everything piercing sound of the statement: *It is done.* We would say; all is over. Everything is ended. History has reached its goal. And the new order of things towards which every former thing tended, now ensues. Yet this pertinent statement is not all. The end itself is now depicted. It is not merely said, as on a program, that the end is come, but we see as before our eyes how it begins and what is brings. So the prophecy follows in vs. 18-21, that there shall be voices and thunders and lightnings, and that amid these awful noises the whole earth will be shaken by so destructive an earthquake as never was known before. Or in the words of the text: "an earth-quake such as was not since men were upon the earth," which means that this last earthquake will be entirely different from any to which we have been accustomed. Common earthquakes were but shiftings of some component parts of our earth. But this was to be different. The world had come to its end, and was to be utterly torn apart, to give place to an entirely new order. This is first applied to the political world empire. The great city (v. 19) shall be divided into three parts. The words "into three parts" are naturally not to be taken literally, for the meaning is that the whole state of things is to be torn out of its relation. And that great city does not refer to Rome or Paris, to Berlin or New York, but indicates that also in that last hour, as had always been before, the centrum of world power would be in one given place, where then a king bears rule and exercises authority over the whole earth. Where this will be, will only appear when the last hour is come. But wherever that world power of the antichrist may be located, it shall suddenly crumble, be scattered and destroyed. In the words of v. 19, it will have to drink and drain to the last drop "the cup of the wine of the fiercenes of God's wrath." And now comes the terrible overthrow of all things. Every island suddenly disappears and every mountain sinks into the deep, and a destructive power from Above descends upon all the earth, here imaged by a great hail whose stones weigh a talent each, so that if one of these stones were to hit a person it would mean instant death. And in conclusion comes the pitiful story that in that dreadful moment there will no one convert himself, for even in that hour of the final issue men will again blaspheme God's name, and thus blaspheming God will go down into the abyss and descend into hell.*

———

* Verse 16 is not examined. "And he gathered them together into a place called in the Hebrew tongue *Armageddon.*" Ar means city and seems to refer back to Megiddon. Leading exegetes agree that this does not refer to any given region or city, but to what we read in Judges 5, 19. With respect to the Consummation this mention of Ar-Mageddon or Ir-Megiddo is of no consequence.

XXIII

"IT IS DONE"

*And the seventh angel poured out his vial into the air;
and there came a great voice out of the temple of
heaven, saying, It is done.* Rev. 16, 17.

From chapter 16, which records the outpouring of the last
vial, we now pass on to chapters 20-22, that in conclusion we
may deal with what lies in between as the final scene. Not that
chapters 17-19 are not highly important, but they bear a different character. When the seventh angel had poured out his
vial, a great voice came out of the temple of heaven, from the
throne, saying, *It is done,* which, as observed before, in Greek
is but the one word: *Gegone.* This indicates that the course
of historical events is ended, and that nothing further would
happen save the end itself in its consummation. And in chapter
21 the same word concludes the course of things. We read in
v. 6 of said chapter: "And He said unto me, It is done", thus
again the word *Gegone,* upon which immediately follows: "I am
Alpha and Omega, the beginning and the end. I will give unto
him that is athirst of the fountain of the water of life freely".
But though both times the same word *Gegone* is used, between
the two times the whole mundane existence has come to destruction. When in Rev. 16, 17 the voice came out of heaven, saying,
It is done, with all its woe and misery the old world was still
intact. Though its end was at hand, it still was in its original
form. But when in Rev. 21, 6 it is again said "It is done" the
end is not only come, but is fully come to pass, is perfected and
consummated.

So *history,* if we may strongly emphasize this word, goes regu-
larly on until the outpouring of the last vial,—that is, up to and
including chapter 16, after which the final events and conditions
ensue. Thus chapter 16, 17 marks the turningpoint in the all-
embracing statement that now "it is done"; which clearly indicates that the normal course of human history, as was begun

in Paradise, is ended. But in chapter 21, 1 an entirely new condition has arisen. The reading is plain: "And I saw a new heaven and a new earth: for the first heaven and the first earth were passed away; and there was no more sea." And though v. 6 of this same chapter repeats this pertinent statement, so that again we read in vs. 5 and 6: "And He that sat upon the throne said, Behold, I make all things new. And He said unto me, Write: for these words are true and faithful. And He said unto me, It is done," yet what lies in betwen the two sayings: "It is done" is entirely uncommon, strange and wholly exceptional, in that it is no longer earthly history, neither is it part of the new state of things on the re-created world, but bears the entirely peculiar character of transition. With the first "It is done" the world passes away and with the second: "It is done" the passing away of the old world and the transition into the new is consummated. Naturally between these two there is an exceptional state of things, an entirely unique occurrence, an attack on heaven and earth, which is no part of our present world history, and can not yet be counted as belonging to the new state of things on the new earth under the new heaven, but is entirely exceptional. After long smouldering the flame has broken out. With roaring detonations everything has crashed down into ruin. And when presently the fiery glow has spent itself, the new earth under the new heaven is come.

And between the last moment of the world history and the first moment of life on the new earth, the stupendous event takes place. A mighty conflagration consumes the old world and all that is therein, and thanks to God's omnipotence out of this ruin arises an unlooked-for new order of things, which constitutes the blessedness of the reborn Paradise. But between these two mighty events there is that transitional state of things, which can neither be reckoned as part of our old world history, nor as belonging yet to the new earth and the new heaven. Things then go on as with a great fire. First the old house stands secure in all the beauty of its noble proportions, and passers-by admire the grandeur of its dimensions. Then the first signs of fire within begin to appear. Soon other parts of the mansion show fire, and before long the whole house is one mass of flame. Also this condition then lasts for a while. Salvage of any part of the structure becomes more and more impossible, until utter ruin can no longer be averted. For a few moments then the frame of the perishing house stands out in the fiery glow of its enveloping flames, till suddenly it all totters and gives way and comes crashing down in utter collapse. Now there is no longer any house. Nothing is seen save the glow of stray sparks, and nothing but a heap of ruins marks the site which the house once occupied.

Yet here this is not so. In the final world conflagration two powers are at work: the destructive power of the everything-consuming fiery heat and the recreating and newly creating Almightiness of God; and when at length the devouring flame is extinguished no heap of ruins remains, but an entirely new creation which is indicated as a new heaven and a new earth gloriously occupies the site where the old world passed away. Not as though thereby the whole past is transposed into splendour and glory. Prophecy of old and Christ and His apostles have pointed to the fact which can not be ignored, that after the old world shall have passed away, aside from the new, there will also be a place of woe, where there will be "weeping and gnashing of teeth." Leaving this dreadful part of the eternal future aside for a moment, the teaching of the Apocalypse is plain as to the coming end of human history in the earth, and to the new creation of a new heaven and a new earth. And this implies a transitional period, referred to above, when what is, ceases to be, and the new is born by the wonder working power of Almighty God.

Thus revelation first gives an insight into the shorter or longer period of Divine forbearance, Divine toleration, Divine patience, one would almost say of Divine permission of demoniacal human injustice. We purposely put the words demoniac and human together. For remember that according to Scripture sin in the earth is not original with man. Scripture teaches that we have to count with three spheres. The holy sphere of the life of God and His angels. The demoniac sphere of the devil and his satellites. And the sinful sphere in which fallen man lays himself open to the influence of Satan, yet by God's grace in Christ is not left unto himself. So the world can not come to an end until first the relation between our world and the world of

demons is brought to an issue. Therefore the closing chapters
of the Apocalypse make it evident in every way that at length
in the final conflict between God and Satan everything concentrates itself in the arena of human life. That last conflict is not
merely two-sided as between God and man. Even as in Paradise,
so also in the final sphere, when everything is to come to an
issue, the relation is *three-sided*. The power that opposes God
is not original in man but in the world of angels, and Satan in
opposing God drags man down with him into that apostasy.
Thus in the final scene the struggle again is bound to be between
these three powers, on one side God, and on the other not sinful man alone, but man and Satan. And the closing chapters of
the Apocalypse show that in the end man's redemption can not
be perfected until that demoniac revolt is broken, and that so soon
as this is broken the new condition of the re-creation ensues.

Just this, however, imparts a still more uncommon and even
an entirely exceptional character to the end of the final conflict,
which should firmly be held in mind. If in the final catastrophe
the reckoning were merely between the holy God and sinful man,
the end of things would have appeared in a much simpler form.
But this was not so, neither could be. Sin is not original with man·
There was sin in Satan and in his satellites long before there was
any sin in man. The angel world was already there, and in that
world of angels from the first the great ethical problem had been
staged. Had no man ever been created, the world of angels
would have brought the mighty ethical problem to an issue. In
that glorious world of angels revolt began. Angels are rational
beings, even in a stronger sense than would presently be the case
with man. Angels were no blind instruments, no thoughtless ma-
chines. A moral world order was operative in them. And the
distinguishing mark in the nature of angels was, that their de-
liberate choice against God settled that matter for aye. No fallen
angel is susceptible of conversion and thus also not of salvation.
The moral choice which angels make, is clear and absolute. With
great difficulty only can we form an idea of the magnificance of
the highest angel before his fall. Luther called him "a brother of
Christ," and that was not saying too much. Satan is a disagree-
able name that fills us with horror, but that very name of Satan

or of head of demons expresses the excellency of his person. Yet from this it follows, that in the final conclusion the conflict could not simply and solely be concerned with man, but in the final conflagration, in which it all would end, of itself three factors would be involved: The holiness of God, and next to this not only lost man but also the final dispensation in the world of angels. And, therefore, in the closing chapters of the Apocalypse these three elements are so strongly intermingled, that we are continually forced to count with God, with Satan and with man.

All this necessarily led the close of the Consummation to be involved in such a complex of events, that the representation of it could easily cause confusion. This made the sharp distinction between the three decisive moments a matter of highest importance. The Apocalypse, which reveals the future, was bound to indicate clearly and plainly where, and at what moment, and by what event, the ordinary historic course of life in our present world would come to an end and in a clearly observable manner be cut off. In the second place then there was bound to follow a transition moment that would be entirely separate from passing history, but in which the new condition of things had not yet come. Only then could the third moment follow, which would usher in that for which the new condition arose, which led to the final issue, which now for ever would endure. Hence to follow the Apocalypse in its course, attention must specially and carefully be centered upon these *three* moments severally. What from the world of demons mingles itself in this, is not indifferent, yet does not dominate the interlinking of the whole. What humanity undergoes is to the last instance of supreme importance. Without in the least desiring to assert that what took place in the world of angels was merely secondary, it must not be disguised that in the Apocalypse man, and the lot that awaits man, is ever in the fore; which of itself was bound to be so, because in Christ, the Son of man had brought us men into the front rank.

But then also inseparably connected with this, is the breaking off of the historic period, upon which follows the world conflagration and the coming in of the new future. Grant that God Almighty is not bound to time, the fact can not be ciphered away that it has pleased God in the creation to bind Himself to an order

of time which we could assimilate. The seven day week is, even
as the change of day and night, a given order in the creation
itself, which we did not invent, but has thus been appointed by
God. Hence in all prophecy the distinction also between past,
present and future had to present itself. And so it has. All history would then run down as in a fixed roster, in days and
nights, in months and years, and so long as the ordinary normal
course of life went on, our human life would go on in the un-
dulation of time. But then there also follows from this, that a
radical modification would be necessary, so soon as the moment
had dawned, when this regular progress of the historic life of
humanity would cease. And this was here bound to be the case.
It could not be otherwise. The collapse of the whole structure
of the creation, as had to take place before the end, would make
the time-piece stop, so to speak, destroy the time-piece, and bring
in an entirely different order, which would still be bound to some
order of progress, but in an entirely new way. However viewed,
it always comes again to the three moments. There must come
an end to the working of the time-piece, on whose dial we had
thus far read the progress of time. A middle period would and
was bound to follow, in which this order of time would no longer
be observable. And from this state of utter confusion a new
condition would arise which would bring a different order of
existence into being. So we would have (1) our present life,
(2) the collapse of the house of the present creation, and (3)
the rise of a new order of things. Just as is narrated in chapter
21, 1.

With an eye to this we had to be told what would become of
demons, what would take place in the spirit world of history,
and also what would happen in the Christian world, for so far as
many Christians, who because of election belong to God, had not
yet entered upon eternity. The latter especially should be carefully noted. There have been elect from the days of Paradise;
think of Abel. There have been elect in every age, not only the
men and the women of whose faith the sacred record has come
down to us, but also those which forgotten of the world were
consecrated to God. Also the little ones which have died in in-
fancy must surely be included in this great multitude, which no

man can number. If this was so before Bethlehem, of course it went on in the same manner after the Manger. Yes, presently it spread in a wondrous way, when even whole peoples and nations were consecrated unto Him by Baptism. The apocalyptic use of the number 144,000 serves exclusively to bring out clearly the very vastness of the number of the elect. If in our limited earthly environment we incline at times to think that only a few will be saved, as even Jesus testifies: Many are called but few chosen, every student of Scripture knows that the Lord's elect of every age and of every land and of every nation taken together is bound to reach a gigantic number.

But it is equally worthy of note that Scripture always sharply distinguishes and, as it were, sets apart from among these innumerable multitudes, those who in times of persecution have suffered bitter hardships in the earth for Christ's sake and have tasted the martyr's death. In heaven these martyrs play a role which is entirely their own. They are continually distinguished from the rest of the dead. Theirs is a different lot. Thanks to their martyrdom they became peculiarly related to Christ, which peculiar relation operates on the other side of the grave. Yet what especially counts in Rev. 20 is, that other class of martyrs who likewise occupy a peculiar place, by reason of the fact, that in the last period previous to the Consummation they have been true to the faith on Jesus even unto death, and in the final tribulation have confessed and maintained their uniquely splendid Christian position. Already in advance it seemed likely that this last group of believers in the earth, which was to persevere in their faith on Christ to the end, would at length have to resist opposing forces in a special way, and when finally the end came would, so to speak, become personally involved in the mighty questions that would be at stake at the time of that end, even to such an extent, that apart from all the rest of the people they would to the death have to defend a position, but also enjoy it, which was entirely unique and could scarcely be compared with the lot of the others. Rev. 20 puts this entirely unique position before us. They are the elect by which the Chiliasts have been misled.

XXIV

ONE DAY AND A THOUSAND YEARS

*Therefore shall her plagues come in one day, death,
and mourning, and famine; and she shall be utterly
burned with fire: for strong is the Lord God who
judgeth her.* Rev. 18, 8.

Between the two positive sayings: "It is done" there is a two-fold world of events. In Rev. 16, 17 we read that now history is ended, that the regular progress of human social life is finished, and that life under Common Grace has ended in general ruin. The end is come, and with surpising rapidity the present world order terminates. Yet this is not the end of what must occur. After the regular historic course of the ages, under Common Grace, has been disrupted, the new order of things is not immediately begun. We only hear of this in Rev. 21, 6. There the great turningpoint is indicated a second time and again we read: "It is done." But though both times the saying is the same, the meaning in Rev. 21, 6 differs from that in Rev. 16, 17. Three successive conditions of things are depicted. First, the condition of our human world at the close of its history, when the end is announced. Everything pertaining to the ordinary course of human history had then taken place, and corruption everywhere had hastened the end of our human social life. Then came the short period of the great upturning of every existing thing. This also covered a fixed period. That upturning served partly to destroy what was, and partly to establish what would *eternally* abide. And only in chapter 21, 1 we learn, that St. John saw a new heaven and a new earth, for that the first heaven and the first earth were passed away, so that there was even no more sea. And when in these words the consummation is depicted, and the new state of things is realized, and all the old is brought to nought and the new world order is begun, in v. 6 we are told again: *"It is done,"* which means that what is to abide forever is now realized, and materialized. Thus Holy Scripture images succes-

198

sively: (1) how the creation came to be; (2) how that creation was ruined by Satan, which brough sin and curse into our world; (3) how Common Grace temporarily made an intermediate state of things possible; (4) how at length this intermediate state of things will come to an end, and give place to the re-creation; (5) how then there will be a short period of revelation of satanic power, and of an overturning of everything that is; and (6) how from this ruin the new world shall arise, and how then everything shall have been done to materialize the new existence on the new earth and under the new heaven.

In connection with all this, however, a most remarkable antithesis presents itself. In the foregoing recital we have come across two highly important events that belong together, but which nevertheless are sharply distinguished from each other by the fact, that in connection with one—as we saw in chapter XXII—a period of a thousand years is indicated, while in connection with the passing away of the world that same period is contracted into the shortest conceivable lapse of time. Thus the happy period of the redeemed, that enter upon eternal life, runs alongside of the period of disintegration of everything that is not under grace, and passes away. At length it all ends in a final separation. The redeemed enter into glory. They who have spurned the offer of free grace go into the place where there is weeping and gnashing of teeth. And while chapters 17, 18 and 19 deal with those that perish, chapter 20 depicts the blessedness of the saved. Meanwhile what perishes gives place to the entire renewal of heaven and earth, as we read in chapter 21. And when both the ruin of the lost and the rejuvenation and renewal of what is destined to abide for ever are consummated, for the second time we read that *"It is done,"* which means that now the last,—that is, the *eternal* period is begun.

But what in this connection particularly arrests the attention of him who traces the relation and the coherence of things that bring about the end, is the fact that two seemingly contradictory things are said about the duration of that particular period. With respect to the saved this transition period is said to last a thousand years, and again this period is spoken of as though it consisted of but one day, yes of one hour. The words that express the one are as simple and plain as the words that express the other. In behalf of the blessed, as regards this transition period, it is literally said that the dragon, the old serpent, which is the devil and Satan would be bound for a thousand years, and that he should deceive the nations no more, till the thousand years should be fulfilled. And after that, he—that is, Satan, must be loosed again a little season. But next to and over against this representation in chapter 20, 2 and 3, in Rev. 18, 19 we read the very opposite, which carries the impression that all the dreadful events that must come to pass at the time of the end will transpire in the shortest possible period of time.

Both the sayings to which we refer occur in chapter 18, the one in verse 8 and the other in verse 10. Both verses speak of the final fall of Babylon, about which it says in v. 8: "Thereupon shall her plagues come *in one day,* death, and mourning, and famine; and she shall be utterly burned with fire: for strong is the Lord who judges her." Babylon that set herself up against God has swayed the sceptre of supreme power among the nations age after age, now in this form, now in that. And so she will do until the end of time. Where she will then have to be looked for, is not stated. But it is positively said that then for the last time the power of an empire such as Babel once was, shall make itself great, and also, that then suddenly this Babylonian power shall perish, and her plagues shall come in one day. Thus the very opposite of what we understand by the millennium. According to Rev. 20 this last kingdom of the saints will go on for a thousand years, and here we have the drawing of an image that as in one single day fulfills itself. One might say that one day merely marks *the beginning* of the final plague, and that nothing is said about the length of its duration, so that also here the duration might be that of years and centuries, but the text allows no such interpretation. However taken, the beginning of a world event naturally takes place in one day, from which ever afterwards it dates. Of course this also applies here, and it would be preposterous to state that the plagues by which the last Babylon will be brought low will not begin in one century, nor in one year, but on a given day. Even as a child is born on a given day, from which he ever afterwards reckons the number of his years, so it is in the case of a great world event. Naturally it begins on a certain day, and for this very reason it is needless to say it in this special way. And since it literally reads that the plagues shall not end but come on a given day, it necessarily implies that Common Grace shall suddenly and unexpectedly be cut off, and that then almost suddenly the end shall come. If one prefers to take the expression *"in one day"* as not referring to 24 hours, but as merely tending to indicate the precipitancy of what will come to pass, we do not object, provided he understands and grants that the expression itself points to an end that comes in with precipitancy.

This is further confirmed by what follows in v. 10, which refers to the same event as v. 8, but with this difference, that what v. 8 says will take place *in one day,* v. 10 reduces to the space of *one hour.* When the kings of the earth shall see the smoke of the burning of that great metropolis, they shall bewail her, and bemoan her downfall, saying, "Alas, alas that great city Babylon, that mighty city! for in one hour is thy judgment come" (v·10). Here too of course Babylon is not the Babel of antiquity, but the great city that in the Consummation is to be the great metropolis, and which then will be destroyed. And it is emphatically said that the destruction of that last great metropolis shall suddenly come upon her, yes so suddenly as to occur in *one hour.* It does not say that at length the hour of her destruction is come, but that the judgment upon this last Babel is come *in one hour.* There is nothing uncertain about this. On the contrary that one hour is indicated as the shortest possible period of time in which God's judgment would come upon the last Babel.

This positive saying in v. 10 also confirms the representation that the saying in v. 8 of one day must be taken in the literal sense. Thus the Scripture emphatically teaches that by disaster and destruction the end will take sinful humanity by surprise. The history of all great cities shows that shame and sin abound in these congested centers of population. It is even difficult to deny that in the course of time the sinful and demoniacal character of the great cities of the world had rather become more vicious than more pure. If this goes on to the end of time, and at length the final appearance of the great metropolis or, if you

will, the sinful Babel has come to development and Consummation, nothing can be looked for save spiritual degeneracy and demoniac life at its worst. And in keeping with this the decline,
the fall and the passing away of this last great metropolis at the
end of time will assume a baffling character and bring a sudden
change into all of human life. Thus in this striking representation there is nothing inexplicable. Ancient Babylon fell, but the
Babel-idea of sinful and criminal usurpation of power has perpetuated itself in human life of all time, yet in no city has the
demoniac degeneration of human life come to its final deadly
acme. So what we are here told is but part of history. From century to century now in this, then in that city, Babel goes on and
on. And also at the time of the end there will be a metropolis in
which the type of sinful Babylon seeks its realization and issue.
Upon that great metropolis destruction will then descend and unexpectedly and suddenly take this last Babel-type by surprise, and
then shall be the end.

Thus it very evident that what in Rev. 20 is said of the millennium, and in chapter 18 of the destruction of Babel, presents
a striking antithesis. Of the last kingdom of the "Israel of
God" we are told that it will be of long duration, and the statement that it will last a thousand years is even seven times repeated (Rev. 20, vs. 2, 3, 4, 5, 6, and 7) ; while of the destruction
of the world power as represented in the great metropolis is said,
that it will take place in the shortest thinkable time. In v. 8 it
says in one day, and in v. 10 in one hour. This clearly shows
that here the computations of time are not taken by the count,
but only figuratively express the duration of what is to come.
However sudden the end of days may be, it is plain that even
the great metropolis will not be taken and destroyed in sixty
minutes. This might be possible, if it merely meant the capture
and surprise of that great city. One can imagine that the metropolis of the end might not be fortified by a girdle of fortresses
or forts, and be entirely in the open. In such a case that city
might well be surprised by a mighty hostile army, and the assail-
ant reach the market-place in one hour. But this would not be
the destruction of such a lost Babel. The capture of a great city
like London, Paris or Berlin, which would end their metropolitan

supremacy, would normally require at least two days, but to destroy such a city in one hour would be out of the question.

Of course fancy can here be at play. One can imagine that such a city is suddenly taken by surprise, that it is not protected by army or fortifications, and that presently the hostile forces occupy an all-commanding position in the midst of or above that city. But here no such representations are in place. Ancient Babylon was taken suddenly by surprise one night by the draining of the Euphrates and by the entrance of the hostile army, but the matter in hand here is the last Babel, which is to be the most gigantic metropolis that has ever been known. If the reference were to a smaller metropolis of lesser importance, no one would take it as an image of the richest and most gigantic and unsurpassable development that would at length characterize the final Babylon. If in your imagination you minimize the last Babel or deem it of less significance, the whole representation is devoid of sense. The question here is the realization of a sinful idea that first in ancient Babylon tried to assume a visible form and tangible appearance, in the course of centuries made constant progress, assumed proportions that from age to age became more and more formidable, till at length it reached that high realization beyond which there was none higher. He who compares the scope of ancient Babylon with that of later Rome and Byzantium, and finally that of New York, London, Berlin or Tokio, sees as before his eyes, how the metropolitan idea does not remain equal to itself, but ceaselessly going on through the ages assumes ever mightier proportions, and realizes that there would be no sense in it, if with respect to the end of time the Apocalypse would refer to what now would be an insignificant capital city like Amsterdam. It must have had in mind a metropolis in its highest conceivable proportions. The great Babylon which Rev. 18 describes far surpasses everything that in a great metropolis ever bewildered the senses and outshone previous metropolitan glory. And when such a gigantic metropolitan city is said to have fallen in one day, yes in one hour, it is evidently no literal statement of fact, but rather the indication of the speed, the hurry, yes the precipitancy wherewith things will come to pass, when the end of the world is come. So we have the same word and the same image used twice. The image of the last period in the history of believers is seen to be that of a millennium, and the image of the fall of the unholy world such as could limit itself to one day, yes to one hour; which makes you realize that both times the language is figurative: one time to make you clearly understand that the destruction and the passing away of the sinful world shall be indescribably dreadful, and the other to make you realize the exceeding richness and excellence of the last experience of believers.

Purposely therefore, we did not enter upon the question of the millennium in the preceding chapter more fully than to show that the 20th chapter of Revelation draws an image which the history of our world's life under Common Grace does not explain. There is something in what the 20th chapter images, that is not of this world, but like the world separates itself, and depicts the end of the life of believers in a semi-heavenly state, as we will explain more fully. For the moment it needed to be made clearly evident that here we face two worlds neither one of which tallies with the ordinary life of our world. The common life of the world, we are told, had been ruined by the invasion of Satan's demoniac forces on a scale unheard of before. This, therefore, in the explanation of the closing part of the Apocalypse, demands special emphasis. As shall have to be shown more particularly, the character of our earthly life shall indeed be modified. It is now perturbed by satanic instigations, yet according to the word of Jesus Satan's power for the present is still bound, and only at the end shall that demoniac power be unbound, loosed and given free rein to work out its abominations in the earth. We can form no adequate idea of what the horror of that period shall be. It will in every way be crushing and overwhelming. But that bewildering period will also be the beginning of the end. There will be no more Common Grace. Satan will no longer personally act upon us by evil inspirations of every sort, as now, but will come down to earth and try to appropriate dominion over our earthly life itself. Everything we read of the dragon and the beast points to this. This entirely modified character of the final state of things in the earth alone will explain the course of the concluding events. What now is still fused and intertwined will then be separated, which will give rise to two modes of existence that are utterly alienated from each other.

For so far as after the fall our life went on from Paradise through Israel, by way of Bethlehem, and Golgotha, and Pentecostal glory, the life of the lost and the life of the blest together formed one human life, and in every way the salvable and the unsalvable continued to be mutually related and associated. But according to Jesus' word, even between parents and children, husbands and wives separation shall once be final. For the present however that final separation still tarries. Beside the Christian religion there is ever yet Common Grace. But one day this will come to an end. Then comes the descent of Satan into our human life. Then powers will arise that are portrayed to us in the beast and in the dragon. And then the final development of the unholy will take a way of its own, which necessarily will cut off every possibility of relationship with the final experience of the blest. Then the two part company. The final history of believers in what is called the millennium will assume an entirely peculiar character, will be entirely separate from the life of the world, and must needs appear as though it places over against the demoniacal final development of the world a heavenly and from above inspired perception of the soul. Thus in the Apocalypse chapter 20 is separate both from what precedes and follows, in order to present itself in a character of its own. And this from age to age has given rise to confusion in the conception of this part of the Apocalypse.

XXV

THE JUDGMENT UPON BABYLON*

And there came one of the seven angels which had the seven vials, and talked with me, saying unto me, Come hither: I will shew unto thee the judgment of the great whore that sitteth upon many waters. Rev. 17, 1.

Chapter 17 begins no new series of revelations. The vials have put an end to the prophecy of what will come to pass. With the vials history ends. "And the great city" as we read in Rev. 16, 19, "is divided into three parts, and the cities of the nations fell: and great Babylon came in remembrance before God, to give unto her the cup of the wine of the fierceness of His wrath." This clearly indicates that the normal historic course is at its end and that the collapse of the whole and the direct passing away follows. This end is here dealt with. Of this the Consummation speaks. All things are now in ruins and utter confusion, and true believers come to stand by themselves, while the whole structure of the world collapses, and a new system of things comes to light in the new earth and the new heaven which take the place of the old. But between this conclusion of history in chapter 16, 21 and the separation of believers in chapter 20 there are three important chapters, 17, 18 and 19, which demand attention. What have these three chapters to say? They can give no continuation of world history, for this is now ended. Neither can they forecast the new state of things, for that is recorded in chapter 21. What then do these three important chapters have to say?

That here a fourth series of judgments by angels should follow, can not be granted. There has not been a fourth series of historic events. The vials marked the end. Neither can these three chapters give an insight into what will be new and eternal, because what they deal with belongs to the old mundane state of

---

*In the original "The Judgment upon Babylon" covers chapters XXV-XXIX.

things. The main difficulty which here we face is that everything is clothed in figurative language. The main mention is of a woman, and yet it soon appears that this is merely symbolic. Not a word is said of an actual woman. Woman is the name that is given to what in the end of days will present itself as the great metropolis. Again we are apt to be misled by what is told of this woman, and in connection with her of the terrible beast and the demon. We are so prone to think that everything here refers solely to what will happen at the end of the world. Yet this is not so. The sinful process which must end in selfdestruction, does not begin when history ends, but began in Paradise, runs through all history and only terminates in the Consummation. So the content of these three chapters harks back to the past, and shows that the destructive line extends all the way from Paradise to the end of the world's life and only there reaches its goal. This would not be possible if given persons in the course of human history were dealt with, neither is there any mention of this. The course and effect of unholy principles here appear in the form of an image, and this hidden movement that governs the course of life claims the attention. The spirit that governs a country, the spirit that rules a people, a city and sometimes a village from century to century is not embodied in one single person, nor does it show itself in any one personal life. And this spirit that rules every people in every land is dealt with at length in the three chapters in hand.

The very first verse of chapter 17 shows that here we have no fourth, new series of historical successions. "And there came one of the seven angels which had the seven vials, and talked with me, saying unto me, Come hither; I will shew unto thee the judgment of the great whore that sitteth upon many waters." So there are no seven angels that are now to speak. For the angel that here speaks is one of the seven angels which had the seven vials. Thus nothing of a new series is said. What here is given but continues the judgment of the vials, not that a new vial is poured out, but that the results of the series of vials are further elucidated. It is the conclusion of the judgment that brings the end, and this judgment is here applied to the centrum of the world's life, as at length it concentrates itself in a given city and which city is represented in the form of a woman. That city, that is headed toward destruction, has in the course of time, as is commonly held, expressed itself in a given form, now in this, and again in that metropolis, all according to the years in which the writer lived, and some given city exhibited moral ruin. We see this in Da Costa's prophecy regarding Paris. The world catastrophe that from Paris had come upon all Europe impressed Da Costa so overwhelmingly that he was convinced that Paris was the city upon which this judgment was to be visited. Such had been the case before with Rome, first with the Rome of the emperors and later with the Rome of the Vatican. There was always some great city that forced itself to the fore and ruled the whole status and mutual relation of the nations and from which those influences emanated that corrupted all of life. As circumstances dictated this was at one time interpreted socially and politically, at another time purely ecclesiastically. When imperial Rome seemed to be the exponent of the general degradation of man, the question at stake was the political power of the Caesars; yet it was equally natural that later, when the issue of the Christian church was at stake the low state of morals in life at large was not laid to the charge of the political power but to ecclesiasticism, and that from this viewpoint the Vatican occupied the attention, because of the inquisitorial persecution of the adherents of the new movement.

But however much the ideas regarding the meaning of these three chapters differed, in the main it always came down, not to what a single person, or a group of persons had achieved or established, but to the general spirit that for a long time had governed the life-view, and had led it into a given direction. For the mutation of that spirit the continual use of the word *whore* expresses most clearly that there is mention here of an *immoral* turn in the trend of life. The ugly word *whore* is not used here metaphorically, but literally. Without hesitation it declares that the social life in so thickly populated a leading city readily resulted in moral degeneration at top speed, which was bound to work moral corruption everywhere. That chapter 17, 1, where this view obtains, speaks not merely of the whore, but of "the

great whore" most strikingly indicates that at the approach of
the Consummation moral corruption shall have increased hand
over hand, and shall have given rise to a demoralized state of
life which directly calls for the last judgment and excludes all
hope of deliverance or salvation.

This "whoring" applies, as is self-evident, in both senses of
the actual and the metaphorical. So we read in v. 2 that this
morally deeply fallen woman is a sinful woman with whom the
kings of the earth have committed fornication, and thereby gave
rise to a city- and a national-life, in which both city and country-
men have been made drunk with the wine of her fornication. In
Scripture marriage is always the all-prevailing image. St. Paul in
his epistle to the Ephesians sets forth the solidarity of Christ and
His believers in the holy image of Bride and Bridegroom, and the
violation of wedlock is always used as image by which to paint
in the most lurid colors the unholy disposition of those who face
perdition. Thus it is entirely in the spirit of the Scripture that
also here marriage is referred to, and that violation of wedlock
is most luridly brought to light in the lewd woman who slights
marriage, and whose one ambition is by her voluptuousness to
draw all men after her. And as these adulterous practices on ever
larger scales poison and corrupt the whole moral state of things,
and inflames the whole disposition and spirit of such a metropolis
and inspires it with false ardour, there is no escaping the banal
results, namely, that adultery infects the life of the body and
poisons it through and through, and that also the social and religious life is in every way corrupted, so that in the end both
physically and spiritually the conditions of such a metropolis suffer ever greater loss. In connection with this it is especialy
necessary to keep in mind that this is not a question of a few
years or of one lifetime, but is generally a dominating question
of many centuries, which as of itself and unperceivably makes
the moral and social condition continually to grow worse.

This was especially observable in the rise of Berlin. As soon
as her population began to enlarge on a scale by which it promptly
ran into the millions, there began to appear also in this previously
staid and sober minded city a phenomenon which had long dis-

graced Paris, London and New York. The several contagious
diseases directly traceable to syphilitic conditions show how rapidly even among the higher social classes degeneracy can progress.
Among the student body alone the cases of syphilitic poisoning
was so alarmingly on the increase as to make every one who
takes life at all seriously mourn. It became more and more the
custom to spend the greater part of the day in bed, so as to devote
long hours of night to the sinful indulgence. We need not go
back to Rome or Alexandria to visualize the evils of a demoralized life. What the Apocalypse here depicts in such dark colors
as the distress of the times of the end, may presently increase in
degree; in kind it has always been known as the natural result
of crowding too many people within the confines of a single town.
No metropolis has ever been able to wean itself from this. Thus
the angel here naturally strikes unsparingly at the heart of the
deeply sinful character of metropolitan life, and plainly indicates
that though in later ages such cities may be called Christian,
moral corruption will steadily go on, and at the time of the end
shall have assumed so universally a vitiating character that the
tone of life will make the impression of being thoroughly demoniacal.

The angel indicates the universal character of this phenomenon
by saying that "the great whore sitteth upon many waters." The
"waters" here signify the many nations that under the ravages of
this sin have succumbed. And note also that the woman makes
a twofold appearance. In v. 1 she appears as sitting "upon many
waters" which indication is borrowed from ancient Babylon and
Nineveh which were generally said to be located on the Tigris and
Euprates, and presently became connected with Tyre and Sidon·
So Euphrates and Tigris indicate the great waters that coursed
through the land of Asia, and Tyre and Sidon recall the waters
of the Ocean which in ancient times owed their glory particularly
to these two cities. But if this could be represented in this way
because as a rule life at sea furthers immorality, yet at the approach of the Consummation it could not be said that the final
catastrophy would limit itself to seaports and sailors. Rather it
had to be made plain that the final catastrophy would affect our
whole race, and while deniers of Christ were to be separated

from believers on His name, all nations and peoples would be more and more corrupt, which would bring down judgment not only upon a given region, but upon the whole world. This also shows why the adulterous woman which at first is bound to the waters of the Ocean and to the great rivers, now appears in the entirely other image of a woman that is carried by a beast from which she derives her leadership. As we read in v. 3: "So he carried me away in the spirit into the wilderness: and I saw a woman sit upon a scarlet colored beast full of names of blasphemy, having seven heads and ten horns." Naturally this is the same woman who was first indicated as the great whore that sitteth upon many waters. Only, here she is given another meaning. At first she was little else than a temptress, but here she is the venomous woman whose object has been attained, and now could really present herself as ruler.

What is said of this venomous woman in her second appearance points to her wealth and splendour. She is no longer the whore standing on a street corner enticing men, and by her sin getting their money, but here she appears as possessing great wealth which by her finery and luxury in every way bewilders the spirits. She is a woman, so says v. 4, "arrayed in purple and scarlet color, and decked with gold and precious stones and pearls, having a golden cup in her hand." But this is not all. It is not merely this extravagant wealth, made by her sin, that distinguishes her, but this wealth goes hand in hand with her cruelty, which it is to her interest to practice on the adherents of Christ, whom moreover in her immoral life she made the objects of ridicule. Both are even circumstantially depicted in her image. Arrayed in all her finery she rides upon the scarlet colored beast, and even the solid gold cup which she holds in her hand is not empty, but rather filled to the brim with the cruelties and immoralities of her whoredom. So she ever retains her original voluptuous character, only now this side of her life also is decked with much greater wealth. Neither is this yet all. She now appears to give full expression to the mighty antithesis between what came up from Satan and what came down from God. For on her forehead she had, according to v. 5, a clearly legible written name, which name was mystery, and that mystery referred to the fact that she is the exponent of the great Babylon, even to bring that Babylon into lurid evidence as the mother of harlots and abominations of the earth. This was one aspect of her appearance, which directly connects her with the great evil of Nineveh and Babylon. Only, this was not all. The urge, the inclination, the disposition which from the demoniacal entered into man, had not only a positive but also a negative side. So everything was drawn toward Babylon, or toward what in the course of centuries some other great metropolis would adopt as the role of Babylon; while this woman at the same time was filled with bitterest hate against the Holy, and particularly against the Christ. So it follows: "And I saw the woman drunken with the blood of the saints, and with the blood of the martyrs of Jesus." It is always again the red blood color that makes her shine in her scarlet cloak, yet in such a way that in this purple tint she shows her wrath against the blood of the saints. The antithesis now showed itself in the most striking manner. And therefore follows the testimony of St. John: "And I wondered with great wonderment."

This does not mean that this woman's evil attitude against the church of Christ affected St. John strangely. The apostolate had already been made keenly aware of the bitter effect of this, as, with the exception of the Seer of Patmos, the apostles at the time had already suffered martyrdom, and he could scarcely look for anything else than to have his exile on Patmos end in the martyr-death. No his wonderment had another cause. He fully expected, that thanks to the martyrdom of the apostles and early believers, the church would gradually obtain such a standing that free and untrammeled she could pursue her course. But he did not surmise a return of the martyrdom of the early years. And what above all had never occurred to him was, what was now imparted to him, namely, that not only would the martyrdom of the early years return, but in the end would be much more alarming, much more cruel and much more terrible than it had been at first. And he recoiled from the dreadful thought, and he showed that he could not enter into this, and that he rejected the very suggestion of it. This is meant by the reading that he wondered with a great wonderment. (Dutch ver.) To wonder here means not to be able to understand, and not to be able to make tally with his former idea what it would be at the time of the end. And the angel saw in the apostle's face the look of pained surprise and almost reproaches him for not having a better insight into the course of things up to the Consummation. So the angel says to him: "Wherefore didst thou marvel? I will tell thee the mystery of the woman, and of the beast," and so only the clear insight into what is to come is imparted to the apostle.

XXVI

THE SEVEN MOUNTAINS UNDER THE
SEVEN HEADS

*For God hath put in their hearts to fulfill His will,
and to agree, and give their kingdom unto the beast,
until the words of God shall be fulfilled.* Rev. 17, 17.

Thus the idea that chapters 17, 18 and 19 of Revelation form
one coherent whole must be put aside. The 17th is a chapter by
itself, and while chapters 18 and 19 report the collapse of the
world, the 17th chapter is exclusively engaged with the organic
coherence of the world's life. The great world-events from
time to time would inevitably be linked with the names and
achievements of outstanding figures, and the insufficiency of this
representation called for supplementation. It could not be denied,
nor said to be untrue, that a few great figures in history hold the
attention of the ages, and that some names are an inspiration
to all the world. Only, when these great personalities are taken
as the sole motive of the world movement, the insight into the
course of things and into given conditions is blurred. For this
is not so. From the beginning there have been in the course of
the world's life two sharply distinguished motive powers, one of
which depended personally upon the individual, and the other is
the organically unifying motive power that in the course of centuries has governed whole generations and whole nations. And
the 17th chapter deals exclusively and purposely with that motive
power which organically unites the whole world's life, and therefore demanded treatment by itself alone. In chapters 18 and
19 the Apocalypse describes how in the final catastrophe the whole
world will be torn asunder till it utterly collapses, and then passes
over into an entirely different order of existence, as is told in
v. 1 of chapter 21. This however was preceded by the terrible destruction of what had thus far been. This was the ruin of the
world that followed when history was ended, and from which

by God's Almighty power the new state and order of things is to be born, which upon the new earth and under the new heaven shall eternally endure.

In the process of this tearing and wrenching apart of the old world, of course what was connected with the organic negotiation was bound to be considered as of paramount significance. This explains why in chapter 17 that organic coherence engages the attention so fully as to divert it for the moment from the personal element. What this chapter reports plainly results almost solely and exclusively from the mutual relation of things, and not one word is said of the mighty appearance of a single person. Yet, while most historiographers have almost never had any glimpse of this organic relation of things, no effort has been spared to explain this 17th chapter, even as the two following chapters, historically, and to discover in it nothing but a series of successive events. This has even been carried so far, that at length not only the correct explanation of what this chapter presents has been lost, but even the authenticity of the whole Apocalypse has been questioned. One knows how the Apocalypse has fared. When St. John first put it in book form it met with unconditional acceptance, and, especially in the early days of bitter persecution, it has guided the steps of the Lord's people and kept them firm in the faith. But there came an end to this. When once the Christian church was fully organized and was given state support, almost of necessity a different order and explanation of this book came gradually in vogue, in the wake of which even the authenticity of the Apocalypse began to be doubted, and from that time on almost everything in chapter 17, after the vials had been poured out, was applied to what the emperors of Rome had done to the early Christians. So also chapter 17 was soon entirely misunderstood. The organic coherence of the end of days with the fundamental trait which after the fall in Paradise had always characterized human life was utterly lost from sight, and consequently the seven mountains of Rev. 17, 9 were soon entirely misinterpreted, and were said to refer to the seven hills which formed the area of ancient Rome, and the seven heads that are mentioned in the same verse were designated as the seven emperors that were in authority in Rome.

Thus everything that was further reported in connection with this could not possibly refer to the time of the end, but only to what had already taken place in the centuries that are gone. And of course there was nothing inspiring in this. It was all a closed chapter of history. It was merely an account of what at the time had been a menace to Christianity and had well-nigh made an end of it, and the only comforting thought one could draw from it was, that even from such harrowing circumstances deliverance had been possible. But it had nothing to do with the Consummation. It was all ended and past. It contained not the slightest apocalyptic notification. In connection with this we referred to the *seven mountains.* Thus reads the 9th verse as a whole: "Here is the mind that hath wisdom. The seven heads are seven mountains, on which the woman sitteth." The Old Testament repeatedly uses the image of a mountain for political greatness,—that is, for a mighty world empire. We are familiar with the representation in Ps. 68 of Bashan "as a high hill" or mountain. "Why leap ye, ye high hills? this is the hill which God desireth to dwell in; yea, the Lord will dwell in it for ever"(v.16). To think of Rome in this connection is what no one should dare to venture. The word hill or mountain here merely designates what lifts itself above the ordinary. And as a kingdom that has attained preeminence presumes to lord it over the neighbouring kingdoms, it was natural that here the word mountain should be used for what had worked itself up to high distinction. Similarly Psalm 125, 1 and 2 speaks of the mountain of Jerusalem and the mountains that surround Jerusalem. "They that trust in the Lord shall be as mount Zion, which can not be removed, but abideth for ever. As the mountains are round about Jerusalem, so the Lord is round about his people from henceforth even for ever."

In like sense we read in Psalm 76 of *the mountains of prey.* Of God's Almightiness and kingly dominion is here said: "In Salem also is his tabernacle, and his dwelling place in Zion. Thou art more glorious and excellent than the mountains of prey. The stouthearted are spoiled, they have slept their sleep: and none of the men of might have found their hands" (vs. 2, 4 and 5). So we read in Jeremiah 51, 25 of Babel: "Behold, I am against thee, O destroying mountain, saith the Lord, thou which destroyest all the earth: and I will stretch out mine hand upon thee, and roll thee down from the rocks, and will make thee a burnt mountain." And in Isaiah 2, 12: "For the day of the Lofd shall be against every one that is proud and lofty, and against every high mountain and against all the oaks of Bashan." In Psalm 46, 2: "Therefore will we not fear, though the earth be removed, and though the mountains be carried into the midst of the sea." Ezekiel speaks in the same way of mount Seir: "Son of man, set thy face against mount Seir, and prophesy against it, and say unto it, Thus saith the Lord God: Behold, O mount Seir, I am against thee, and I will stretch out mine hand against thee, and I will make thee desolate." And in Zechariah 4, 7 also the world power is called a *mountain.* "Who art thou, *O great mountain?* Before the face of Zerubbabel thou shalt become a plain."

If from this it clearly appears what significance in the East and especially in the Hebrew process of thought is attached to the idea of a *mountain,* one will have to acknowledge at the same time that the idea, the word *mountain* lends itself much better to this sense, than to what at Rome was attached to the seven hills which constituted the territory of this great metropolis. Without emphasizing too strongly the difference between the words: mountain and hill, as they are sometimes used interchangeably, yet it can not be denied that the word mountain naturally and most unaffectedly indicates something that is high and awe-inspiring and represents great power. And since the apostle John was of Israel, and mainly wrote for the converts of Israel, there is no warrant, in the exposition, without a definite direction to the contrary, to take the expression *seven mountains* in chapter 17, 9 to mean anything else than something mighty, awe-inspiring and overwhelming. If it read: " the seven heads," it might be said to refer to well known and solidary powers. But also this is not so. It reads without the article: "The seven heads are seven mountains, on which the woman sitteth." So the idea that this refers to the seven hills of Rome must be dismissed. When St. John in his Apocalypse writes as a man of Jewish origin, so that in this instance the peculiarity of the Jewish use of language must be retained, the expression: *seven mountains* can not refer to the

seven hills of Rome, but must refer to seven independent powers,
which are here taken together as one idea.

We can not enter upon the further particulars of what follows
in connection with v. 9. A summary treatment such as the subject of the Consummation requires does not lend itself to this.
We did not do so in our treatment of the book of Ezekiel, neither
in that of Daniel, and will not do so here. The main point is
that in chapter 17 we have an organic world view, and that from
this angle the entire coherence of what is here described must be
viewed. It always comes again to this, that historic events come
about by given persons, and that at the same time all history is
dominated by trends of public opinion, which, independently of
individual persons appear each time anew to dominate the course
of history. In both of course the Divine ordinance has a voice.
Almighty God governs and directs the public appearance of individual persons whom He clothes with the required authority and
power by which to fulfil their task, according to His ordinance.
And in the same way comes the recapitulation on the part of
God of what is divided and heterogeneous into one mighty grand
organic whole, and herewith you realize in a very special sense
that it is not man that sets the whole in motion and directs it,
but that God holds the one great whole in His power and in His
hand, and disposes the outcome of the ages. We only reckon with
persons, and in our dispositions and actions we have merely to
do with them. This in part applies even to princes and heads of
state. But the Lord holds both the individual persons with all
their peculiarities of character and proper talents in His hand,
together with the nations in their coherence as a whole, which
last action on the part of God does not depend upon a few years
nor one day but usually upon the course of centuries. Here it
concerns what endures and maintains itself.

Hence that here the mysterious woman appears, who seated on
the beast influences the life of the whole world, and rules it with
a firm hand. And of course in connection with this the dominion
of feminine power, sitting upon the beast, in the course of all
history leads to an ascendency. One can not say that the action
of this woman, wherever it may be, begins in history. When
once the fall had done its part and human life had been given

its false bent, this influence of woman also began at once to be corrupt. The influence and action of this woman which poisons and corrupts everything it touches is not apparent only when the Consummation sets in, neither did it have its beginning when Christ was born and His church went out into the world. Rather from the beginning of the world this deadening and God-defying influence of woman has been abroad, disennobling, deadening and corrupting the world's life. So the seven heads and seven mountains in v.9 of the chapter in hand may well be said to indicate the succession of trends of the times and drifts of public opinion, which under this unholy influence would present themselves in the world's life. Yet this repetition would not remain equal to itself. Also in this disennobling and poisoning influence upon the life of the world there would be a process, a development, a growth in power, and according to the development of this process the unholy influence of this woman would assume increasingly dangerous proportions.

This had gone on step by step during the long centuries of history, until at length the day came when this unholy power had reached its culminating point. On one hand sin on the part of individual persons would become more sinful. The whore would become "a great whore" which in most shameful self-abandonment and in sharpest antithesis against Almighty God would strengthen her forces to the utmost. And simultaneously with this the personal life would become more and more degraded and gradually show its antichristian character more and more openly. Yet all this had been going on from hoary antiquity. This gnashing of teeth of the unholy against Almighty God had been heard in Egypt, in Babylon. He, therefore, who would understand and fathom this dreadful antithesis must from the beginning trace the steps in history by which every thing that is noble in man has become ignoble and alienated from the life of God. Then the different periods would naturally present themselves. One would see as before his eyes how from age to age the conflict between God and Satan has gone on. And now the dawn of the end characterizes itself by the fact that the revelation of Satan in the beast and in the dragon assumes so much more dreadful a character. It now becomes outspoken opposition of the satanically infected world against God, in terms of vehemence as have never been equalled before. Satan is now come to the final combat with the Lord. He will venture one more violent assault and with this will see his power for ever vanquished. And this process is consummated in the seven mountains under the seven heads.

XXVII

THE ROMAN EMPIRE AND THE TEN HORNS

*And the woman which thou sawest is that great city,
which reigneth over the kings of the earth.* Rev. 17, 18.

However complicated and figurative the second part of Revelation 17 may be, in connection with the foregoing it presents no unsurmountable difficulty to the exegete. Only, it must not be taken as a new oracle which adds a new series to that of the vials. As indicated above this is excluded by the saying that it is one of the vial-heralds who here speaks. The first verse says this so plainly as to leave no room for doubt. It is not an aside, but the introduction to the whole apocalyptic vision: "One of the seven angels which had the seven vials, came and talked with me, saying unto me, Come hither; I will shew unto thee the judgment of the great whore that sitteth upon many waters." This is all plain. We are still under the spell of the vial-vision, and now the working of this vision is more minutely shown. There is even nothing problematic here about the significance of the woman. The "many waters" are the heathen world, the sum of the numerous peoples and nations that will be in the world until the time of the end; which, as the end draws near, will grow in numbers and in prestige, and will array itself against Almighty God. Now comes the great separation. Believers withdraw from public life, as they are pushed, so to speak, into the corner by the rest of the population of the earth. They themselves, on the other hand make themselves master of everything that represents brutality in the world. Thus at first there is a state of high tension. This tension turns into radical estrangement, and the worldly power soon lays claim to the whole earth, repulses true believers, and forces separation. It is no mere shifting but gradually an absolute separation. The compassion of God withdraws itself. The final issue brings the judgment near. And so the outcome is twofold: Believers isolate themselves, and in the great powers of the world the power of the beast, as it reads, takes a new lease on life. This is all plain reading, provided the beast here is not taken as an actual beast, but as a human spirit which has so abandoned all those higher things that ennoble man and spiritually exalt him, till at length there is nothing left save what puts man on a level with the beast.

Moreover in earthly life the relation between the holy and the unholy has been radically modified. This can be explained from more than one viewpoint. This is seen in its strongest colors, when one considers the absolute change that has taken place in the relation between Satan and this world. If one counts from the great miracle of Pentecost, the cross of Golgotha had not wholly stripped Satan yet of his ruling power in the earth, but had so hedged him about, that presently the church was able to establish herself in the earth, to lengthen her cords, and even obtain such supremacy among the nations as to break the demoniacal influences if not in individual persons yet in the system of nations as a whole. In this matter Common Grace in the course of time led to glorious results. Not only did it break for many centuries the ascendency of the demoniac element, but worked a more and more historic progress among the heathen nations, which removed the offensiveness of this heathen life at least in part, and gave rise to a more tolerable state of things. The external power over the world had now passed into the hands of Christian nations which had been able to develop themselves along the lines of a higher civilization and nobler sense, and what specially counted, they, naturally, as it were, became mutually related. Christendom was the honorary title that was now applied not merely to the churches, but also to the outward life of the nations. Especially the Mohammedan apostasy, and the Crusades to which this gave rise, had imparted to the Christian nations, also politically, a great solidarity which, if it did not avert the dominion of war, reduced and mollified it. Thus a condition was born that gradually put a restraint upon the heathen nations, made them recognize the supremacy of the Christian nations, and at length proved commerce with these christianized nations to be the means by which to take a place in the real and only actual world of men, which had to be counted with in behalf of the world as a whole. The rest of the world went its way as before, but had become in popular esteem less significant and as of a lesser sort, and Satan could no longer use it as an instrument by which to revive the demoniac power anew.

The Apocalypse emphatically indicates that the demoniac power which in former times had enabled the heathen world to tyrannize over the faithful in Israel, was now shorn of its former superiority, and though it still operated on a small scale, it was of no great significance. But it must not be inferred from this, that this power had been entirely broken and subjugated. On the contrary the angel of the vials emphatically indicated that this beast—for so he called this satanic power—after he had ruled for a time, had been brought low and had almost been brought to nought; but that nevertheless this beast had at no time ceased to exist, and to exercise power, though as it were more covertly behind the scenes. This however would not go on. Rather this beast would not only regain his former power, but would see his power increase, so as at length to enable him to turn the whole state of the world's life into its opposite.

This is the meaning of the 8th verse, which is so singular when taken by itself. "The beast which thou sawest was, and is not; and shall ascend out of the bottomless pit, and go into perdition: and they that dwell on the earth shall wonder, when they behold *the beast that was, and is not, and yet is.*" Verse 11 further explains this beast as follows: "And the beast was, and is not, even he is the eighth, and is of the seven, and goeth into perdition." It could not be more positively stated that this beast would be a man. He is even said to be a *king*. When it says that this (king) is of the seven, and goeth into perdition, it refers back to v. 10 which reads "And there are seven kings: five are fallen, and one is, and the other is yet to come; and when he cometh, he must continue a short space." This is mostly taken to mean persons who wore the crown, and so it is said that here successively the emperors of Rome are indicated. But this idea must be discarded as utterly incorrect. He who so interprets this goes astray, and is bound at length to conclude that what here would stand as the record of what took place in St. John's day, was still unknown history, so that the Apostle John could not have written the Apocalypse. But when we take these seven heads and seven mountains as indicated, it becomes wholly different. If then we read in v. 10: "There are seven kings: five are fallen, and one

is, and the other is not yet come"; this does not refer to personal
princes, kings or emperors, but to chapters, parts or periods in the
great history of the world. This then began in Egypt, in Assyria,
in Babylon, in Persia, in Greece, was continued in Rome while
St. John was alive; hence this was the sixth period, and the kingdom of the antichrist was to be the last. So it always comes
down again to the relation between the government of God and
what in the course of history springs from created life. The
latter is subject to change and never remains the same. Rather it
always assumes a different form. The difference between these
successive forms is clearly recognizable. With Rome we are in
the sixth period, and in Rome's form it goes on unto the end,
and then there is nothing more to come and nothing else can
come, except the antichristian appearance which, while still in the
form of a man, is so deeply fallen a man that he must be called
the beast. Thus when it reads: "There are seven kings," this
must not be understood of royal persons, but of kings as though
it read: "There are seven kingdoms, that will succeed one another," and to this is added that of these seven kingdoms at the
time five had already fallen, while the sixth still prospered, and
by this must be understood the Roman empire; yet to these six a
last kingdom is to be added of an entirely different origin and
this seventh or last kingdom will be the kingdom of antichrist.
And so it reads that this kingdom is not yet come, and that when
it comes it will not survive long, but will continue for a short
space.

Thus the exception is that in vs. 9 and 10 the number seven is
not used in the broad, but in the literal sense. It actually means
that seven empires have successively exercised, or will exercise,
dominion over the whole world. And when it comes to this
seventh empire,—that is, to the kingdom of the antichrist, the
history of mankind shall end, and the earth will be wholly
changed, so that now what is prophesied in chapter 21, 1, must
come to pass, and the new heaven and the new earth shine forth
in their eternal glory. Then follows the prophecy of the ten kingdoms that shall arise. The antichristian king is said to be the
eighth ruler, but this does not mean the completion of the number eight. For it reads: "The beast that was, and is not, even
he is the eighth, and is of the seven, and goes into perdition";

this but merely indicates that there will be a transition, which will be so striking as to leave the impression that the king who makes this transition shall appear twice, first in the original form, and afterward in the new form, which will be the result of the transition. The last Napoleon was president of the republic before he was emperor. Yet both times he was the same person, and in counting up the rulers of France, though Napoleon was but one person, he can be named twice. This is done in v. 11 when it says: that the antichrist is of the seven, and yet in a sense is the eighth, and that afterward he went into perdition. Thus, if one takes vs. 9 and 10 as referring to successive Roman emperors, verse 11 is absolutely unintelligible, while, as it were, it explains itself when we take it as referring to the seven successive periods in the government of the world which must end in the antichristian period, and which of itself would make the passing away of the world in its present state seem like the beast that was, and is not, even though it is.

In the main, however, it simply means that in the normal course of history the Roman empire is the last. What will come after as the seventh or eighth empire will be of a different kind, and forms no part of the history of this world, but depicts its bewilderment, decline and destruction. With an eye to this, note carefully that the ten kingdoms which are mentioned for the first time in v. 12 are not ten new kingdoms that are to come after the Roman empire, but the parts into which the Roman empire was to be divided, or if you will, expand. Such has been the understanding for twenty centuries after emperor Augustus in whose reign Christ was born. It makes no difference under which emperor Mary brought her child into the world. Yet chapter 2 of St. Luke's Gospel begins the story of Jesus' birth by saying that it took place in the days of Caesar Augustus, and by giving the name of the governor who at the time exercised the imperial authority over Syria, and thus over Palestine and Jerusalem. Thus from the outset it is told, that what took place at Bethlehem took place in the Roman empire and under the highness of Caesar's governor. Moreover it is said that the decree for the enrollment did not apply to Palestine alone, but to the whole world. "There went out a decree that *all the world* should be enrolled."

This understanding of the matter has never been abandoned, and though it should not be overlooked that the Teutons ventured to displace the Roman administration of justice by Germanic law, and that the leaders of the French Revolution tried to displace the present administration of justice by an entirely different one, even as now again the Maximalists and Bolshevists in Russia labor to introduce yet more radical changes and to overturn what has always been counted as right,—yet all this can not undo the fact that Roman law has in all these ages been the basis of all administration of justice in our part of the world.

At times it seemed that this was even exaggerated, as for centuries it was customary to speak of the "Romischer Kaiser," now more often in Austria and again more frequently in Germany. "Romischer Kaiser" was not a mere honorary title, but an historically coined manner of speech which always meant to have it understood that though Roman rule had undergone a radical re-creation and change, it had in nowise passed away. Not only the solidarity but the identity of Rome's administration of justice with that of Christian states has for many centuries been so deeply felt, that in the edition of Roman law after Constantine the Great even in the title, the highness of God, as the source of that law, was and still is indicated. That there was exaggeration in this can not wholly be denied, but through the centuries it was firmly held that not only private but also public law had its historic development in ancient Rome. This met the more readily with consent for so much as it can not be denied that ancient Rome was called of God for this purpose, and was equipped for that sacred task with a clearer insight into law than any other people. The gift of the artistic sense that was imparted to Greece was withheld from Rome, even as what Rome received, Greece had to go without, and that gift to Rome was lustrous in the exceptionally profound elaboration of the administration of justice.

Moreover the Roman empire was the last in the series of the great monarchies of the world. The previous empires in course of time passed away, but the Roman empire had no successor It was the mightiest and also the last in the series of the six, and shall not be superseded, except by the empire of the antichrist. Hence the later rulers always took pride in calling themselves the heirs, successors and substitutes of Roman imperialism. And to

this the Apocalypse points, when it speaks of the ten horns. So
v. 12 reads: "And the ten horns which thou sawest are ten kings,
which have received no kingdom as yet; but receive power as
kings one hour with the beast. These have one mind, and shall
give their power and strength unto the beast." It needs scarcely
be observed that ten here is not a number, but indicates the whole
group. The purpose is to indicate that however long the Roman
empire may yet maintain itself, it shall yet be forced to surrender
its dominion to other nations; provided it is well understood that
this does not mean that an entirely new power shall arise, but
rather that the superiority of the Roman empire, under the abiding administration of justice shall be shifted and moved about
from place to place. This even in a very onesided manner still
goes on. Aside from the ancient Romanic insertions which ruling
monarchs still carry in their titles, with respect to the administration of justice it must still be acknowledged, that in all jurispru-
dence Roman law stands highest, and that as ancient Greek art
rules the world of art, so ancient Roman law is still clothed with
a historic power which from ancient Rome has come to us.

The ten horns in v. 12 indicate that the great Roman empire
will not always go on as a mighty unit. Rather it must prophetically be announced that the mighty unity will be lost, but that
though broken as a unit, in a modified form Rome would perpetuate herself in groups of mighty states which here are indicated by the ten horns. When it reads: "These ten horns are ten
kings," the ten horns only mean the powerful weapon wherewith
bull and goat assert themselves. They do not refer to personal
kings but to kingdoms. And the prophecy is that the Roman
empire shall give place to several kingdoms or empires in Europe,
which competing for world power will fail of obtaining the same,
but still after each other and by the side of each other will be of
sufficient strength and significance to exhibit anew the image and
type of ancient Rome. Of course all this was part of Common
Grace. From of old Almighty God has distributed among the
races of mankind the gifts that govern human life. This disposition and natural bent is God's gift, which determines what the
development of any such a nation is to be. When therefore, with
the great migration of the nations Europe was entirely differently

divided, necessarily under the pressure of constant change one people after another would force its claims upon the rest, in order to proclaim itself as the substitute of ancient Rome. This is here indicated by the number ten,—that is, by a certain number of kingdoms which would come up like horns, by violence secure supremacy, and once having acquired this supremacy would in different ways herald themselves as the divinely appointed rulers of life

Hence it is out of the question that these ten horns or kings or dynasties indicate a seventh world empire, as successor to the ancient Roman empire. With the rise of the power of these ten horns or kingdoms, history would merely witness an after-glow of what had perished with the fall of Rome, or, if you will, with the fall of Byzantium. Thus what was revealed to St. John with respect to these mighty events was pure apocalypse. Of all this nothing could have been foreseen in the current events of those days. When St. John received this revelation, the Roman emperor was still the absolute ruler in all the known world of that day, and no political competitor had yet vied with him for the supremacy of the world. This makes the Apocalypse so extremely rich and far reaching. Of course St. John wondered greatly at this forecast of the future, which made the angel say to him: "Wherefore didst thou marvel? I will tell thee the mystery of the woman and of the beast that carrieth her, which hath the seven heads and ten horns." For in these seven heads that refer to the successive monarchical periods which will finally end in the kingdom of the antichrist, and in those seven horns which refer to the life of the nations, we have the advance announcement of the historic events that would dominate the life of the nations until the coming of antichrist. To the angel this was clear and perspicuous, St. John however was ignorant of all this, and wondered at it. And this prophecy affords him an outlook upon the future down to the days of antichrist.

XXVIII

BABYLON THE GREAT IS FALLEN

For God hath put in their hearts to fulfil his will,
and to agree, and give their kingdom unto the beast,
until the words of God shall be fulfilled. Rev. 17, 17.

Thus the series of the mighty empires of the world ends with the Roman empire. What came after the fall of Rome was not, as was seen above, any new power, but the development of the power of ancient imperial Rome. And this power of Rome, vested in Caesar Augustus and Pontius Pilate, came in immediate conflict with Christ. The conflict that affected the whole world broke out on Gabbatha and Golgotha. It could not have broken out more concretely and definitely than it did there. The birth of Christ in Bethlehem during the Roman governorship partly accounts for this. This predominant combination was confirmed moreover by the fact that Pontius Pilate sentenced Jesus to die on the Cross, and again that the Roman power under Titus besieged Jerusalem and took it; and so actually made an end of Israel's political career, and made Jerusalem succumb. These are but the bare facts, and the ruling thought that was couched in all this went much deeper.

With Jesus also it became at length a question of justice (Recht). This is strikingly evident in the fact that when Pilate sat in judgment on Jesus he was greatly troubled in his conscience by the sense of justice, which made it incumbent on him to set Jesus free. Pilate's contention with the Sanhedrin on this point was an event of marked import. Rome had been divinely called to a noble, honorable task. Rome was to make justice (Recht) the subject of closest scrutiny and develop it most richly. The calling of the other nations also had been highly significant. Egypt had had the honor of vanquishing the power of nature in the Nile. Babylon had been privileged to make advances in astrology and to bring the Tigris and Euphrates into their renown. The Greek world had brought out the glorious possibilities in art. But in loftiness of sentiment and import the "might of right" far excelled all the rest, and the sounding of the depth and the elaboration of this power had been entrusted of God to the Romans. This was the richest and noblest development among the nations thinkable. Religion had been entrusted to Israel, and thus was quite outside of this, but setting for a moment this singular privilege of Israel aside, to consider solely art as in Greece, and law as in Rome they had reached their highest and richest development, it is needless to say that the trust committed to Rome was far superior to the trust committed to Greece, and that there was none higher in all the world. That Rome was given this title-deed was not because the Roman people were of so much nobler standing than other people, on account of which they were thus highly privileged; rather on the contrary it must be confessed that from the first the Roman people had been endowed of God with these noblest gifts, for the express purpose that they might fulfill this so entirely unique a calling. It needs no reminding that, alas, all too many still estimate the Greek development of art as of greater benefit to the world at large than what Rome was given to achieve, yet who can question but that, however much by way of beautiful adornment we owe to art, the life of the world has uniquely been ennobled and led up to a higher standpoint by the Roman study of law. The great question of the antithesis between Christ and the world, which He came to save, was not about the products of art. Rather it must be acknowledged and confessed that in Jesus' life art, with its hidden treasures, has scarcely so much as a hearing. In Christ's contention with the world the question was not one of beauty or of ornamentation, but purely of *religion* and *justice* (right). Religion was the great conflict that by Christ over against Israel has been fought out to the finish; while that which between Jesus and the world had to come to an issue, was justice (right). And this latter conflict has been fought out between the Messiah and Rome's governor. Caiaphas and Pilate are the two exponents of the great problems which in the essential conflict were at stake. Between Christ and Caiaphas the truth of God, between Pilate and Christ justice.

The objection, that aside from religion and law there is morality, as a third spiritual power, can not be sustained. Morality owes its origin on one hand to religion and on the other hand to law (Recht), and from these two morality springs even as an offshoot from both, and by no means as an independent power that is capable of governing both. A morality that lacks a religious foundation, is a weakened revelation of law (Recht), and a morality that does not count with justice, and refuses to be governed by law, throws its nobility to the wind. We see in the Gospel how autonomous morality in no way achieves union. In the ministry of Jesus, religion and law (Recht) are the two predominant and inspiring factors. This shows itself in the attitude which Christ assumed toward *the Law*. The perfect fulfilment of the law would have been the satisfaction of strictest justice; and the undeniable fact that Israel was indeed put under the law and in every way fell short in the fulfilment of that task, made morality weaken in religion, and so it is not the Law, and not morality, but the highest development of religion, and the highest satisfaction of law (Recht) on Golgotha, which in the end offer reconciliation and satisfaction. So it can not be maintained too strenuously that for our human life there is no richer and higher development conceivable than that of law (Recht), and that by having been endowed with the equipment for that development of law, and in having achieved the highest success in the support of the idea of justice, the Romans have reached the highest round of human development conceivable. After what had come to maturity in the life of the Roman world no higher sphere could be realized. Israel for religion and Rome for law, were the two great salient points that governed our human life. Religiously nothing can surpass Israel, and as to law no more deeply penetrating idea could be inculcated at the time than was then given to Rome. In Rome it did not depend upon certain forms of law which in many respects were far below the ideal, but in Rome justice had the preference. The profound import of the law of Right (Recht) was realized in the Roman state as nowhere else. The Roman was endowed with the gift to grasp the law of Right, to feel and to appreciate it. Nowhere in the world did the appreciation of the

law of Right surpass the reverence wherewith in Rome they
looked up to it. Not that also elsewhere justice was not studied
and law formulated in ever clearer terms, but it was an experiment as far as possible with a system of forms, which in reality
had no practical bearing on life. But that wherein Rome had
been favored above every other nation was that, in the Roman,
there fomented and operated a sense of justice which from
within himself made the inner reality of the law of Right take
shape. See how Caiaphas and with him the high priests as with
one thrust at the expense of Jesus put justice aside. The moment
it seemed to the priests that His assertion did not tally with
their own religious insight, Jesus is struck in the face. And compare with this the tumult in Pilate's breast when he realizes that
in Jesus there is no guilt, no violation of the law of Right, while
at the same time he can not persuade the Jews to pay homage to
this innocence of Jesus. Even his wife is disturbed in her dream,
as in her also the supreme claim of the law of Right rebelled
against the possibility that Jesus should be a prey of the religious
hatred of the Sanhedrin. Of course after the Romans had taken
so high a stand as this, no nation in the world could take one
higher. And by the rise, the development and the decline of the
Roman state the series of nations had come to an end. No nation
could have a higher calling than had come to Rome, Israel with
its religious supernatural dispensation always excepted. In the
earthly dispensation nothing surpasses the law of Right (Recht),
and this law of Right in its deepest sense had been entrusted to
Rome, the mysterious exposition of which in Rev. 17, 7-12 is the
perspicuous and deeply significant elucidation.

In this clear and distinguished administration of justice the
highest mission of Common Grace had of God been entrusted to
the heathen nations. This does not say that not in Egypt also,
in Babylon, in Persia and in Greece treasures of knowledge, of
dominion over nature and of development of character had been
entrusted; but so much was evident each time that, among all
the forms of civilization, the richer development of the law of
Right was highest. In having this richer and higher law of
Right, Rome attained to the highest conception of human life;
and thus Common Grace never unfolded itself more successfully

than in the Roman state and among the Roman people. Of necessity therefore when the end came, and at length in the life of the peoples the law of right melted away and lost its binding power, Common Grace was withdrawn, justice became a lost art and nothing could remain, save universal ruin, dismemberment and destruction of that understanding of human life which once had been our honor, and had afforded the deepest satisfaction of life. With the last vial everything at length perished, and it is worthy of note that this destruction had really already begun when the life of the ten groups, according to v. 12, undertook to dominate Europe; and, while it divided Europe into several parts, yet strung it together in its ancient Romanic connection; something which was to continue until the beast and the dragon were to introduce the closing scene, and with it the final dissolution of the whole drama.

Already with the last trumpet (ch. 10, 6) it had been solemnly declared on the part of God that the normal course of time would be broken up, even in the words: that there should be time no longer; which fact was fortified by this most solemn assurance: "And he swore by Him that liveth for ever and ever, who created heaven and the things that therein are, and the earth, and the things that therein are, and the sea, and the things which are therein, that there should be time no longer." This is too solemnly announced not to be the proclamation of an event of high importance and a considerable alteration in the course of things. This saying that there should be time no longer does not yet imply what presently, after the last vial is poured out, the "It is done" will mean. Here it merely means that Common Grace is ended, and that now the destruction of the Universe begins. This indeed is what went on in chapters 10 to 17. The end drew ever nearer step by step. The saving ordinances of Common Grace fell away. Everything became loose and disconnected. The saving hand of God was now withdrawn, and, left to itself the whole creation, above and here below, was devoted to self-destruction. Now indeed it is already a matter of the past, not merely that there will no longer be a normal development of time, but also that "It is done" (ch. 16, 17), and that now the general destruction and solution of the creation as a whole begins. Of course in connection with this it must be borne in mind that a world-shaking event had taken place with respect to the world of demons. The two transitions which this new order of things called into life were mutually related. The demoniac world underwent a predominant change and the life of the world consummated its moral self-repudiation.

The beast, the dragon and the false prophet impart the peculiar character to this new state of things. In thinking this through, however, we must retrace our steps to Paradise. There Satan had succeeded in causing man to fall. Yet only in part. The fall in Paradise was such, as still to admit of grace to save the human family and perfect God's plan regarding our race. Partly Common Grace and partly Particular Grace made this possible. When the whole future of our human race seemed cut off, it pleased God to check the power of Satan, whereby, even though human life was fundamentally impaired, to make a rich development of it possible. What that power of Satan still signified, only became evident again in Jesus' temptation in the wilderness. But also there Satan was vanquished, and with an eye to the approaching Cross Jesus said to His disciples (John 14, 30): "Hereafter I will not talk much more with you: for the prince of this world cometh, and hath nothing in me." Thus after Jesus' Resurrection Satan has not been able to practice his demoniac power to the full. The prayer: "Deliver us from evil" could day by day in all parts of the earth be addressed to the Father, and be heard. But not forever. For when the time of Common Grace is past and the end of the world is come, the demoniac power of Satan will be let loose and then the outbreak of his unholy wrath will be terrible. The beast also will then appear and the dragon will lay hold on dominion. The normal state of things that has prevailed from the days of Paradise (after the fall) will then be ended. The absolutely abnormal will then ensue. This will bring about the final conflict when at length the unholy elements among the peoples will entirely wander away from God and array themselves against the Holy. This will give rise to a persecution of believers. And thus in the midst of the mighty life of the world believers and unbelievers will part company, and when the scythe or sickle of separation has once begun its unsparing work, Christ will consummate the separation. What opposes God will pass under curse and doom, and what unto the uttermost, yes even unto death, remains faithful to God will wondrously be taken up into heaven.

The angel did not reveal to St. John what then will occasion the rupture, neither how many centuries must elapse before all human society will be disrupted and scattered. It may fairly be assumed, therefore, that St. John had not the least idea that twenty centuries would elapse the whiles the regular course of things would ever yet go on. All that for certain is foretold and, as it were, shown to him is, that on a day and at an hour which even Christ did not know, and was known to the Father only, the ordinary course of life would be broken up and give place to the dreadful period of the end. Even a period that would end everything that thus far had been normal, that would disjoint all things, and in a short time would work so radical a change, that everything that dominated the common state of things would fall away, that would separate absolutely the holy from the unholy, that for a while would permit demoniac superiority free rein, and thus bring about the final cleavage that would consign all that sided with Satan to perdition. Then the beast would be arrested and with the beast the false prophet. For these two were to be cast alive into the lake of fire.

Where "that great city" of chapter 17 and v. 18 will be located is not indicated, but it certainly will neither be Babylon nor Rome. Naturally it will have to be a city of gigantic size and of staggering proportions not only, but at the same time a city in which a very highly philosophical and artistic life shall have been developed, so that from her leading elements an intellectual, moral and artistic superior power shall go out, which at length will dominate the life of the whole world. It will be peculiar, in that a strongly colored human life will flourish in "that great city" and also that her military strength and what belongs to it will gradually represent a power and exercise a military-political supremacy that will vanquish every other power, and little by little subject the whole world unto itself. This power now presents itself in the image of a woman. "And the woman which thou sawest is that great city, which reigneth over the kings of the earth" (v. 18). Thus here would be materialized what also in our days sometimes engages the spirits. It would no longer be one free country by the side of the other, but rather all countries and peoples of the earth would be fused into one bond and federatively united under one government, which by a gigantic police power would hold all peoples in subjection. The beast supported by the dragon would create this all-inclusive political military world power, to which as a social figure would correspond what here is presented by the woman. Of Gog and Magog we make no mention here. Prophecy always presents the colossal mass of mankind as divided into two groups; that of the leading nations which make history unto the end of time, and that no less great a part of humanity that lives more isolated and by the name of Gog and Magog presents a series of nations which do not lead, do not dominate the current of human life, but drift along by themselves, such as especially appeared to be the case with the negroes in Africa.

As a result of this liberation of Satan's power by the suspension of Common Grace, and of the urge to the end which will then arise in nature as well as in human life, the historic life of the peoples will no longer be possible, and even this urge to the end also among unholy peoples shall from God go out among them. So reads v. 17: "For God hath put in their hearts to fulfil his will, and to agree, and give their kingdom unto the beast, until the words of God shall be fulfilled." In connection with this it should finally be observed that according to v. 14 these peoples at length will unite in a war against Christ. "These shall make war with the Lamb, and the Lamb shall overcome them"; for that Lamb is now the "Lord of lords and King of kings," and not only the angels but also they that are called, and elect, will take part in His triumphant victory. Upon this the final conflict will begin. On one side will be the mass of people that surrender their future to the beast and to the false prophet. These are the lost, and to them presently will be apportioned the weeping and gnashing of teeth. But over against this beast with his unholy power will stand the Christ with His holy multitude of believers. This struggle will give rise to the final conflict, in which Christ shall triumph, and the beast, Satan and the false prophet, having come to the end of their career, under the sentence that is passed upon them, will succumb.

In chapter 18, 1 the actual state of things to be sets in, by the appearance from heaven of another angel who with a mighty and strong voice announces what will immediately come to pass. This angel was said to have "great power" and wherever he appeared and made his approach to the earth, the earth was lightened with his glory. The comment that this angel had "great power" clearly expresses that he not only announced the fall and ruin of the great Babylon, but that he himself had a hand in the destruction of the "great city" that ruled the whole world. To what else would his "great power" have tended? Nothing special need be said of an angel which appears merely to announce something. In Revelation we read of several angels who merely appear to make an announcement, having done which, they return to heaven and disappear. It is quite different, however, when an angel appears in order to discharge a weighty mission and to execute the same. What in v. 1 of chapter 18 is said of the great might of the angel, makes it evident that he has to do something more important than make an announcement, and that something like an exhibition of power is to ensue. This angel not merely appears but "comes down from heaven"; he has "great power"; and radiates such glory that St. John beholds the earth, as far as he could see, lightened with the brightness of great splendor.

Thereupon follows an extremely important event. Again in an imposing manner this angel is now the instrument or servant in God's hand, who effects the fall of the renowned and glorious Babylon of that time. Note how here also the "great" is emphasized. Not only is the final lot of the reigning Babylon at the time proclaimed, but with still greater emphasis is added that the dreadful ruin that here is effected concerns the "great" Babylon. Thus here we have an angel "having great power," abundantly able therefore to accomplish this mighty work, and to make one realize that nothing less than a mighty angel would be equal to this, it is emphatically added that it not merely meant the destruction of an ordinary abode of men, neither an ordinary city like Pergamus or Athens, but of a metropolis which is called "Babylon the great." Babylon the great here means the greatest of all the cities that will then be in the world. That mightiest of cities would suddenly be besieged in a dreadful way and, as of the ancient Babylon on the Tigris and Euphrates, nothing would be left but ruins and wild beasts. The great metropolis of super-abounding wealth, which by her diplomacy and military power ruled the whole world, succumbed, collapsed, sank away in ruins, and now (is added that she) is become the habitation of devils, and the hold of every foul spirit, and a cage of every unclean and hateful bird. This mighty Babylon is reduced to a heap of ruins. The great metropolis which had harboured the antichristian power and had deemed herself safe, breaks in pieces, as dust and refuse comes to nought, and the image of the ruin is borrowed from the scene of horror that had once been witnessed on the Euphrates.

Nor is this all. This last great metropolis is not only punished, but there is also a judgment passed upon her. As the holy apostle writes, he heard yet another voice from heaven, which addressed not only the discomfitted Babylon, but also struck the note of warning to the believers which at that time still dwelt in the great world empire. It is not at all certain that these believers lived in the ruined metropolis. For the world empire was one with the metropolis. In case those Christians who as last believers were still in the earth, dwelt in villages or in more distant parts of the world empire, for them also the hour of decision had come. They had to withdraw and separate themselves. In that great Babylon the temptation might become too bitter and too grievous, so that they might become partakers of the sin of that metropolis, and hence also would have to share her judgment. In v. 3 of chapter 18 it is therefore emphasized that this metropolis has poisoned the whole world. All peoples have been bewitched by her. They have all drunk of the wine of the wrath of her fornication. And, note this especially, the kings of the earth and the mighty merchants of the earth had waxed rich by the charms that the great city had worked. Therefore, postponement of the rupture is no longer thinkable. The sins of the metropolis, or if you will, of the demoniac Babylon, were heaped one upon the other. They had, as it were, come up heaven-high before God. And God had become mindful of her iniquities. So the breach had become irreparable. Reconciliation was no more possible between a world that had become demoniacal and believers that were still in the earth. Separation between these two was now imperative. The end no longer tarried, it was there.

XXIX

THE SEPARATION OF THE REDEEMED

And I heard another voice from heaven, saying, Come out of her, my people, that ye be not partakers of her sins, and that ye receive not of her plagues. Rev. 18, 4.

As to clearness the division of chapter 18, especially in the first ten verses, leaves nothing to be desired. In the first three verses a mighty angel from heaven announces to earth the fall of Babylon, even saying, not that it is to fall, but is fallen. Not of course in the historical sense, as though the great and mighty fact had already happened; but in the sense that prophetically the announcement makes us see how, when it comes to the Consummation, it really will take place. This was not heeded, when by Babylon the ancient Babylon before its fall was understood. Then they harked back to olden times and one had even to imagine that all this had preceded the Bethlehem Birth. At least with respect to things to come at the end of the world this representation was without rhyme or reason. It was soon understood however that Babylon was used in a figurative sense, and that the name was applied to the great metropolis, which would be in the period of the last days what ancient Babylon had been in the days of Daniel. As ancient Babylon had diametrically opposed everything that pertained to Israel and the Kingdom of God, so the Babylon of the latter days, be it in Europe or America, will carry godlessness, immorality, yes antichristian wickedness to the nth degree and, having corrupted everything, at length also herself will perish and be destroyed.

The end of the metropolis is now come. This predominant event is begun and carried through by one of the greatest and mightiest angels of God, who came down from heaven not merely to announce God's counsel and ordinance, but to execute the same. So he does not say: "Babylon *shall* fall," but; "She is fallen, is fallen the great Babylon, and is bcome the habitation of devils".

Immediately thereupon and connected therewith, in verses 4-10 Christ Himself the Son of God from heaven gives a most striking order. That it is not an angel, but Christ Himself who here speaks is clearly evident from the words: "Come out of her, *my people*". No angel could thus have spoken of "my people" as though either Israel or the collective multitude of believers could have been *his* people. If what here follows referred solely to Israel, one might take it to mean that the witness intended to say: Israel is the people of the Messiah, and as such the people of witnesses of God, and thus also of the angels. But in the nature of the case, this can not be the meaning. The inspired writer here deals with the end of the world and thus of the period immediately preceding the last judgment. Presently it will be manifest, who are the Lord's people and who have made choice of the antichrist. So it is plain that the witness who here speaks, saying "my people," can be none other than Christ Himself. And this speaking as Christ Himself is here entirely natural, as the war is on against the antichrist, and in the nature of the case Christ Himself, and no one else, is to inflict the final blow upon antichrist, the effect of which would be the destruction of the satanic. No angel here would have been in place. The deadly conflict is between Christ and antichrist, and therefore neither the connection nor the commanding manner of speech permit any other explanation than that which, in v. 4, makes the Christ Himself to appear. So everything is perfectly plain. The Apocalypse is now come to the fall of Babel,—that is, to the judgment and destruction of the antichristian world-power, and no one but Christ Himself can execute this last act. The words: "Come out of her," —that is, out of the demoniacal metropolis, "O, my people," must refer to the last moment when the Consummation comes in, and Christ Himself executes the final sentence upon the demoniac antichristian world.

The appearance of Christ here imparts special significance to the turning-point. In what in vs. 4-10 is said by Christ, one no longer recognizes the Saviour. No note of grace is sounded. You do not recognize the good Shepherd. Now everything is come to the issue. The Lamb of God that taketh away the Sin of the world is, as it were, vanished, and in place of the Reconciler, Re-

deemer and Comforter, the Messiah now appears as the One that
brings the irrevocable judgment. Not that even in this latest
hour he who turns to Christ should not be saved; but it is no
longer the note of seeking and reconciling love. Everything that
Christ says in these seven verses points to the final judgment.
It is either *for* or *against;* and all they who do not with full conviction and resolute purpose choose for Christ, face almost immediately their final doom. It now comes to the ultimate separation. "Come out, my people!" is the call that is heard, and this
even as the means of escape from having anything to do with the
metropolis and thereby from sharing in every way the judgment
of the world. Time for deliberation is no more. Action must
be drastic, and on the spot one must break with the antichrist and
with everything that is his.

Stronger still: All indulgence, all forbearance, all suffering
compassion is now ended. True believers must now so make
choice of Christ as to make a formal break with the world with
her iniquities and with her wicked machinations against God.
See it in v. 6: "Reward her even as she rewarded you, and double
unto her double according to her works. How much she hath
glorified herself, so much torment and sorrow give her. Her
plagues shall come in one day, death, and mourning, and famine".
And the end shall be that this perishing world "shall be utterly
burned with fire". Also the kings of the earth shall share her
sorrows and the vengeance upon the lost world. So it is said of
the kings: "And the kings of the earth, who have committed fornication and lived deliciously with her, shall bewail her, and
lament for her, when they shall see the smoke of her burning,
standing afar off for fear of her torment, saying, Alas, alas that
great city Babylon, that mighty city! for in one hour is thy judgment come." This implies no suggestion here of anything that
once characterized the Saviour and Redeemer of sinners. Of the
"Come unto me, all ye that travail and are heavy laden," no
faintest echo is now heard. There is nothing that reminds one of
the Christ of the parable of the lost son. A wholly different
Christ here stands before you. Grace is past. The final issue is
come. Christ turns in holy wrath against all those who, inspired
by the antichrist, set themselves against God; and the final divi-

sion of our race into those who believe and those who turn themselves against Almighty God is so absolute, that Christ calls
upon every one that has made choice of God to turn from the
attitude of grace and mercy to that of wrath and the spirit of retribution. And the finishing touch of it all is, that this final decision is a matter of sudden occurrence. It reads so impressively
at the end of what Jesus says: *In one hour is thy judgment come.*
It is, so to speak, the last drop of the last vial that, in accordance
with vs. 1-3, is here, as it were, poured out. And this was bound
to be so, because the last vial, and with it the last outpouring of
unmitigated distress, could not be consummatd by any other than
Christ Himself. Only after Christ has made His appearance and
has taken from the angel the bitter, terrible role, and has not only
announced the final destruction, but also begun it, does the world
process come to the final thrust into the eternal perdition, and
now can be said: "Thy judgment is not merely come in one day,
but thy judgment is come *in one hour.*" There is no more mention
of duration or lapse of time. One terror overtakes the other, and
Christ, who now has laid aside every remembrance of the lost
son, in sorrow and bitterness Himself consummates the final task.

To this corresponds what now follows in the second part of
this chapter regarding the dreadful lot that awaits the busy and
pleasure loving world. The next nine verses express the spiritual
experience of the people. The world that here speaks occupies no
high vantage-ground. Not a sound is heard from a temple, not
an echo from a house of prayer, no spiritual utterance of a higher
order from the school of philosophers. On the contrary everything that is dealt with in these nine verses belongs to the mer-
cantile world. Among those whose complaint is now heard.
navigation and commerce occupy the center of the stage. In v.
11 this is plainly indicated. "The merchants", so it reads, the
"merchants of the earth shall weep and mourn over her calamities," but for no profounder reason than that sales decrease and
finally cease. They shall weep and mourn because no man buyeth
their merchandise any more. Commerce always thrives on rich
cities that proudly develop themselves. If this great metropolis
has become *the* city where all sorts of treasures have been col-
lected, of course navigation and commerce owed their thriving

business to its wondrously prosperous condition. As was the case with Tyre and Sidon, where once all navigation and commerce had concentrated itself, and where, when the wealth of Alexandria and Rome had vanished, bitterest destruction had followed, such would be the case here. Only with this marked difference, that whereas the moral and presently the material decline in the great cities of the world, together with that in navigation and commerce, had always been gradual, now it would suddenly burst in upon the richest city of the world, as in one hour her ruin would come in and be consummated.

And to make it clearly evident that in the great metropolis everything ended at length in material wealth, without the faintest suggestion of any higher spiritual life, the speaker recapitulates what the luxury of commerce and trade had become. It was no ordinary commerce in food-stuffs and wearing apparel, but in all sorts of expensive luxuries. "Merchandise," so he says, "of gold and silver, and of precious stones and of porcelain, and of fine linen and purple and silk and scarlet. Furthermore all manner of vessels of most precious wood, and of brass, and iron and of marble." And then there were all sorts of merchandise of cinnamon and perfumes and frankincense and wine and oil, and fine flour and wheat of the best, all sorts of animals and bodies and souls of men. And now by what overtook the great, rich, all dominating metropolis, at once and suddenly all this superabundance of wealth had sunken away into nought. There is no more call for it and it can no longer be brought to the market.

Bitter complaints and cries of woe are heard among the shipmasters and merchants and artists. The merchants of these things, so reads v. 15, which were made rich by her now idly stand afar off for fear of the torment that awaits them. So they stand deserted and forsaken, weeping and wailing and saying: "Alas, alas that great city, that was clothed in fine linen, and purple, and scarlet, and decked with gold, and precious stones and pearls." It was so immensely rich, and now "in one hour so great riches is come to nought." Not the princes and conquerors of towns, but the manufacturers, the warehouse keepers and treasurers raise a bitter cry. And the captains and mates and sailors in the ships, the crews and all that do business in the sea, suddenly facing this terrible catastrophe are utterly overcome, as it were, by fear and dread. They stand no longer, as before, in the foreground, but withdraw to the rear, and abandon all hope, and as they see the sudden demolition and the overwhelming fall of the mighty metropolis, they remain standing afar off, and cry, saying, "What city was like unto this great city?" Nor is this all. They cast dust on their heads, and crying and weeping and wailing, they shriek, as it were, saying: "Alas, alas that great city, wherein were made rich all that had ships in the sea by reason of her costliness! for in one hour is she made desolate."

Thereupon follows in vs. 20-24 of chapter 18 the absolute change from mercy and compassion to wrath and unsparing destruction, as now the martyrs cry for vengeance. This is first seen in v. 20 and again in v. 24. Where thus far gold and precious stones and the things that minister to the luxury of life have been dealt with, v. 20 calls attention to what they who made choice of God and His Christ have suffered. There we read: "Rejoice over her, thou heaven, and ye holy apostles and prophets; for God hath avenged you on her." The antithesis could not be more striking. Two sorts of enthusiasms have inspired and impelled the children of men. One part of the children of men has been delighted with pearls and diamonds, and the much smaller part of mankind has rejoiced in the higher, though unseen, realities of heaven. The great majorities of people have found their treasures in the earth; the superlatively rich treasure of the blessed consisted solely in what they, as belonging to Christ, had received from on High by the Holy Ghost in the soul. The first large group included the princes and superrich owners of the treasures of the world; the second small group had its mighty point of attack not on the earth, but in heaven above. Apostles and prophets, rather than earthly princes and rulers, were their holy spiritual allies. With the princes and the great of the earth every attraction was downward and God was forgotten. Here on the other hand God was the all in all; and all spiritual life drew one up to the throne of the Lord above. This antithesis is fully expressed in v. 20: "Rejoice over her, thou heaven, and ye holy apostles and prophets; for God hath avenged you on her, that is to say, according to the wrong she has done you the great metropolis is judged."

But with this also comes the final encounter. The strain has been endured. The antithesis has now shown itself in its very strongest colors. There can be no more tarrying, and the blow that brings the end must immediately follow. Therefore already v. 21 reads: "And a mighty angel took up a stone like a great millstone, and cast it into the sea, saying, Thus with violence shall that great city Babylon be thrown down, and shall be found no more at all." This seemingly contradicts what is said in v. 2, namely, "She is fallen," and a second time: "She is fallen." In v. 21 this same metropolis is still intact, is not fallen at all, and only now another angel inflicts the destructive blow that utterly vanquishes her. Stronger still. Verse 21 does not say that the great metropolis *is* fallen. It gives a symbolical comparison. A prodigiously great millstone is lifted up by a mighty angel, is held over the sea, and is now cast into the sea, where it tracklessly disappears. After this symbolic act it does not say: "So Babylon is cast down, but, in the future tense: "thus shall that great city Babylon be thrown down, and shall be found no more at all." Yet there is no confusion here. Only, it must be kept in view that in the Apocalypse is not told what has taken place, but always what *shall* take place. St. John had not the least idea what of all this he would live to see, and what would occur after his death. And so he is bound to write as though what he records has already happened, and yet again he must extend his witness to far distant ages. It is always again the struggle between the two leading thoughts: "Even so, come quickly, Lord Jesus!" and the centuries that might yet have to elapse in between.

In closing the striking antithesis makes its appearance again. The great and mighty metropolis is once more magically, as it were, thrown on the screen before eye and ear with the wealth of her great palaces and the voice of the players on harps, and then also as sinking away in the stream of her corruption that drags her down. V. 22 speaks of the voices of harpers and musicians, of pipers and trumpeters, and says that this play of sounds and songs is come to an end. All this wonderful music "shall be heard no more at all in thee." "No craftsman, of whatsoever craft he be, shall be found any more in thee," and also in the domestic sense "no sound of a millstone shall be heard at all in thee." Even, and this goes still farther, when neither sun nor moon can illuminate life and one tries by candle-light to banish darkness, even then the light of a candle shall shine no more in that metropolis. Social and family life shall end. No voice of bride or bridegroom shall any more be heard. The merchants with their wealth have corrupted everything, and by their sorceries have poisoned all earthly life. And what will now be most terrible of all? In these same cities that now by their wealth die the social death, the dreadful antithesis between the wealth of the world and the blood of the martyrs shall openly be shown. So the closing verse reads: "And in that city was found the blood of prophets and of saints, and of all that were slain upon the earth."

XXX

CHRIST'S COMING AS JUDGE*

*And I saw heaven opened, and behold a white horse;
and he that sat upon him was called Faithful and True,
and in righteousness he doth judge and make war.*
Rev. 19, 11.

When it comes to the Consummation there is on one side the
wicked, the unholy power which finally can not hold out, and
however much enlarged and relentless, has the worst of it and
perishes. But over against this unholy perishing power appears
the royal majesty of Christ who triumphs over all the unholy, and
by the majesty of God Almighty makes Himself to be glorified.
As in chapter 18, 21 we had the turning point, so here it occurs in
v. 11 of chapter 19. In the former we saw the unholy power
which from the first had struck root in Babylon, and each time in
a different form, as ages ran, had shown itself opposed to God.
The future alone can tell in what metropolis and in what kingdom this unholy Babel power shall undertake to insure its
triumph. Yet when it shall have reached its highest pinnacle of
glory and make the most brilliant showing of itself, the end will
be at hand.

But before it comes to this pass, that unholy world shall have
become demoniac. This was previously indicated by the coming
to the earth of the beast and the dragon, and finally of the antichrist. With this Common Grace had come to an end. The demoniacal had been given free course. The demoniac, the dia-
bolical, and finally the antichristian had so invaded the world,
that all earthly power had been lost in it. The struggle between
this perishing earthly power and the really demoniacal had already progressed in such a way that the antichrist repulsed every
other power, and even triumphed over the powers of nature. But
this too had reached its end and v. 21 of chapter 18 depicts the

*In the original "Christ's Coming as Judge" covers chapters **XXX**
and **XXXI**.

final issue in the image of the great millstone, which the angel cast into the sea, saying with a loud voice: "Thus with violence shall that great city Babylon be thrown down," even in such a way, that "she shall be found no more at all." So this is the final issue of one side. The power that opposed God has finished its course, has turned from Common Grace into the demoniac, and in its antichristian form is brought to nought. This could not be told in more forcible terms than that this power "shall be found no more at all." The triumph of the holy over the unholy is now accomplished.

This is directly connected with what is told in v. 11 of the 18th chapter, namely, that as now the unholy metropolis and with it the power of the antichrist is vanquished, the triumph of Christ and of his cause bursts into view, becomes actual and perfect. Now Christ again appears, not in His suffering form of the Lamb of God and dispensing mercy, but as the Exponent of the glory of God, and as the One who is called to achieve the victory of the Kingdom of God. So He is seen as a horseman, seated on a white horse, and bearing the honorable title of the "Faithful and True". He now comes not to save and reconcile but to judge and to wage war against every unholy thing in the earth. "And I saw heaven opened, and behold a white horse: and he that sat upon him was called Faithful and True, and in righteousness he doth judge and make war" (v. 11), which last expression means to say that mercy now gives way to the stern and inexorable claim of the Divine law of Right. In these two concluding catastrophies lies the finality. On one side the passing away of all earthly de- moniac power, of which it is said that it "shall be found no more at all." This does not mean that unholy angels and men, who were the exponents of the same, shall cease to exist. All they are consigned to the place of corruption where there will be weeping and gnashing of teeth. Only they will no longer be a power. They will no more have power, nor in any wise be able to exercise power. Unending woe will be their portion, in which woe of the unholy the rightousness of God will reveal itself in glory.

Between these two,—that is, the destruction of the unholy and the triumph of Christ, there is a song of jubilant rejoicing, which some have tried to make part of chapter 18, and others have taken

as introduction to the triumph of Christ. To us it seems that
there is no need of either the one or the other, and that it is
more natural to take this glorious song as the middle part that
stands between all these decisive events and so forms the transition from the one into the other. Were there need to add these
ten verses to either of the two, undoubtedly with Kliefoth we
would sooner reckon them as part of chapter 18. The jubilant
song that we now hear divides itself into two parts. Verses 1 to
6 of chapter 19 deal with the triumph that has been achieved,
while verses, 7, 8, 9 and 10 take another turn. So verses 1 to 6
contain the main matter. Now it must be noted that this song
of praise is not sung by the redeemed that are still in the earth,
but is a song that directs itself from heaven toward the earth.
"And after these things I heard a great voice of much people in
heaven, saying, Alleluia; Salvation, and glory, and honor, and
power, unto the Lord our God" (Ch. 19, 1). It does not read:
"They are the Lord's," but they are ascribed "unto the Lord."
Hence to this extent these words do not refer to what precedes
but rather to what follows. And still again these words do refer
to what precedes as we learn from v. 2: "For true and righteous
are his judgments." Also here, however, the song touches what
went before as well as what follows after. The triumph-song
celebrates the victory that has been won over the unholy world
power, but what is inferred from this points to what now in
Christ as Victor is about to appear. So what here presents itself
is the connecting-member. It starts out from the fall of Babylon
and from the fact that the unholy world power is no more, and
then points to Christ from Whom now the glory proceeds.

The Alleluia that now follows makes one feel that the issue
of the one side,—that is, of the side of the world—is already
come, and that at the same moment from the side of Christ it begins. The judgments are no longer to come, but in part are already here, and for the rest are in course of process. As v. 2
reads: "For true and righteous are his judgments: for he hath
judged the great whore." That "great whore" naturally points
to the metropolis that takes everything by surprise, that is become the instrument of the antichrist, and now has been destroyed. Judgment has been executed upon her. She can do
nothing more. All her doings are ended, even to such an extent

that the metropolis in which this power concentrated itself, and from which it went out, shall no more be found at all, and the only thing that would still be found would be a reminder of her godless cruelty as shown by the blood of the prophets and of the saints and of all those who "for the faith's sake were slain upon the earth" (18, 24) ; even as also in v. 2 of chapter 19 is repeated that God the Lord "hath judged the great whore"; not that He *shall* judge, but that He *hath* judged the great whore, which did corrupt the earth with her fornication, and, for this must be added, hath avenged the blood of his servants at her hand. Thus the representation now before us does not deal with prophecy, but with accomplished facts. It is still prophecy in a sense, in that it still must come to pass, not only when St. John wrote this, but even yet now. John understood that the antichrist had not yet been routed and vanquished, and that the great metropolis had still to be laid low. Yet while this is so, in the representation that is given here everything is ended and consummated. Hence we do not read that God *shall* avenge the blood of His servant, but (see v. 2) that He *hath avenged* the blood of His servants at her hand.

The same is evident in the twice repeated *Alleluia* that sounds from heaven down to earth. It is here said again that the Alleluia which went out from heaven was in every way overwhelming. It was an Alleluia that was sung from heaven, as it reads, "by a great multitude, with a great voice·" Already the introductory prophecies spoke of those vast numbers of the angelic host which run up to the thousands of millions. And also here in the nature of the case by this speaking of the *"great multitude* with the voice as of many waters" these thousands of millions are again purposely referred to. The idea that the number of angels is calculable had here also to be set at naught. Anew the impression of the Alleluia that resounded from above had to be overwhelming. And though the numbers of millions and millions are not repeated, yet the impression is overwhelming, when we hear anew that this first Alleluia with majestic intonation from heaven resounded in the world. This is confirmed by what follows in v. 3: "And the angel said a second time, Alleluia. And her smoke rose up for ever and ever." However strangely the last expression may affect one, it is perspicuous. The end of the great metropolis was that it was burned to the ground, so that nothing was left of her. Of course during the burning, smoke went up. This smoke is now even metaphorically referred to in the sense, that rebuilding Babylon is for ever out of the question. It is always and for ever done with her. This is indicated as follows, that the smoke of the smoldering of her destruction goes on for ever, so that restoration is impossible.

If with this the second Alleluia has been sung, the context shows that now in the heavenly world the song of praise again ascends and assumes its most perfect form, as the "elders" and the "beasts" also are introduced anew. So follows in v. 4 with the Presbytery in the lead: "And the four and twenty elders and the four beasts fell down and worshipped God that sat on the throne, saying, Amen; Alleluia." And as though this were not enough, a call goes out from above to everything that is privileged to know the glory of God, and to all that have ear and voice, to join in with this chorus of heavenly jubilation. For so we read in v. 5: And a voice came out of the throne, saying, Praise our God, all ye his servants, and ye that fear him, both small and great." The words: "Praise *our* God" show that they are creatures from whom this voice came forth in order that every sanctified creature shall take part in that impressive Alleluia. For the fact that now at last the decision is come, that Satan is vanquished, and hence the triumph of the Son of God is achieved, is in every way predominantly glorious and striking.

This call meets with immediate response, for St. John testifies that he heard the voice of a great multitude which gave its re-action to the Alleluia. This was so strikingly evident that it seemed that from heaven and from the earth, yes from every place where creatures dwell which made choice of God and against Satan, a call of world-wide reach went forth, to give due response to this Alleluia. In connection with this is heard: "Alleluia; for the Lord God omnipotent reigneth," (v. 6); and it is so impressively stated that this song of rejoicing sounded as "the voice of a great multitude, and as the voice of many waters, and as the voice of mighty thunderings." And that all things in heaven and on earth must join in this triumph song in which they jubilantly celebrated Babylon's fall and now awaited the appearance of the Christ.

Quite unexpectedly, and yet in part of necessity, there is now between this twice sung Alleluia and the descent of Christ for judgment, a reference to the marriage of the Lamb, in the words: "Let us be glad and rejoice, and give honour to him; for the marriage of the Lamb is come, and his wife has made herself ready." We call this an insertion, because the great antithesis is here formed by the antichrist and the Christ, so that one would almost think that the congregation of the blessed were here ignored. Of course the sanctified and the blessed were represented by the four and twenty elders or presbyters, who before God's throne represent the reconciled and redeemed church of Christ. Only, the great congregation itself, the mighty church of Christ which presently on the new earth is to constitute the new and redeemed humanity does not appear herewith in its innumerable multitude. She was merely represented by these elders. Thus actually the innumerable host of the redeemed was left out of account, and it seemed that the antichristian element which is cursed and faces ruin, alone was dealt with, even in this way, that now none save Christ and antichrist stood face to face. As well however as the antichrist does not stand alone and cannot appear merely personally alone, but as the unholy head of the unbelievers that are lost, so Christ could not be reckoned with apart from the multitude of believers that are His; and this end is served by the insertion in v. 7 to and with v. 10. In these four verses, quite outside of the struggle of life and death that between Christ and the antichrist together with his satellites and demoniac hosts here faces the end, the bride of Christ makes her appearance.

These multitudes which Christ has won and which are His now sing the song of rejoicing, not as fellow-combatants with Christ in the deadly conflict, but in honor of the marriage. So the redeemed are counted with in a very real sense, though not now as themselves involved in the struggle of life and death. Christ Himself brings the deadly struggle against the antichrist to an issue. With an eye to this struggle it can even be said that these multitudes of believers are set aside, and in this conflict do not count. To them it is the hour of triumph, because to Christ it is the hour of complete victory. As will be further seen in chapter 21, the lot of the redeemed is involved in what the end brings to pass, but it is between Christ and antichrist alone that this struggle is to meet its final issue. And therefore between the Alleluia-song of the angels and of the Presbyters and of the four beasts the joyful song of the redeemed and reconciled, as a jubilant song of the marriage, is here inserted. Between Christ and His church that is for ever united to Him it must come to a holy utterance of joy, just as, with a coming marriage, there is a day of festivity before the marriage is consummated. Those happy days preceding and including the actual wedding-day are what we call the marriage, and as the marriage of the Lamb had been referred to before, so now it is introduced, not as the marriage of the warring and triumphing King-victor, but as the marriage of the Lamb.

However strangely this may sound, yet it could not be presented in any other way. The redeemed and the reconciled do not owe their triumph and their festal joy to the conflict of their conquering King. Without the fall in Paradise this might have been thinkable, but not now. As the fall in Paradise had dragged down all the elect, from the first to the last, it was absolutely inconceivable that without atonement and without atoning sacrifice the blessed could have been liberated from sin and saved unto life. As king and antagonist Jesus triumphs over His unholy opponents; but the elect whom He brings unto life, can only come to that eternal life by means of the atonement, which is not the gift of the King, nor of the Wrestler, but solely of the Reconcilor who on the Cross makes a sacrifice of Himself in behalf of God's elect. So here it is again the Lamb that works the mighty miracle of grace, and not the victorious King. As King He overcomes in vanquishing His enemies. As Christ He overthrows the antichrist. But as Reconcilor He always is the Self-sacrificing Lamb of Golgotha Who draws His own unto Himself. Thus when the angel introduces the Bride and starts the Bride's song of rejoicing, the King anew gives place to the Lamb, so that now it can be said: "Let us be glad and rejoice, for the marriage *of the Lamb* is come, *and his wife* hath made herself ready."

XXXI

THE FINAL DEFEAT OF HIS ENEMIES

And the remnant were slain with the sword of him that sat upon the horse, which sword proceeded out of his mouth: and all the fowls were filled with their flesh.
Rev. 19, 21.

The appearance of the Bride of the Lamb is in the nature of the case of such unique significance, that one can not repress the feeling of surprise that it is here inserted merely as an aside. The whole course of what chapter 19 forecasts lies, if we may say so, outside of Christendom. We see the rise of one worldly power after another, which, each with increasing fierceness, and at last especially in the antichrist, makes war against the Christ. So the main point in what follows is the superior power of Christ wherewith He not only faces all these bitter attacks, but at length Himself becomes the aggressor and foils every form of opposition. It even seems that Christendom stands apart, and has nothing to do with this. The opening verses of chapter 21 truly show that Christendom reaps the benefit of it all, and wonderfully revels in the blessing which it brought, yet when the awful struggle of life and death comes to an issue, we only see the destructive power of Christ awake in all its fulness and at length gloriously triumph. In all this the church remains in the background and to the death it all ends in the astounding opposition which Christ directs against paganism. For a moment it really seems as though the church of Christ has no part in this and as though the gigantic struggle between Christ and the antichristian power is the only thing that counts. If then for one moment verses 7 to 10 were taken out of the context, it readily would seem that both what precedes and follows after v. 10 has nothing to do with the reborn humanity, that shall presently inhabit the new earth. Chapter 21 introduces the redeemed again, who, after every opposition has been overcome, take possession of the new creation, yet the most momentous part of the work of destroying the paganistic and antichristian powers seems to be accomplished entirely outside of the people of God. Yet this makes it so much the more impressive, that here in verses 7-10 the Bride is not only introduced into the scene, but that this is done in a way, which, as from aside and in the background, presents the church of Christ shining forth in the glory of her relation and closest intimacy with Christ.

What is presented here does not impress one yet as being the *perfected* salvation. Hence that here quite unexpectedly *the Lamb* appears again, and that only in v. 11 is told how the Rider on the white horse at the head of his mighty army begins the deadly assault. Also the image of the marriage intimates that the matter is not yet consummated. Marriage precedes actual wedlock. Thus it is not the king who with his consort takes possession of the abode of God. On the contrary everything rather bears as yet a provisional character. Christ still appears in the form of the Lamb, and is not yet the triumphant King, and Christendom appears not yet as the mistress of the new heaven and the new earth. Of all this there is as yet no mention. Only with v. 11 does that glory come in. And therefore verses 7-10 still confine themselves to the Lamb that seeks and atones, and so draws the church to Himself as His bride, which only later will be entirely his. Yet this depiction that presently vanishes could not have been left out. Presently Christ in His glory shall victoriously attack the antichrist, but here it seems as though this still awaits a later period, and so Christendom which during the deadly conflict will almost seem to be of no account is here, as it were, intentionally introduced, lest for one moment it might be thought that she were of no consequence. In full accord with this the bride is very beautifully arrayed. "To her is granted that she should be arrayed in fine linen, clean and white," which metaphorically is meant in the spiritual sense, for, so follows in a tender way, "that fine linen is the righteousness of saints." The angel who said this to St. John went on to say: "Write, Blessed are they that are called unto the marriage supper of the Lamb." And, as if to emphasize this still more fully, he adds: "These are the true sayings of God." This affected St. John so greatly, that he fell at the feet of the speaker and folded his hands as though to worship him. This shows that he must have thought that these words were spoken by Christ, or perchance by God Himself. But the angel at once removes this incorrect impression, and bids him to stand up and not to take him for anything but a fellow-servant. And so ends this, as it were, inserted revelation; it is suddenly broken off; and now Christ appears immediately to bring in the final judgment. Heaven now quite unexpectedly opens and Christ descends on the white horse to carry the last judgment into effect.

In whatever way the interlude of the marriage of the Lamb be taken, by common consensus v. 11 of this 19th chapter begins the great event that makes an end of the existing order of things, and brings to pass the great onslaught which does away with what is, and not merely announces the new state of things, but begins it. This 11th verse: "And I saw heaven opened, and behold a white horse, and he that sat upon him was called Faithful and True, and in righteousness he doth judge and make war," indicates the great turning point. Here the break in the historical course of earthly life is final, and now comes in what shall eternally abide. In part this break had already taken place, when it said: "that there should be time no longer," and more emphatically still when the voice said: "It is done"; but even then in the ruining process of things it was ever yet a transition, and only now is that transition ended. Now St. John sees heaven opened and Christ come down from heaven, not as Redeemer and Saviour, but to bring in the final break; to destroy what exists; and to put in place of it the blessed glory. Only in v. 1 of chapter 21 that new and eternal state is consummated. When St. John can say: "And I saw a new heaven and a new earth: for the first heaven and the first earth were passed away; and there was no more sea," then it is ended, then the great process is consummated, then what is doomed to perish has perished, or is appointed to doom. And what then the eternal future offers God, the angels and believers, now presents itself in a new form on a new earth and under a heaven that with new splendor overarches the rejuvenated earth.

Of course when St. John wrote this, it was not yet really so. It was as yet but a representation of what it was to be, and thus as yet simply in image. Yet in the holy vision this representation exhibited what would come, is visualized as real, and in the image that St. John caught of it, it now went ever forward to the final end. Purposely we do not refer yet to what chapter 20 presents, which is better dealt with by itself alone, when first we shall have followed the straight course of the Consummation in its main stages. All we can do here is to take the given representation from v. 11 f. as what actually and really thus takes place. When in chapter 21, 1 it reads that St. John saw a new earth and a new heaven, it is evident that he was still on Patmos, yet at the same time, that in the vision that came to him, and in which he completely lost himself, an entirely new reality had come in, and that in that visionary world, into which he entered with his whole soul the transition from the old into the new dispensation or new order of things was really taking place. As regards that transition of the vision, everything depends on v. 11 and on what follows after. Ever since His Ascension Christ had occupied the seat of honor at the right hand of God. After the Ascension a period of waiting had come in, during which Christ had performed His prophetical, priestly and kingly task. He had sent out His Word to gather His church, priest-like He had prayed for the application of the atonement to those that believed on His Name, and as King he had borne rule to keep His church standing in the face of unbelief. All this had now come to an end. The last conflict was on hand. And Christ comes down to the earth that was giving way under doom and curse. As once in Bethlehem amid the song of angels He had entered into this world's life, as the Lamb of God to redeem and to bless, He now comes down a second time to our earth in a different form and with a different purpose. Not to make atonement but to judge; not to make an offering of Himself in behalf of our world, but to put an end to the sinful life of that world; not as Saviour, but as Judge. The day of salvation had run its long course, and the hour of doom had come.

The whole representation shows that Christ now comes, not again as Saviour but, as Judge. Visualize the manger of Bethlehem with the song of the heavenly choirs in the fields of Ephrata, and here the heavenly Judge, who sitting on the white horse announces His arrival. It is again the white horse that was spoken of in Rev. 6, 2: "And I saw, and behold a white horse: and he that sat on him had a bow, and he went forth conquering and to conquer," yet here the representation is different. We see again the "white horse," but the representation as a whole is different. In Rev. 6 there were four horses, one of which was white as here, on which sat the Son of God, but of the other three one was red, another black and the third pale. Here, however, in chapter 19, 11, *f*. nothing is said of those three other horses, but we see the Son of God seated on the white horse, and with Him great armies of heaven likewise upon white horses following Him, to execute His judgment on the world. The difference between then and now also shows itself in this, that while in chapter 6 Christ handles a bow from which destructive arrows fly, so that it remains an attack from a great distance, here Christ handles the sword, a weapon that strikes near at hand, wounds and kills. Also in the name which the Son of God bears in Bethlehem and here, the divergence shows itself. In the fields of Ephrata it was the Babe of Bethlehem, here His appearance is expressed in the two laudatory terms of "Faithful and True". And lastly the difference between then and now shows itself also in that now He comes not to save, but to judge, not to forgive, but *in righteousness to make war*. This shows that all forgiveness and remission is ended and that now everything is done in constant and absolute justice.

This stern, unsparing character of Jesus' coming to judgment and casting down everything that is unholy is then told in broad and striking terms. He does not look invitingly or tenderly into the faces of those who appear before Him, for His eyes are "as a flame of fire." He is no more the Man of Sorrows, for many royal crowns are the mark and indication of the omnipotent power wherewith He now comes. And in all this He is ever an impenetrable mystery to the world. For on His kingly crown (v. 12) a name is written which no man knew, but He Himself, while by the hosts that follow Him He is hailed as "The Word of God" (v. 13); which of course was not a name but the expression of His hidden being. Thus in one way a mystical divine name which even the angels did not understand, and in another way a rich name which was the mystery of His own knowledge. But this is not all. The outward appearance of Christ also shows itself in striking colors, as v. 13 reads: "He was clothed with a vesture dipped in blood." And that trait of blood always points back to Golgotha, and each time brings out anew that the triumph which at length shall be the part of the Victor is neither favor nor gift, but wage and outcome of what on earth the Man of Sorrows has fought through. *Blood,* taken as human blood, in this connection not only retains its name, but also fulfills its original role. Christ came on earth to redeem forfeited life, and that human life, from the creation and from birth, always depends upon the blood. This is not accidental but essential. The life is in the blood. The Saviour gave His life only when for us He shed His blood. It must here be told therefore in so many words that "He was clothed with a vesture that had been dipped in blood." In case of accident or by an injury of the skin or of the veins, bleeding is possible. But here it must not be taken in this way. In the last instance the life is in the blood, and death shows itself very obviously in the blood. Thus in this instance blood is not taken as the blood of a wound. Not as blood that could have been shed without attacking the life. As is indicated in the Gospels the Saviour is attacked in the *blood of His life,* and only by this attack on the life in the blood, both the death has ensued, and the shedding of that blood has obtained its high significance. So the two are taken together. His vesture was dipped in blood and He Whose blood thus sealed His death is Himself and in His own person, the Word of God. In his Gospel the apostle John fully emphasizes this: "In the beginning was the Word, and the Word was with God. The same was in the beginning with God."

The finishing stroke in this vision is that the Son of God here does not appear alone, as with a word of rebuke to cast down the whole pagan power. On earth the armies of the antichrist consisted of innumerable hosts, which, together with the armies of Gog and Magog, were prepared to engage in the deadly struggle against the Messiah. If single-handed and alone Christ, as with Divine almightiness, had attacked and cast down this unholy military power, the mention in v. 14 of those armies that followed Him would not have been necessary. But such is not the mode of procedure. The unholy world power is not repulsed as by a word of magic. Rather power is pitted against power. A war is begun, and as the antichrist draws up all his demoniac armies together with those of Gog and Magog in battle-array to vanquish the Son of God, naturally the Christ does not appear alone, but in His turn calls upon His armies to follow

Him and under His leadership engage in the deadly conflict. Thus we read in this 14th verse: "And the armies which were in heaven followed him," and these, even as Christ Himself, were seated upon white horses, clothed in fine linen, white and clean. And as the thousand times ten thousands of angels, as an irresistible military power, from heaven come down to earth, to engage in battle, yes, in mortal conflict with the pagans under the leadership of antichrist, a sharp sword goes out from the mouth of Christ. But the might wherewith Christ attacks the heathen, antichristian forces does not confine itself to this. So we read in v. 15: "And out his mouth goeth a sharp sword, that with it he should smite the nations." With a rod of iron shall He attack them, and to come back to the old image of Rev. 14, 19 and 20, it is added, that he not only "treadeth the winepress of the wrath," but also "of the fierceness and wrath of Almighty God." Thus almost literally as had previously been announced in Rev. 14. There it was said that "the angel gathered the grapes from the vine of the earth and cast them into the great winepress of the wrath of God." And to bring out clearly and plainly the glory of the Victor, there follows in closing: "He hath on his vesture a name written: King of kings and Lord of lords."

So only does one understand what follows in v. 17, that John saw an angel standing in the sun. This reference to the sun shows that now the whole structure of the universe is to be attacked. What we read in v. 1 of chapter 21, that everything is renewed, so that our earth not only undergoes an utter rejuvenation, but the heaven also shall pass away and re-appear as an entirely different heaven, is also found here in v. 17 of chapter 19. The sun as the center of our solar system is involved in this universal change· Even St. Paul in 2 Thess. 2, 3 f., and no less St. Peter pointed to the fact that in the end the whole cosmos would undergo a radical change, no mere change such as in this dispensation large regions in ocean and mountainous country have undergone. In all reality it is to be a *new* earth surrounded by a *new* firmament. And in the vision of St. John it is now come to this radical and universal modification. An angel standing in the sun cries with a loud voice, saying to all the fowls that fly in the midst of heaven: "Come and gather yourselves together unto the supper of the great God." And what for? For what else than that now the moment is come when everything earthly that glittered and shone forth in majesty, is suddenly cast down and perishes. Kings now pass away together with their generals. For so we read in v. 18: "That ye may eat the flesh of kings, and the flesh of captains over thousands." Yes, the superior power of Christ now directly attacks all earthly power. Therefore it says so emphatically that the flesh,—that is, the external power of everything that opposed God, is destroyed, not alone the Kings and captains, but even "the flesh of horses, and of them that sit on them, and the flesh of all men, both free and bond, both small and great." And now the enemies of God appear again in their antichristian combination and organization, and in both these they are brought to nought. St. John sees the beast appear again, followed by the kings of the earth and their armies, and he perceives that now that whole organized and united demoniacal world power sets itself in battle array to wage war with Christ, still deeming itself sure of victory.

Yet now comes the absolute point of turning. V. 20 reads: "And the beast *was taken,* and with him the false prophet that wrought miracles before him, with which he deceived them that had received the mark of the beast, and them that worshipped his image. These both were cast alive into a lake of fire burning with brimstone." With this the great battle is ended. Everything that by the antichrist and demoniac forces, and by the beast and Gog and Magog was planned and carried out against the Holy, is now suddenly and as with one blow utterly routed. And after that herewith the leaders and tempters are doomed to impotence and in their inner being are disrupted, there now follows a general slaying of all that had dared to exalt itself against God. For so reads v. 21: "And the remnant were slain with the sword of him that sat upon the horse, which sword proceeded out of his mouth: and all the fowls were filled with their flesh." So everything is ended. Everything earthly or from the world of demons or from the sphere of the beast, together with the dragon and the antichrist, that had arrayed itself against God and His Anointed, is now mortally wounded and stripped of all power. What is doomed to perish has had its day, and the moment is come for the new condition of heaven and earth to come in.

XXXII

THE MILLENIUM*

And I saw a great white throne, and him that sat on it, from whose face the earth and the heaven fled away: and there was found no place for them. Rev. 20, 11.

The first part of the 20th chapter of Revelation presents such almost insurmountable difficulties to the expositor, that it is still a question whether the correct explanation of the first ten verses has been found. To appreciate the intricate character of what is here presented one needs but to connect what precedes with what follows. If the thousand years spoken of in vs. 2, 3, 4, 5 and 6 be taken literally, what here is taught can not be naturally connected with what precedes; for then the Return of Christ to judge the earth would only be possible after the expiration of these thousand years, which is irreconcilable with what precedes in chapter 19. In chapter 19 it is clearly stated that Christ had already come for the last judgment. "And I saw," so St. John writes, "heaven opened, and behold a white horse; and he that sat upon him was called Faithful and True, and in righteousness he doth judge and make war." Also the further description that here is given of Christ confirms the impression that His session at the Right hand of God was ended, and that now he came to make an end of things. So we read in v. 12 *f.* "His eyes were as a flame of fire, and on his head were many crowns; and he had a name written, that no man knew, but he himself. And he was clothed with a vesture dipped in blood: and his name is called The Word of God." And what indicates still much more strongly his coming to judgment is read in v. 14 *f.*: "And the armies which were in heaven followed him upon white horses, clothed in fine linen, clean and white. And out of his mouth goeth a sharp sword, that with it he should smite the nations: and he shall rule them with a rod of iron: and he treadeth the winepress of the

---

*In the original "The Millennium" covers chapters XXXII-XXXV.

fierceness and wrath of Almighty God. And he hath on his vesture and on his thigh a name written, King of kings and Lord of lords." Even though for the moment we leave what then follows aside, we have already in these verses the picture of Christ, as he goes forth to judgment and to materialize the end of things.

But of course we can not rest content with this. The announcement of the Return of Christ, as this is portrayed in chapter 19 with so much definiteness, is immediately connected with what is set forth in chapter 6 to chapter 19. Though we leave the first four chapters from 2 to 5 aside for the moment, in the following chapters there were first the seven *seals*. Upon these followed the seven *trumpets*. This carried us into chapter 16. Then came the seven *vials*, which really extended to chapter 19. Only after these seals, trumpets and vials had successively announced a series of twenty-one horrors, and the whole state of human life and of the earth had undergone a radical onslaught, so that the normal condition of earthly life had experienced the effect of the curse and earthly conditions had given place in part to misery and wretchedness, came at length the dreadful judgment, to which all the former plagues had been but preparatory, and now it was most clearly indicated that the last judgment was at hand and judgment from on high would be executed not only upon the earth but in part even upon the whole universe. Regarding all this chapter 19 leaves not the least doubt. The Son of God has already left the seat of honor at God's Right hand. Ordinary time is no more reckoned with. The end is come and judgment began.

But more still had come to pass. As we read in v. 17 of chapter 19, an angel of God had taken his place in the sun, and had cried with a loud voice, saying to all the fowls of heaven, "Come and gather yourselves together unto the supper of the great God." This indicated that the flesh of kings and of captains and of mighty men, together with the flesh of horses and of all civilians and servants, great and small, would become a prey to the destroyers. This led to a last conflict. For we read in v. 19: "And I saw the beast and the kings of the earth and their armies gathered together to make war against him that sat on the horse, and against his army." With this the deadly conflict began, the end of which was, that the beast and the false prophet, and all that were subject unto them, were taken. All were then cast alive into the lake of fire that burns with brimstone. And the remnant, so ends chapter 19, the remnant were slain with the sword of him that sat upon the horse—that is, with the sword of Christ, and all the fowls were filled with their flesh. Thus this is not a judgment, that merely threatens to come and is announced, but a judgment, even a divine judgment that is in course of accomplishment. The successive steps even follow quickly upon each other. There is nothing said of a pause in the narrative, that would change the scene. The end is come. Everything that was to be subjected to the judgment has been brought to nought and robbed of power and life, and from the reading of chapter 19 one can only gather that now the final decision is begun, and that now the Son of God is in the act of executing His judgment. There is indeed nothing more left to destroy. Everything that still had the appearance of greatness has been brought to nought, and in His last judgment Christ has triumphed over the misery of sin.

If this stood by itself alone, one might think that up to this last moment the ordinary condition of earthly life had still retained its old form, that nothing had yet been changed, and that now as with one stroke all human life on earth were destroyed· But, as observed before nothing is said of this. The plagues that had been visited upon the earth with the seven seals, trumpets and vials, had not attacked human life spiritually only, but also nature and her products had thereby been entirely disrupted. One calamity after another had overtaken mankind. Violent disturbances in nature and ravages of disease had lifted human life out of its grooves. So distressing had the terror been already with the realization of the seals, that death itself had been courted, and despairingly people from highest to lowest social ranks had called upon "mountains and rocks, saying: Fall on us, and hide us from the face of Him that sitteth upon the throne, and from the wrath of the Lamb" (see chapter 6, 15 v. v.). Thus there is nothing to indicate that, at the time of the judgment in chapter 19, human life had still retained its former attractiveness. Instead of this, already before the trumpets had ominously sounded, earthly life had been filled with terror and anxiety. It may even be taken for granted that the succession of the seals, the trumpets and the vials had not been slow, but with some rapidity had followed one another. In any case it is certain that what chapter 19 records of the judgment that the Son of God was to execute upon the unholy world, would be terrible and destructive. It must be borne in mind that what chapter 19 depicts is the concluding result of everything that had gone before by reason of the seals, trumpets and vials. So it can not be said that ordinary normal life had meanwhile undisturbedly gone on. Words can scarcely be found to describe the dire distresses that had already come upon this earth and the human race, and what chapter 19 portrays as concluding result is so positive an outbreak of the last judgment, that after it was ended, normal human life on this earth was no more possible.

So from chapter 19, one would rather pass on at once to chapter 21. There was not a moment's further doubt about the triumph of the Son of God. After everything that by the seals, trumpets and vials had become manifest in all the world, it was evident that the triumph belonged to God's Son. The sin-ravaged and lost world could have reverted into nothingness, and the new earth under the new heaven have become manifest. And of itself the one would have joined on to the other. All that was unholy had been slain by the sword of him that sat upon the horse, and "then I, John, saw a new heaven and a new earth: for the first heaven and the first earth had passed away; and there was no more sea."

If now the Chiliastic representation were in agreement with this view, one might reasonably imagine that the last conflict, which is not to be fought out with the sinful children of men, but must be fought out with Satan, should take place after this initial victory of Christ, and nothing would prevent the visualization of a short period during which Satan is overpowered and the last battle is fought to the finish. But this is not the view that is forced upon us. Bear in mind that Chiliasm has presented itself in many forms, and in the course of centuries has borrowed from the prevailing conditions of the ecclesiastical life ever changing and diverging forms. Even now it can not be said that Chiliasm presents an entirely uniform aspect. This will be emphasized later on. But in this first approach to chapter 20 it is of utmost importance not to break or abandon the connection with chapters 6-19. We can not yield to the untenable representation that in his approach to the judgments in chapter 20 St. John set the contents of chapters 6-19 aside as of no more account. And as this can

not be laid to the charge of the apostle John, it is far less thinkable that the Spirit of the Lord by Whom he was inspired, at the
20th chapter would suddenly have set aside the preceding 19
chapters, as though they had not been revealed. Unless the several
parts of Revelation are properly connected with one another, how
can the book as a whole be accepted as a sacred writing inspired
by a higher Spirit? Hence the content of chapter 20 must cohere
in good order of succession with what lies back of it.

We have no desire to exaggerate. We readily admit that in
this last part of the Divine revelation, which came to St. John,
there is a lapse of time and a division of time and reckoning,
which departs from our common representation; but this will
never let the divergence turn into absolute nonsense. This is so obvious that the Chiliasts themselves direct attention to this, and by
legitimate modification escape in part the impossible snags into
which the ultras among them fall. More than one has stumbled
upon the number of the thousand years. Yet this does not remove the main difficulty which irresistibly forces itself upon us
when the content of Rev. 6-19 is actually set aside, or to say it
better still, is taken as though it had not been written. Grant
that this preceding revelation had not been written, and that
chapter 20 stands independently by itself alone, and there is nothing to prevent the representation of the literal meaning of Rev.
20, 1-10 as legitimate prophecy. The great difficulty one faces,
and which radically cancels this interpretation of these ten verses,
lies in what precedes. One can not, and ought not to, sanction the
representation that what chapters 6-19 announce as close at hand,
should take place, and that then it should be followed by a period
of a thousand years which announces itself as though the content
of these earlier chapters fell away. However taken, this always
means a play with the Return of the Lord, which, in all seriousness, must be guarded against. Much ought and also can be
settled here by 'give and take', but to confess that Christ has
returned, accompanied in His descent to earth by the armies of
heaven, and immediately thereupon welcome the idea, that long
centuries again are to intervene between this descent of Christ
and the end, were intolerable obliquity of judgment.

Undoubtedly according to human reckoning something could
be said of a definite course of time, but Revelation indicates that

time, in the ordinary sense, would be no more. Naturally there would be *duration*, progress and transition from moment to moment; but with the Return of the Lord the narrowness of our earthly chronology of itself fell away. This works, so to speak, in two ways. That which has relative duration can contract itself as into one moment of time, and again that which takes place as with lightning speed can obtain some duration. The main point here, however, is, that what in ordinary life takes days and years, contracts itself as into the twinkling of an eye, and yet can acquire an important effect. Especially what here is the main point, to wit: the action of Satan and his demons on our earthly life requires no long duration of what we call *time*. Think of the apostasy of Satan and of his demons, when the creation was young, and it is clear to the thoughtful person that the dreadful events which were implied therein were lived through as in one moment. Of Adam and Eve this can not be understood otherwise. Our first parents have not agonized days and weeks to come to their decision. The venomous assault of Satan on their heart came to an issue in one moment; first with Eve and presently with Adam. And though some moment of inner conflict must be admitted, yet the decision whether they would remain faithful to God or whether they would let Satan beguile them, was plainly made in one single moment.

Also the reverse of this is the rule. A soul, which from the life of sin is translated into the life of holiness, makes this transition in one moment of time. It is God who brings this to pass in us; and it is one single moment in our life that decides with respect to this. In this connection it is not all necessary therefore, that what Satan intends to do at the approach of the last judgment must take long days, months and years. Obviously also in that final decision, the evil working of spirits and the opposition thereto of good spirits, could reach a result in a very short period of time. Here too it meant final decisions in the disposition of spirits. Though one admits that it took some time before this turn in the spirits had carried its effect from people to people, yet here too with respect to the satanic influence it narrows down to one drastic assault. And while we do not undervalue the fact that, when it came to this turningpoint, Satan suddenly had tremendous power at his command, and has used that power, yet this does not imply that it deferred or held back the Return of the Lord. So there is no reason why here a spiritual warfare of ten centuries should come in. And though in these verses the expression of "a thousand years" repeatedly occurs, it must not be inferred from this that these thousand years mean ten centuries. The insertion of ten centuries here renders the content of chapters 6-19 untenable. If then one bears in mind that frequently in Scripture, and especially in the book of Revelation, numbers can not be taken literally, but must be understood metaphorically, there is no reason why in this instance the expression of "a thousand years" should be taken to mean a lapse of time of ten centuries.

XXXIII

THE UNTENABILITY OF THE CHILIASTIC CLAIM

*And he laid hold on the dragon, that old serpent,
which is the devil, and Satan, and bound him for a
thousand years.* Rev. 20, 2.

It can not be emphasized too strongly that the part played by
the angel of v. 1 in chapter 20 is not finished until v. 9 of chapter
21. Indeed this angel is one of those that poured out the vials,
but this outpouring is now ended. For so we read in Rev. 21, 9:
"And there came unto me one of the seven angels which had the
seven vials full of the seven last plagues." Hence this concludes
the preceding act, and a new act begins. From v. 1 in chapter 20
to v. 9 of chapter 21 everything proceeds as a coherent whole.
These chapters, therefore, should have been differently divided.
As one unbroken whole, the representation should have
run from chapter 20, 1 to chapter 21, 9, and in this
modified division the complete representation should have
been evident. The futility of the several attempts that have
been made to take the "thousand years" of vs. 2, 3, 4, 5,
6 and 7 in chapter 20 as periods of ten centuries would then have
been realized. Even the idea that these "thousand years" should
count from a much earlier date has long proved more and more
untenable. These divergent interpretations have given rise to
three views. St. Augustine, whose view Beda shared, counted the
1000 years from the death of Christ on Golgotha; others, especially Keil, thought the thousand years to have begun with
the conversion of Constantine; while Hengstenberg counted
from Charles the Great. In the face of all this, the Chiliasts were
right when they contended, be it with a difference, that the thousand years had not come to pass, but are still ahead of us. If
from the context it appears that what we read in Rev. 20, 1 to
the 9th verse of chapter 21, is not merely mutually related, but
will only come to pass after the Parousia has begun, obviously

the 1000 years also can not be taken in the numerical sense. The idea that the parousia will be succeeded by a new historic period of 1000 years contradicts itself.

In the first place do not forget that the purpose of these Patmos revelations was to bring cheer and encouragement to the churches of that day. They abound indeed from first to last with the comforting and inspiring words that the cruel oppression will soon be at an end, as the testimony: "Surely, I come quickly" is answered by believers with the prayer: "Even so, Come, Lord Jesus!" The very peculiarity of the Apocalypse is, that it can lengthen, and in the course of history, stretch to centuries, and yet all along admit of the future of the Lord as being close at hand. It holds out no suggestion of safety to those who defer the end to a future that is far distant. Christ had always emphasized the sudden coming of His parousia. And with an eye to this it is the peculiar character of the Apocalypse that it lends itself to this twofold view, as well that of an almost sudden and immediate coming of the end, as that of an agelong preparation for the same· Again and again we are surprised by expressions and indications that Christ might come at any moment; while again these indications undergo such modifications that these past twenty centuries do not contradict the revelation of St. John. If then one abandons the direct connection which must be maintained between these 1000 years with what follows after, and thus also with the Consummation, it is natural that, as especially St. Augustine recommended, one locates the 1000 years before, rather than after the parousia, and so ignores the coherence between what precedes Rev. 20 and what is presented in Rev. 20, 1—Rev. 21, 9.

This false impression has led to the fact that either without more ado the several parts of the Apocalypse have ruthlessly been disconnected, or that after the parousia a new historic period has been inserted, which then after the lapse of ten centuries ends in a second parousia. But this does not satisfy him who for his soul's welfare sake seeks vital contact with what Christ Himself enjoins regarding His Return. Christ's teachings with respect to this both in St. Matthew 24 and other parts of the Gospels, contain nothing that even remotely suggests any such an interval, and directly contradict it. One does not tally with the other. In

the Gospels and apocalyptical writings the parousia is not presented as the succession of a series of events of long duration, but
as a drastic action which is immediately connected with the resurrection of all the dead, with the last judgment, with the destruction of this world and the rise of a new world on a new earth
under a new heaven. It is inconceivable therefore that between
the parousia of Christ and the Consummation there would again
ensue so tremendous an interval of a thousand years.

The parousia and the judgment with the Consummation belong
together and form one whole. The insertion here of long centuries is impossible. The whole representation in the Gospels connects the parousia most intimately with the resurrection of the
dead and with the last judgment. It betrays haste that savors
of surprise, rather than suggesting the insertion of 1000 years
between the parousia and its final effect, and every attempt to
make these 1000 years mean ten centuries conflicts irreconcilably
with the teaching of Christ respecting the Consummation. Neither
do the perspectives of Ezekiel and Daniel lend themselves to such
an extended period of ten centuries. Both prophets solely depict
what had symbolically been presented to their mind; and he who
compares the teachings of Christ regarding the things that await
us in the Consummation with what these prophets forecast, feels
that they merely present in figurative language what would be
realized in a different way.

Neither is the relation tenable, which then, according to some,
there would be between the glory of Christ that would reveal itself in the renovated Jerusalem among the multitudes of the
blessed, and that ordinary state of things which would prevail
among the heathen nations outside of Jerusalem and the
holy land. It is then made to appear, as though the state of things
in Jerusalem and Palestine were of an almost heavenly character,
while in the other parts of the earth, where the tradition of Gog
and Magog still survives, the reign of sin would go on, and missionary zeal would know no languor. This would present an irreconcilable duality. Life in Jerusalem and Palestine can not be
heavenly, while everywhere else in the world it is sinful. Those
"thousand years" would have to show a history which should
clearly indicate what purpose that long period of ten centuries
would have served. On the new earth under the new heaven life

will be sinless and spiritual, and the eternal duration of a perfect, holy state of things can be awaited; here on the other hand no reason would be thinkable why this period of waiting should last ten or more centuries. If the hour of the consummated mission had come, and Israel also were converted, the execution of this final act would not require a period of centuries, but merely a short epoch; and there would be no reason why the parousia of Christ would century upon century have to assume a character which is altogether contradictory to what He has prophesied regarding His parousia and the Consummation.

Also to the kingly dominion of the blessed, for which appeal is made to v. 4 of chapter 20, no wrong significance should be attached. There we read that in his vision St. John saw thrones, and the blessed sat on them, and judgment was given unto them; "and I saw" so he goes on, "the souls of them that were beheaded for the witness of Jesus, and for the word of God, and which had not worshiped the beast, neither his image, and they lived and reigned with Christ a thousand years." This reigning as kings must not be misunderstood. It does not indicate that as kings they excelled in splendour and bare rule. The more recent exegesis came to the conclusion, that this does not refer to a reign that is celebrated for splendour and glory. For this would be absolutely incompatible with the reign of Christ, Who now took everything under His charge. Thus it can only mean that the blessed take part in the judgment upon the unrighteous. For how otherwise would a people of kings only, without subjects be thinkable? All this acquires, by misinterpretation, an image which has no corresponding reality. It would simply be a kingdom of kings, nor would there be any record of a history of that kingdom. It would begin and end, but what it would effect and establish in a period of a thousand years would remain an absolute mystery. The making of new, sacred history could in no wise be indicated. It is in fact incomprehensible that, when the end arrives and the parousia of Christ is in process of coming to pass, this all decisive action would suddenly be arrested and the Consummation be deferred, not for a short, quickly passing period, but for a thousand years, at the expiration of which literally nothing would have happened and nothing would have been accomplished to justify this uncommonly long delay. In the nature of the case when the end is so near at hand the redeemed long for the fruition of the same. Such a delay of a thousand years, even if it were marked by holiness of life, is necessarily far inferior in glory to that which the Consummation shall bring. And this lesser state of things would have lasted a thousand years before it would have given place to the full blessedness. The portion of the Saints would thus not have become an increase but a lessening of blessedness. This period of a thousand years might be possible, in case it would afford an opportunity for something to happen or to be established. But there is not one word of reference to this. There is nothing, therefore, to justify the prolongation of such a futile interval. Moreover, after Jesus' parousia time in the real sense is no longer reckoned with. We must reckon of course with the binding and letting loose of Satan. Even after the parousia we face two successive events. Satan is first made impotent, and later he is set at liberty to invite his own defeat. But though this can not be represented except in two distinct and successive periods, there is no reason for extending these periods into a multiplicity of years. Neither in the world of angels nor in the world of demons is there a reckoning with our idea of time, and the three acts, (1) the binding of Satan, (2) the letting loose of Satan and (3) the final judgment upon Satan, can begin, go on, and consummate themselves in what can not be told in terms of years, months or days. There is here no room, therefore, for a thousand years of our reckoning.

The only point that can still be advanced is, that the final outbreak of the barbaric nations of Gog and Magog, their war against the ordered civilized nations, and the final triumph of those civilized nations over the primitive peoples must have covered a period of time. When, however, we call to mind in how short a time Alexander the Great brought Asia to his feet, it is readily seen that it will require no thousand years to put an end to the last conflict with Gog and Magog. From whatever angle this is viewed, there is no explanation of those 1000 years, which would have been stretched in a literal sense for no other purpose than of making an event, that at most might cover a period of ten years, cover one a hundred times as long. There is no reason, no cause for it. And every serious study of the matter always leads to one of two conclusions: either verses 1-10 of chapter

20 are a chapter of pseudo-history that has been inserted at some later date, or the 1000 years must be understood in a symbolical sense.

Thus in the end it is always again the question, whether the "thousand years" in Revelation 20 are or are not to be taken as normal years; which question presumably will never bring a unanimous response. For the fact can not be set aside that the reference to those 1000 years is not casual, but is repeated with special emphasis as many as six times. How is this to be explained? If the Revelation of St. John were a book in which numbers were used in their normal sense as in ordinary prose, we would undoubtedly have a six times repeated expression which definitely refers to a period of ten centuries. Yet in the Revelation of St. John we may not reckon thus. Doubtless the number 1000 occurs repeatedly in Holy Scripture in a literal sense. At the miraculous feeding the miracle took place to the good of the thousands that both times were fed. Especially in the Old Testament, where there is much more reckoning with particulars and with numerical strength than in the New, the number 1000 occurs again and again in the literal sense. In the division of the army the mention of the thousand men in the battalion may not always have been strictly accurate, yet wherever it concerns the strength of the army this number thousand is used in a real, ordinary and normal sense. But nothing can be inferred from this in connection with what we find in Revelation, especially in those texts which do not deal with human actions, but with what is done by Almighty God. To the Jewish mind the word "thousand" meant a supremely rich fulness, and in that sense was applied to the doings of God, to indicate—not the numerical, but—the general idea of the Divine majesty and greatness. Psalm 90, 4 here always gives the keynote. It emphatically states: "A thousand years in thy sight are but as yesterday when it is past, and as a watch in the night"; and in his second epistle the apostle Peter refers to this volatilization of time, where in chapter 3, 8 we read: "But, beloved, be not ignorant of this one thing, that one day is with the Lord as a thousand years, and a thousand years as one day." And in verse 10 he observes again: "The day of the Lord will come as a thief in the night, in the which the heavens shall pass away with a great noise."

In view of these inspired sayings it can not be denied, therefore, that both what Jesus Himself foretold, and what occurs ir
the apostolic literature, refers, not once, but many times, to the
fact that the "thousand years" in connection with the Consummation are not a literal but a symbolical indication. Why then
should the 1000 years in Apoc. 20, 1-10 suddenly obtain a significance, which elsewhere in the Revelations they never possess? In
other writings a six-fold repetition of a thousand years would require a careful explanation, but such a necessity can never apply
to the doings of God, and hence in the book of Revelation, where
it concerns not the doings of men, but of Almighty God, it is out
of the question. To do this, one must attribute to this expression
of a 1000 years in the Apocalypse a significance and a sense,
which otherwise it never has in this last book of the New Testament. The literal interpretation here is even something obtrusive,
which is rejected and contradicted by the whole structure of this
writing. Even from the six times repeated use of that expression
"thousand years" in a writing such as this, nothing can be inferred. When we have a writing in hand in which the rule applies
that the numbers have no numerical, but a symbolical significance,
one has no right to surmise the opposite use of the number, unless
this modified use is very clearly indicated.

If then we had to do with a prophecy which gave a minute description of these thousand years, so that it were evident that
what was to come could not eventuate in less than ten centuries,
we would be bound to accept it, and conclude that these ten centuries will ensue after the parousia, however much this might actually reduce the first parousia to a mere semblance, or, that what
verses 1-10 of Rev. 20 present, not only precedes chapter 19, but
even the trumpets and vials. It was necessary to emphasize,
therefore, that these ten centuries which are deemed here to have
been inserted are empty, without meaning, and furnish no
history, as nothing pertaining to them is recorded. If this undeniable fact is taken in connection with what precedes chapter
20, together with what follows in chapter 20 and chapter 21, 1-8,
we have no right to tear this closely articulated connection apart,
and it must be taken as together forming the vision of one angel,
which comes after the prophecy of the destruction of the earthly
powers at the close of chapter 19, and now as one whole precedes

the Consummation. Thus without in the least disguising the fact that a superficial reading here might divert and readily induce us to substitute the precise historical for the symbolical interpretation of Rev. 20, 1-10, yet upon closer investigation it increasingly appears that he who abandons this symbolical way ignores the language, tone and style of the Apocalypse for the sake of an idea that is in conflict with the whole tendency of the same. In every other writing the construction of the first ten verses of chapter 20 would require a literal interpretation, but as in Revelation the idea "thousand" is *never* taken literally, and also here merely expresses the exceeding fulness of Divine action, the precise, literal and historical understanding can not be imputed to God, and the exegete is duty bound to interpret what as Divine language comes to us according to the claim of the exegesis that is adaptable to it.

XXXIV

THE LITTLE SEASON

*And he laid hold on the dragon, that old serpent, which
is the Devil, and Satan, and bound him a thousand
years.* Rev. 20, 2.

Going back to the particulars which, after the judgment upon
the beast and the false prophet preceded the conclusion of the
Consummation, the main division of the content ends with v. 10
of chapter 20, and the exposition runs from there on to v. 9 of
chapter 21. Upon closer study it appears that each time there are
three subdivisions.   With respect to the transition from the
parousia to the Consummation we have in the first place chapter
20, 1-3, pointing to the binding of Satan; then come verses 4, 5
and 6 which relate the resurrection of the martyrs; and in verses
7, 8, 9 and 10 the subjugation of Satan, who shares the lot of
the beast and the false prophet and is tormented for ever and
ever. What precedes then covers the thousand years, while the
subjection of Satan and the conflict between the blessed and Gog
and Magog take only "a little season," yet always "a little season" distinct from and subsequent to the "thousand years." And
if this marks the beginning of the Consummation, what takes
place in connection with this divides itself again in three groups.
(1) Verses 11-13 which announce the resurrection of the rest of
the dead; (2) verses 14 and 15 which tell of the utter destruction
of the unconverted; and (3) verses 1-9 of chapter 21 which depict the destruction of the old world and the appearing of the
new, which under the new heaven shall for ever manifest God's
glory. As has already been observed, these pericopes, three before
the Consummation and three attendant upon the Consummation
itself, are not divided, but together form one inwardly connected
whole. In v. 1 of chapter 20 an angel introduces this vision and
does not conclude the same till we reach v. 8 of chapter 21. Then
in v. 9 of chapter 21 we learn that a second angel appears who
carries the vision over into a new realm. So the sixfold division

278

must strictly be maintained and equally strictly must the unity and the connection of these six parts govern our representation.

One realizes at once how strange and baffling it is that these two periods, which in one coherent vision follow upon each other, should differ so widely as to their content, and that the first is said to cover a very long extended period of time, while the second is said to last merely "a little season." This antithesis is strongly marked in v. 3 of chapter 20. The two things here foretold are, that Satan would be bound, and again that he would begin his final struggle which, in the conflict of the nations, would lead to his utter defeat. Thus two periods, one of which has nothing to mark it, as Satan is impotent, and is to last ten centuries, and the other in which Satan is free again, and is to fight a great battle, and which is to last only "a little season." So we read in v. 3: The angel "cast Satan into the bottomless pit, and shut him up, and set a seal upon him, that he should deceive the nations no more, till the thousand years should be fulfilled." And of the second period—in which Satan is to gather the peoples of God and Magog together for the final and gigantic conflict with the holy people, hence a historic period of well-nigh incomparable importance—it is said in this same 3rd verse that it will cover only "a little season." If these thousand years are taken literally the singular contrast presents itself between two successive periods—and such in one and the same vision—one of ten centuries and of no historic significance, and the other of "a little season" which witnesses a succession of mighty and overwhelming events which, as to form and mutual relation, entirely modify both heaven and earth. One feels that there is no balance here, no harmony, no concurrence, and yet as a vision by one angel it must form one coherent whole, closely articulated in all its parts.

Going back to the particulars of the 1000 years period, we are told in the first place that the influence of Satan and his action on mankind is suddenly wiped out. Not weakened, nor moderated, no, but ended by the destruction of Satan's power even in such a way that he could no more deceive the nations. So verses 1-3 of chapter 20 read: The angel had the key to the bottomless pit and a great chain in his hand, and thus armed this angel laid hold on Satan, and bound him a thousand years. No servant of Satan can here be thought of, for it reads, that what the angel laid hold on was Satan himself, "the old serpent, which is the Devil, and Satan, and bound him a thousand years." Thus the mention here is of a very mighty angel. Do not forget that before he fell, Satan himself was one of the mightiest of angels, and so in the nature of the case the angel that here appears with the key of the bottomless pit and the great chain must be mighty enough to overcome Satan and so to shut him up that he lost all his power over the world of spirits. He was not only bound, but according to v. 3 he was doomed to absolute inactivity. For the angel cast him into the bottomless pit, and sealed it above him, "that he should deceive the nations no more, till the thousand years should be fulfilled." And only after the expiration of these thousand years would he be able to resume his unholy action for a short time, which in "a little season" would result in his utter ruin and doom to perdition. Naturally this was connected with what had been told before, that Satan had been thrust out from the high world and doomed to dwell in the depths of the miseries of earthly life. We also must admit that the impotence of Satan here is indicated especially with respect to *the nations,* which does not exclude the possibility that *personal* temptation was continued, but only in the sense which Jesus indicated when He in John 14, 30 said: "The prince of this world cometh, and hath nothing in me." But this aside, it is here clearly stated that this mighty angel had been sent of God to break Satan's influence on the nations as a whole and thus on the final development of the life of the nations.

This binding of Satan was no experiment to see how life on earth would go on, in case the satanic influence were temporarily suspended. This binding had of itself a given purpose with respect to the new-born state of things. That condition had arisen by the first judgment that had come upon Satan, when from his high estate in the world of angels he had been cast down into the depth of the lower life. The relation between this world and Satan had thereby suffered a radical change. This changed position of Satan gave rise to the danger that he would taint all earthly life, and bring it into entire subjection to demoniacal domination. In other words the danger was what now is told in v. 7 *f.*: "And when the thousand years are expired, Satan shall be loosed out of his prison, and shall go out to deceive the nations which are in the four quarters of the earth, Gog and Magog, to gather them together to battle: the number of whom is as the sand of the sea"; as though all this already now immediately took place. This could not be permitted since it would have broken the natural course of the judgment. Hence a pause must needs precede Satan's outbreak. To this end Satan had to be bound. When by his expulsion from the high world he had come down to our earth and was able to exert a dominant influence upon life here below, his power had at least provisionally to be arrested, lest he should have paralyzed the latest inclination toward the good among the nations. Hence the impotence that was imposed upon him was for a given purpose, and with an eye to a given final struggle, which was going on, but which could not be a matter of centuries, but at most a matter of delay and transition from state into state, whereby the latest effect of God's Word would not be broken. What here is told should not be separated, therefore, from what was recorded already in chapter 12. There we read in v. 7: "And there was war in heaven: Michael and his angels fought against the dragon; and the dragon fought and his angels, and prevailed not; neither was their place found any more in heaven," which "heaven" naturally does not mean the sphere around God's throne, but the high sphere in which the incorporeal dwelt. From that high sphere Satan and his demons were then cast down and relegated to the lower levels of the material life. So reads v. 9 in chapter 12: "And the great dragon was cast out, that old serpent, called the Devil, and Satan, which deceiveth the whole world; he was cast out into the earth and his angels were cast out with him."

This strong statement in chapter 12 had to be recalled, because apart from this connection the beginning of chapter 20 is unintelligible. The decision is actually reached already in Revelation 12, and not in Revelation 20. Read what in Rev. 12 immediately follows upon what has been quoted. The then receiver of the Apocalypse wrote in v. 10: "And I heard a loud voice saying in heaven, Now is come salvation, and strength, and the kingdom of our God, and the power of his Christ: for the accuser of our brethren is cast down, which accused them before our God day and night." Thus already in chapter 12 the song of triumph is begun: "Therefore rejoice, ye heavens, and ye that dwell in them," and now is added that the Devil who had come down into the world, already then had great wrath, knowing that he hath but *a short time*. This indication from chapter 12 must always be taken in direct connection with chapter 20. What is visualized in chapter 20 refers back to chapter 12, joins itself to it, and is the immediate result of it.

So one understands why Satan had to be restrained, and his magic power to deceive be broken, until that which was to accompany the parousia, and was immediately to proceed from it, could begin. In what chapter 12 narrates, the die was already cast, but the parousia of Christ demanded that a last effort should be put forth to bring the unrepentant to repentance, before the final separation between the holy and the unholy could take place. This requires a hiatus between the first approach of the parousia and its progress. Therefore Satan could not be permitted to engage immediately in his final struggle. The last stage in the dispensation of grace must be given time in which to consummate itself. So Satan had to be arrested in his mad career until the time of judgment had come, and this came immediately after what the parousia itself invited had been realized.

What the parousia invited was in the nature of the case a last appeal to the conscience of the nations, including the Jews. For now the tension of the spirits would come to its highest. The heart of all people would be stirred with the sense that now indeed the end had come, and because of this not only missions would exert their utmost powers to reach the last ends of the earth, but those that in home lands might still be won would be so overwhelmingly pricked in their conscience, as to come to a final decision. Always in such a way, however, that everyone everywhere was in high and holy tension. As appears in chapter 19 the Lord had returned, and the first judgment upon the beast, the false prophet and their adherents had already been executed. Only one more final devision was still awaited. People everywhere would be terror stricken, and, pending the parousia, a final opportunity to repent would be given, which would save what was still salvable, and cast down those who, persisting in their apostasy, set themselves against God and against His Christ·

By itself it is nothing incredible that this final call to the unconverted would occasion a pause in the parousia, so that the parousia really goes through some transition. The parousia comes unexpectedly and suddenly, and when it comes a last appeal goes out to the consciences of men, and this appeal Satan is not permitted to frustrate and render ineffectual. Satan, therefore, is shorn of his power, he is doomed to impotency, and to impress it on all hearts, what wondrous grace God still imparts to the children of men, Revelation depicts this momentary arrest of Satan as a binding of Satan with a great chain. Satan had been hurled from on high down to this earth, but his presence here must not hamper the last effort to save what is still salvable. Hence the sudden arrest, while the parousia is already in progress. Hence that in these lower spheres Satan is in a striking manner deprived of his power for a thousand years, and is forced to witness at this late hour the continued increase of the Kingdom of God. And hence also the antithesis between chapter 20, 1-3 and what immediately follows. The judgment does not tarry, it takes place at once, yet in such a way that the gains of the Kingdom are still gathered in.

But this direct connection between chapters 12 and 20 shows conclusively how impossible the insertion here of an actual hiatus of ten centuries is. In the case of an actual lapse of ten centuries all connection and memory of social life is utterly lost. From old records we may learn what took place in our ancestral families ten centuries ago, but apart from royal and a few noble families the ordinary man knows nothing of how his forebearers lived as long as a thousand years ago. He does not know the names by which his ancestors were known. He no more counts with it. Thus if it were just a question of kings and noble families, some relation with the past might be probable. But since it concerns nations, many millions of people in private life and in forgotten places, this is out of the question, as no memories outlive a thousand years. It is not within reason therefore to insert the generations of ten centuries between the first and second phases of the parousia. Life in any period must have a motive, and a purpose, which must harmonize with the prevailing data. In this instance the paramount datum is the parousia of Christ. This needs no more waiting for, it is here, and chapter 19 not only states this fact but also relates its immediate results. But between the parousia and the Consummation an important datum can well appear which can not be computed after our order of time (for this does no more count) but according to the claim and course of the eternal. So while here one can no longer speak of *time,* obviously there must be some succession of highly important events between the first stage of the parousia and the concluding stage of the Consummation. Judgment must prepare itself, the last claim in behalf of those that are called unto life must be met One can scarcely imagine what telling effect will accompany the final call to conversion. With those that will still be saved it will be an effect unto salvation, but also one of hardening with all the unholy who then, as never before, will resist the Holy. Do not forget that judgment shall not come upon a few, but upon all, and shall be applied to everyone's whole life. Such an exhaustive judgment requires therefore the probing into the secrets of life and its varied experiences, which precludes all superficiality. And so the coming to consciousness of the past in those that rise from the dead must take hold of them and inwardly move them, in such a way as they have never been moved before. Hence it is not a matter of surprise that with v. 4 of chapter 20 there appears a middle-period that demands a special study all its own. Yet that this should be a period of 1000 years, as is ever yet asserted, can not be true. If such were the case it would be incomprehensible why the first part of the parousia should have come so soon. Obviously the coming of the parousia was not arbitrary, neither was it an experiment whether it might now begin. The beginning of an end, the concluding phase of which would only appear a thousand years afterwards, would not even among wise men be thinkable. No continuous investigation is so instituted anywhere. If the parousia were so divided by ten centuries into two parts, why then should the first part of the parousia also not have been postponed? With our human limitations we might make a mistake in the marking off of such periods, but this is not possible with Christ as He leaves His throne to judge the earth. Christ must have known from the first and must clearly have forseen what was yet to take place, before the Consummation could finally come in.

Thus in whatever way one views chapter 20, in connection with chapter 19 it is not possible that Christ could have made the mistake of having hastened His parousia at a wrong time.

One understands why it has been so strenuously tried to disconnect chapters 19 and 20, and not to count these 1000 years from Christ's Return, but from His Cross, or from the first converted Roman emperor. But if one has no sympathy with such a distortion of Scripture; takes due notice of the fact that the content of chapter 20 to v. 9 of chapter 21 forms one vision which admits of no division, so that it must be understood that chapter 20 follows upon chapter 19, and that thus the parousia had already taken place; he realizes that there is no intimation here of an interval of 1000 years' duration; that here, as elsewhere in the Apocalypse is the case with numbers, the number "thousand" has a symbolical significance, and as the highest mystical number is the only one that could have been applied to the secret doings of God between the two parts of the parousia. For this is the number that indicates, not what men, but what God in His Almightiness begins, carries through and consummates.

XXXV

THE FIRST AND SECOND RESURRECTION

And I saw thrones, and they that sat upon them, and judgment was given unto them: and I saw the souls of them that were beheaded for the witness of Jesus, and for the word of God, and which had not worshipped the beast, neither his image, neither had received his mark upon their foreheads, or in their hands; and they lived and reigned with Christ a thousand years. Rev. 20, 4.

So it appeared from chapter 20, 1-3, that the insertion of the 1000 years merely indicated the duration of the arrest of Satan's violence. Satan faced his defeat, but mankind on earth was not to be the victim of this. The people who persisted in their unbelief would be lost, but man as such was not to be the victim of Satan's expulsion from the higher spheres and of his being cast into the depths that are connected with our earth. Some duration of this arrest of Satan's violence is indicated. This was necessary. According to the 19th chapter the end had come, history was ended, normal time could no more be reckoned with. It had all become eternity's moments and eternity's progressions, and to give expression to this period of duration the holy revelation resorted to the Divine and infinite, and spake of "a thousand years," referring thereby to a Divine pause, to a transition and progression in God's holy doing. There could be no return to our human chronology. With the Consummation everything was drawn back from human doing into the doing of the Divine life, and to indicate the Divine action in distinction from our human progression, the duration of a Divine action was narrowed to a thousand. This had been done in the 90th Psalm, and throughout the Apocalypse, and so it had to be done here. It had to be put in words that, entirely apart from human chronology, the progression of the final process would not take place after the human standard, but after the Divine, and to express this, naturally the Divine formula of duration was chosen, and that formula had always been, and so had to be here, the number thousand. With us the course was from 1 to 3, from 3 to 10, and thus was ever progressing and ascending; on the level of the Divine, however, at once and solely the number of Divine duration is named; that number had ever been a thousand, and so it was here, even in this sense, that this thousand did not indicate a precise number of years, but at once and in the large the transition that took place in the Divine doing.

In this connection the 4th verse of chapter 20 begins an entirely different event, in which likewise the number thousand is involved. This is the more strongly emphasized, because the literal understanding of the thousand years would lead to an utterly unthinkable representation. See, what verses 4-6 contain: "I saw thrones and they—that now came to be considered—sat upon them, and judgment was given unto them: and I saw the souls of them that were beheaded for the witness of Jesus, and for the word of God, and which had not worshipped the beast, neither his image, neither had received his mark upon their foreheads, or in their hands; and they lived and reigned with Christ a thousand years." And then we read in vs. 5 and 6: "But the rest of the dead lived not again until the thousand years were finished. This is the first resurrection. Blessed and holy is he that hath part in the first resurrection: on such the second death hath no power, but they shall be priests of God and of Christ, and shall reign with him a thousand years." Naturally this refers back to what from chapter 12 on had been prepared and announced, and is here merely introduced into the end which God prepares for His creation, that He might bring in a new creation. Here especially the record shows very clearly that the thousand years can not mean a period of ten centuries. Here we are told of a middle link in the great concluding event, and obviously a period of ten centuries here would deprive what has been sketched of all sense and significance. To oppose this view appeal has been made to the early patriarchs, of whom Methuselah and Noah lived close to a thousand years, but to no avail. That ancient patriarchal lifetime of about ten centuries had at the time a selfevident purport. Human life was exposed to dangers which in a later period would be out of the question. Unless human life were wondrously lengthened mankind was threatened with extinction. Hence so soon as the population in the earth increased, longevity declined, and the span of human life approximated 150 years, as is still measurably the case in Russia. It is absurd, therefore, to refer back to this in connection with the approach of the end. When the end comes there will be many millions of people in the earth; and for the preservation of mankind there will be no need of lengthening the span of human life or of sparing life.

Here then we face the wondrous event, that a radical distinction is made between two classes of the dead. One of these classes enjoys an exceptional privilege, and in v. 5 we learn what shall overtake the other class. This second class are the ordinary dead, that is to say the millions upon millions which in the course of time have died either in the natural way, or have perished at sea or otherwise. This class had entered upon the state after death. Of course their condition was such as became their spiritual state of being when they died. They that died *in* Jesus had entered upon a state which in the Father's house enjoyed its provisional glory, and they which had died in unbelief had gone into the state of which we are told in the parable of Lazarus and the rich man. But while the representation in the parable led one to think that the resurrection of the blessed took place simultaneously with that of the lost, here in v. 5 of Revelation 20 a separation is made, and the dead are divided into two classes. As first class appears the great multitude which only in the general resurrection returns to life, while as second class appears those who regain life at an earlier period, and thus have part in what v. 5 calls *the first resurrection.*

When the interval between this first and this second resurrection was understood to be a period of ten centuries, this extremely important communication naturally gave rise to all sorts of untenable representations. The more deeply one sounded this mystery, the less able was he to say just what really would take place. The text undoubtedly reads that there are to be two resurrections. But the difference is great, when the interval between the first and the second resurrection is taken to be short, or one that is to last a thousand years. Yet as long as the latter view, which takes the thousand years between the two resurrections in the literal sense, was accepted, the first and the second resurrection were entirely disconnected, as an agelong chapter of history was

inserted between the two. This was to be a chapter of human history of a higher order, which we readily concede. Yet if one
thinks of the first risen saints as residing all those years in Jerusalem and other parts of the holy land, the two resurrections are
always ten centuries of human life apart from one another, and
though as was observed before, these ten centuries of sacred history of Jerusalem and the holy land were marked by neither
change nor progress, yet they must be ten centuries of long, if
uninteresting, history. This bears emphasis the more because no
one can deny, that those saints who were alive in this sacred
phase of history gained nothing by it, but rather were deprived
of the much fuller and richer life which otherwise they would
have enjoyed upon the new earth. And apart from this it must
be kept in view that these saints who by this exceptional grace
had part in the first resurrection, went on living, and presently,
within the fixed period, which the angel of chapter 20 to chapter
21, 9 takes together as one whole, disappear in the new humanity.

For in the end this is what counts. If the content of Rev. 20
to 21, 9 does not form one whole, is not inseparably connected,
does not form one interwoven, closely connected relation,
there might be mention here of an historic period of
many centuries; but then—and this must always be iterated again
—Rev. 20 to 21, 9 must have been inserted in the Apocalypse
at some later date, and if so, does not belong between chapters
19 and 21, 9. And upon this the whole interpretation depends. If
here we are free to follow our own inclination, and have no need
to ask what immediately precedes in the closing part of chapter
19 or immediately follows in chapter 21, 1-9, Rev. 20, 1-10 can
be interpreted as ordinary human history, with ten centuries at its
disposal, yes, one can elucidate our ordinary historic life by it,
as St. Augustine and after him most exegetes have done. But if
one reaches the conclusion that with chapter 20, 1 the adumbration of the end begins, so that ordinary human life already here
comes to its end, and that from now on there is no chronology,
but an adumbration of the timeless doing of God, the second
resurrection follows immediately upon the first, and the effect of
the first resurrection is but a transition-phase between the beginning and the finished effect of the Consummation. Hence it will
not do to overlook that unity of chapter 20 and 21, 1-9. For it

must be well understood that here both the first and the second resurrection, coincide, with but the required difference of duration, to make the first and the second resurrections appear successively in their necessary mutual relation and immediately after one another.

Yet, if these two resurrections are not centuries apart, nevertheless, a real difference marks what Revelation calls the first and the second resurrection. In chapter 20 are put in a separate class "the souls of them that were beheaded for the witness of Jesus," which are the martyrs of the last period. Of these martyrs we receive the impression that they did not pass through the ordinary way of death, but together with the latest living witnesses on earth entered at once upon the spiritual state which was no longer subject to death. Thus the attention here is called to two classes of believers: those who did not die in the ordinary way, but entered at once upon the other state of existence; and the martyrs, that were killed, and from death were immediately re-called to life. Espcially Kliefoth has sharply emphasized this difference by saying that the blessed which at once entered upon the new, higher life are thereby excluded from the judgment and are not presently subjected to the same anew. Of course if in the meantime there were ten centuries to elapse, this would be out of the question, and hence this is the wrong idea that must radically be opposed. The first resurrection is no mere semblance, in order, as in the case of Lazarus and the young man of Nain, to bring also these sanctified persons as from death back to life. What characterizes these saints is, that they are immediately translated into the state and condition which for the rest of mankind only begins with the second resurrection. We readily grant that what Kliefoth, in distinction from his exegetical contemporaries, here asserts, is a strikingly daring piece of exegesis. For it really means that they who have thus been called unto life, no longer share the common lot of the rest of mankind.

In the nature of the case this is a matter of serious thought. If according to the old representation we have to do with a period of ten centuries, the representation that is here given, becomes utterly untenable. Even if it applied to a comparatively small group of elect and those who were particularly endued with grace, it would in no case be tenable that these should enter ten centuries before the end, into blessedness and literally be exempt from the judgment to come, except as one ventures upon the almost ridiculous attempt of attributing to them a lifetime like that of Methuselah. But the matter assumes an entirely different aspect when the course of Revelation is taken as it is depicted in chapters 20 and 21, 1-9. If this part of the Apocalypse, as given by one angel, is not divisible into parts, if it forms one whole, and if it begins and ends in the transition period of the immediately thereupon approaching end, then one obtains a different representation, and every effort to stretch what is here recorded, and to take it by itself, as something that stands outside of the relation with the approaching end, is absurdity itself.

The brevity also wherewith all this is dealt with in ten verses shows the way out. He who feels his way through the book of Revelation and carefully notes the minute description of the first course of what is to come, even so minutely as frequently to detain the mind and divert it from the main matter in hand, is nonplussed that so mighty a series of events, as is said to be presented in chapter 20, 1-10, should be disposed of in six verses. For it should not escape notice that vs. 7-10 refer to another event, which necessarily requires some duration of time. The conflict ending in the defeat of the peoples of God and Magog naturally covers a given period. But leaving this aside for a moment we confine ourselves to vs. 4-6 of chapter 20, and careful notice of this further division convinces the thoughtful reader that the first resurrection is but a short action in advance, on the part of Christ, in the course of what is to happen. Christ has already brought down the beast and the false prophet, and has also cast down Satan and his demons from the high spheres into the depths of the bottomless pit. Judgment is begun, and once begun, goes on. The doing of Christ does not return to the common formula of historic human life. The judgment is begun and runs through its natural phases, one of which is, that Christ takes His holy martyrs unto Himself, by their earlier resurrection restores their life, and together with them hastens what is to come.

Thus nothing is said of a new condition which the Lord calls into life. He takes His martyrs, His latest faithful ones unto Himself, gives them the precedence in the regaining of life, and by this first resurrection of His faithful ones He surrounds

Himself with a magnificent retinue which assists Him in carrying
out the judgment and so makes an extended development of power
possible. But of course all this is meaningless, if there is to be an
interval of ten centuries between the first and the second resurrection. When however the first and the second resurrection are understood to occur, and to end, in what even no normal measure of
time can express, and rather form the beginning of the last
judgment, the whole course not only becomes natural, but at the
same time rich. Now there is no entrance first upon the high and
the eternal, from which to derive a ten centuries' history of a
new life, but a process in the Divine doing subsequent to the beginning of the Consummation. Hence that this whole vision is
shown by one and the same angel, who does not stop until he has
brought into full view the new heaven and the new earth. We
can not reckon here with years, yet if for one moment we might
indulge in a play of the imagination, we might readily picture to
ourselves that the binding and incarceration of Satan were to last
but a few days, during which selfsame days the blessed martyrs
and those believers in the earth which still exalted the honor of
Christ, are raised by an act of separation to a higher state of
existence. This would be the first resurrection. Meanwhile the
process of the Divine Consummation would go on and, when
those that were raised first have entered upon life, the general
resurrection would follow shortly after and the process be consummated.

The last struggle with Gog and Magog presents no difficulty
here. Verses 7, 8 and 9 refer indeed to the final struggle which
Satan with an eye to Gog and Magog will undertake; yet—and
note this well—there is no mention of a long drawn out conflict
to which this would give rise. We read that Satan and his armies
will compass the camp of the saints about, and the beloved city,
but it does not say that this will lead to a deadly conflict. Rather
it is summarily stated that as with one deadly blow fire from God
out of heaven shall come down, which shall devour Satan's might.
Thus also here an actual period of time is not to be thought of.
It all goes on in an entirely uncommon tempo, almost suddenly
and with conclusive results. They who cherish the mistaken view
of having these thousand years literally mean ten centuries according to the almanac, naturally do not understand this. This,

however, renders the announcement of the last angel, as he prophesies concerning the old world, absolutely inconceivable. The thousand years are the measure of divine symbolical appearance. And if, having this in mind, one abandons the literal sense of the number thousand throughout this prophecy, and realizes that the number thousand here merely refers to the process of the Divine action, then naturally the duration of this process narrows itself, so that everything, taken together as one coherent whole, ends in quick succession. Thousand then merely means that there is no more reckoning with human data, and that in the course of things the immediate action of God is indicated. In our small way of doing we reckon with numbers of 3, 10, 12 and so forth; but with God these limiting groupings do not count, and therefore the only number that is used for this Divine doing—provided it is used symbolically—is always again the majestic number thousand that indicates its Divine character.

XXXVI

THE FINAL CONFLICT

And when the thousand years are expired, Satan shall be loosed out of his prison, and shall go out to deceive the nations which are in the four quarters of the earth, Gog and Magog, to gather them together to battle; the number of whom is as the sand of the sea. Rev. 20, 7 and 8.

We now come to the last four verses of this short, but comprehensive chapter of Revelation. Even this last part, however small, is rich in content. It begins with referring back to Satan, to show that his incarceration is at an end, and that his impotency turns into a last outbreak of hellish wrath. So we read in v. 7: "And when the thousand years are expired, Satan shall be loosed out of his prison." But immediately after this release he goes out among the nations to deceive them. So we read in v. 8: "And he shall go out to deceive the nations which are in the four quarters of the earth, Gog and Magog, to gather them together to battle, which he will undertake against the people of God, and the number of those far off dwelling peoples is as the sand of the sea." The vast multitude of these brutalized nations will then go out to the "breadth of the earth, where they will compass the camp of the saints about, and the beloved city." But when the battle is to begin, and the conflict to ensue, Almighty God shall suddenly make an end of it. Fire shall come down from heaven and shall immediately devour all this power of the nations. Thus there is no more mention of a new, last struggle. There is to be no fighting, for the Lord shall cast the Devil, who tempted these nations to make this assault, into the lake of fire and brimstone, in which the beast and the false prophet had disappeared; and there the nations that were inimical to God "shall be tormented day and night for ever and ever." And so shall the final issue be reached, and heaven and earth shall pass away, to give place to the new earth and heaven that shall endure for ever. Even this short and hasty exposition shows that also here nothing is said of a revival of history again. As of itself also here the process of the Consummation goes on. All that is added is, that it will take "a little season"; but such only, because the nations, the cast off peoples, will have to come up from their far distant regions, and gather themselves together, and in one great onslaught begin the attack which shall end in their utter discomfiture.

Thus here, as can not be ignored, a short duration must be admitted, such however, that it all depends upon the time when this event will take place. With the supposition that this gathering together of the brutalized peoples took place already in the days of Constantine, the difficulty is, that the means of quicker communication and hasty mobilization were almost entirely lacking, though we did observe that the history of Alexander the Great shows that in those earlier years, under pressure, ground could be covered with extreme rapidity. But here it is different, since thus far this gathering together of the brutalized peoples has not yet taken place, and thus at least is deferred to a time when communication of these peoples, by means of railroads, would be shortened ten times. Supposing that this gathering together of these nations will increase yet for some time, and that meanwhile communication and intercourse between Japan, for instance, and Europe shall again have become more rapid, we can well imagine a future when the gathering and the marching of these peoples against the Christian nations might be effected in a still much shorter period of time. Thus the saying that all this will take place "in a little season" is already now much better understood than St. John could understand it. We observed above that it all might come to pass in some ten years, but if the development of these countries continues at the rate maintained during the last quarter of a century, the armies of these peoples can well be brought togther for battle at a given point over against the cultured peoples and Christian lands in two years' time. What formerly was so inaccurately grasped is, in consequence of the change in circumstances, now much more clearly understood. It will all come up and be consummated in a short time, and it now appears that two years or less might cover it. When we first came to this point we took pains to show that especially the more recent development of these nations renders the description in

chapter 20 of the coming course of events the more understand-
able. At the same time it throws an altogether peculiar light
upon the prophecy of this same chapter. The end which the Consummation brings is, if we may so express it, at the door, and
even in such a way that the whole final end is summarized in this
one vision; which forbids the introduction here of ten centuries,
for only when the process is taken as passing rapidly, and is seen
as immediately leading up to what chapter 21 relates of the
appearance of the new earth under the new heaven, the whole
coherently unites itself.

Above, when dealing with Ezekiel's and Daniel's oracles, we
indicated how what these prophets prophesied regarding the Consummation likewise eventuated in a final struggle, which the nations of spiritual alienation would undertake against the holy
people. Here we see that what the Apocalypse reveals, coheres
with this ancient prophecy. For thus reads Ezekiel 38, 2: "Son
of man, set thy face against Gog, the land of Magog, the chief
prince of Meshech and Tubal, and prophesy against him." Ezekiel's prophecy eventuated at length in this, that the land of Israel
would be restored to order again and should be given back to the
people of God, but so modified in form that even the sanctuary
would be removed from Jerusalem to another part of the land.
Already with this the question arose, whether it would prove the
case of a real return of the people of Abraham to Canaan, or
whether what Ezekiel portrayed were to be understood in a more
metaphorical sense, and already at that time we indicated that
the literal interpretation of Ezekiel's prophecy would empty it of
its serious and far reaching significance. If now in Rev. 20, 7-10
the reference to Gog and Magog evidently harks back to the ancient Ezekelian prophecy, it, likewise, must not be taken literally,
and the appearance of the nation of the brutalization against the
people of the Lord can as well be imagined toward the side of
Russia and Asia Minor, as toward the side of the Jordan and
Jerusalem. All this is highly significant to those who favor Chiliasm, and quite naturally the temporary ocupation of Palestine
by the British troops is looked upon as a confirmation of the Chiliastic idea. But obviously here it solely concerns the question,
how this heathen power of the brutalized nations could really
have undertaken the last attack upon the people of the Lord, *yet*

without any success, and with the bitter result that this very attack became the cause of the utter overthrow of their power.

Therefore it must strongly be emphasized that the attempt of conquest emanated from the backward, brutalized nations, and had as motive not only the age-long struggle with the baptized nations, but with the cultured nations. This contrast between the cultured nations and the brutalized backward peoples can not be over-emphasized. Not, understand this well, as though these backward peoples had not measurably developed and become civilized. He who examines even to particulars what still remains of the civilization of the ancient Indian peoples in America, can not escape the impression that the ancient American Indians, compared with the cultured nations of Europe, are extremely backward; yet even this gives one no right to represent them as utterly without any civilization. The same applies to conditions in Asia, with the exception of course of the States in Central-Asia and British-India, which rather took the lead in the higher culture. In the last instance Central and Southern-Asia stand even higher than what Europe can pretend. Man was created in Central-Asia, and there the first development of human life took place, as well as that of the holy people; yes, Christ did not come, neither did the rise of His church take place in Europe, but in Asia. Do not confuse, therefore, the two very different parts of Asia with each other. Central and Southern-Asia are the regions of the world in which all higher life has germinated, and if here we must refer to what is called Gog and Magog, which means the nations of lower standing, it points to the masses of people that more and more over-ran North and Eastern-Asia. Already Ezekiel had those nations in mind when he wrote of Gog and Magog, and in Rev. 20 they are the peoples from the four quarters of the earth which now, under the name of Gog and Magog, are gathered together to make war against the people of the Lord. This group of nations was already at the time notorious for its numerical strength, which accounts for the saying in v. 8 that their number is as the sand of the sea. This is still characteristic of the Chinese, while of the Japanese too it can be said, be it in lessser measure, that they steadily and surprisingly propagate themselves. In distinction from the nations of Central and Southern-Asia, these nations are taken in Rev. 20 as a group of peoples that are naturally inimical to the people of God. And so here it narrows down to the same distinction and antithesis, which we see in all history, between cultured nations and backward peoples. The Apocalypse enters into no particulars here. Nothing is said of Negroes and the African population. The main distinction of importance here is, that the cultured states occupy a position of their own, and that the lands of Gog and Magog, though they can pride themselves on some form of civilization, have no count in cultured life, and in the end rather stand directly over against it.

One might readily incline to speak here of Christian nations, rather than of cultured peoples, and though this might do with respect to the period of the seventh to the seventeenth century, yet on the whole this would not be correct. One must keep hold of the idea of the higher culture. Especially the past necessitates this. It can not be said that in Old Testament times the higher civilization or world culture emanated from the Jews. Undoubtedly the Jews enjoyed first the culture of the Egyptians, and later that of the Persians, Greeks and Romans. Their *spiritual* treasure was unique; but in the centuries before Christ the higher culture was not developed from this. Rather the people of Israel remained backward in this respect. In part the Sanscrits and presently the Persians and Babylonians, the Greeks and the Romans surpassed them. From these peoples we borrowed the already matured culture, and only afterward, when Rome went down and the Christian lands in Europe and overseas in the colonies began to take the lead, a new and higher culture developed itself, which culture afterward in Humanism enriched itself anew with what the tradition from the heathenland revived. So we speak of culture, because in this expression the two elements are combined: namely, the historic development of the European nations, and in a later period the Christian civilization that spread over Europe, and in part over America. But though the Christian element firmly established itself in those cultured countries, and there advanced culture to a higher development than had ever been attained before, yet even so it will not do to identify culture with the Christian religion. Especially when it comes to the time of the end, distinction must be made between the two. In the final conflict and decision culture will not bring the backward development to nought. It must rather be said that culture will more and more separate itself from the Christian element; that culture will not prove capable of further and higher development; that consequently also the backward nations, as in China and Japan, will borrow improvements from the outworn culture, and that at length the struggle will end in this antithesis, namely, that the many nations of originally lower standing shall force themselves to the front and shall increase in might, while the Christian group shall dwindle in numbers, and at last as the chosen people of God shall stand over against the unholy mass of people which shall be as the sand on the shore of the sea.

Greater disparity than between the Christian group and the hordes that as the sand on the sea-shore for numbers are ready to destroy her, will not be thinkable. This disparity will be so final as to put a life-and-death struggle out of the question. Hence this final conflict is actually nothing but an intermediate incident. Real battle does not ensue. All that happens is, that the unholy powers gather themselves together, mobilize and undertake the assault; but even to this assault it does not come. As to the people of the Lord, they have not a ghost of a chance to muster an army which could possibly face this stupendous world power. But to the fight itself it does not come. The innumerable millions of the hostile army have been brought together, mobilized and prepared for battle against the faithful of the Lord; but at the moment of attack all is ended. Not that the Christians engage in battle against the armies that are as innumerable as the sand of the sea, but that God awaits these hordes, and the moment they begin to show their power, destroys them. Tersely and definitely the text states: "And fire came down from God out of heaven, and devoured them." There was not even the beginning of a fight; there is no intimation that so much as one drop of the saints' blood was shed. All that God did to bring in the final issue,—that is, the Consummation—was to lure these armies to this particular place where the decision would be made, which decision in that very moment in the most absolute sense came to pass. The countless hordes were *devoured;* and with this the battle was ended, before it had begun. Nothing more follows. The conflict that began in Paradise is now fought out to the finish. No sign of life can remain. Everything perishes, and all that is left is the company of the saints that kneels before Christ as her Lord and Saviour.

Yet this is not all. Not for man's sake alone, but for that of the whole universe, it must now come to the final issue. The Consummation must no longer tarry, but in the full sense come to the finish. And its characteristic is, that both the world of man and the world of angels, and not each by itself, have to take part in the final issue. This harks back to Paradise. The mighty spiritual conflict did not begin with the rise of the world of man. Before man had made his appearance in Paradise history had been made in the world of angels. Hence when in the story of Paradise Scripture refers to this, this original connection must needs again be recognized, now that the final conclusion is at hand. To say that everything began with the creation of Adam and Eve, and with the appearance of the world of man, is not correct. The world of angels was first, and the world of man came after. And not only did that world of angels precede that of man, but that world of angels had already come to the great issue. Satan had torn himself loose from God, and his demons had participated in the apostasy. Thus history did not begin with man, but with the angels; and furthermore sorrow and sin and misery did not have their origin in man, but in Satan; and always with this difference, that because the fall of man was not original with man, but the result of temptation, it admitted of redemption, deliverance and reconciliation; while sin in the world of angels did not admit of this, but was bound to end in final retribution. This is why Rev. 20 which tells of the beginning of the Consummation could not refrain from referring to the world of demons.   In the world of man deliverance was still possible, and becomes at length a fact; but such was not possible in the world of angels. By itself already reconciliation for the world of fallen angels was not possible, but apart from this, angels had not been tempted by man. Hence these two results were bound to be arrayed over against each other. Grace would provide a chance and open an outlook upon salvation for fallen humanity which had been tempted by Satan, while for the world of angels which itself, without any temptation, had turned away from God, reconciliation was not possible. That world had to suffer total perdition, yet its perdition could not come before the work of redemption and of pardoning the sinful world of men had been accomplished. Hence that the final punishment could not be inflicted immediately after the fall in Paradise, but had to be deferred to the closing period of the conflict, when the Consummation was to ensue.

It is not surprising, therefore, but entirely natural, that the final reckoning with Satan and his satellites takes place only just before the Consummation. God had always held Satan and his demons in leash, and after the temptation in the wilderness and the Cross of Golgotha, redeemed humanity had come into God's possession, and had been protected against the superior power of Satan. But this could not always go on. Satan's final overthrow was bound to come. Hence the statement that at last Satan with his demons were cast into the depth of the unholy. This would then already have at once been fatal to our human race, but according to Rev. 20, 1-3 God has prevented this by rendering Satan and his demons impotent. Of course not for long, but rather even for a short time only; and as soon as the re-animation of the martyrs and the first resurrection had taken place, Satan began his assault again, that if possible he might even then poison our human existence and destroy it. And though God allowed this last attack to be made, Satan was immediately and inexorably foiled in this last attempt, and as we read in v. 10, Satan was utterly defeated. "And the Devil" who tempted those hostile nations to attack the people of God, "was cast into the lake of fire and brimstone, where the beast and the false prophet are." Immediately upon this the final judgment follows: "And they shall be tormented, day and night, for ever and ever." This ends all. The enemy who has always put temptation and misery in the way of men, is now for ever impotent. Nothing further can be feared from him. And now Paradise discloses itself anew, this time in its sanctified and consummated state, from which all danger of temptation is averted. Hence that now the end, yes the perfect Consummation is called in. The old, sinful world sinks away into nothingness. Under the new heaven a new world dawns, and the redeemed race of the children of men enters upon glory.

XXXVII

THE LAST JUDGMENT

And whosoever was not found written in the book of life was cast into the lake of fire. Rev. 20, 15.

With the 10th verse of chapter 20 the Consummation begins, in order directly to reach its final goal. According to v. 20 of chapter 19 the beast and the false prophet have already been cast into the lake of fire burning with brimstone, and now the same lot overtakes Satan. So reads v. 10 of chapter 20: "And the devil that deceived them was cast into the lake of fire and brimstone, where the beast and the false prophet are, and they shall be tormented day and night for ever and ever." In this same vision, and thus with the preceding one forming one solidary whole, follow three parts which must be carefully distinguished. First chapter 20, 11, then chapter 20, 12-15, and finally chapter 21, 1-8. In part one we see the old world wholly come to nought and perish; in part two follows the judgment; and in part three the new world makes its appearance. This tallies exactly with what is taught elsewhere in Holy Scripture regarding the Consummation. Especially Isaiah prophesies surprisingly clearly as to this. "For, behold," so reads chapter 65, 17, "I create new heavens and a new earth: and the former shall not be remembered, nor come into mind." And in like spirit Isaiah writes in the following chapter (66, 22): "For as the new heavens and the new earth, which I will make, shall remain before me, saith the Lord, so shall your seed and your name remain." To this Old Testamentish prophecy the apostolate immediately joins itself. Writes the holy apostle Peter (2 Pet· 3, 12 and 13): "Looking for and hastening unto the coming of the day of God, wherein the heavens being on fire shall be dissolved, and the elements shall melt with fervent heat; nevertheless we, according to His promise, look for new heavens and a new earth, wherein dwelleth righteousness," predictions, to which the profound content of 2 Thess. 2 joins itself.

In the second epistle to the church of Salonika the holy apostle Paul state emphatically that when the full development of iniquity starts in and the apostasy strikes root, "the man of sin" shall reveal himself. He characterizes that "man of sin" as "the son of perdition; who opposeth and exalted himself above all that is called God, or that is worshipped; so that he as God sitteth in the temple of God, shewing himself that he is God." This is not the first time that Paul communicates his insight to the Thessalonians; for he adds: "Remember ye not, that, when I was yet with you, I told you these things?" And then he continues: "And now ye know what withholdeth that he might be revealed in his time. For the mystery of iniquity doth already work: only he who now letteth will let, until he be taken out of the way. And then shall that Wicked one be revealed, whom the Lord shall consume with the spirit of his mouth, and shall destroy with the brightness of his coming." To which, for the sake of elucidation, the apostle adds: "Even him, I say, whose coming is after the working of Satan with all power and signs and lying wonders, and with all deceivableness of unrighteousness in them that perish; because they received not the love of the truth, that they might be saved. And for this cause God shall send them strong delusion, that they should believe a lie: that they all might be damned." This broadly elaborated prediction of St. Paul echoes in full what Isaiah already had indicated, and what is most clearly presented on Patmos to the apostle John in the vision of chapters 20 and 21. It is always indicated that sin and iniquity in human degeneration and in satanic opposition against God will increase to the uttermost, and when unrighteousness shall have broken out in its most corrupting manner, God's Almightiness shall in the most unexpected way put an end to Satan's unholy action upon the children of men, and thereby end the struggle that was begun in Paradise. Then the wholly new condition shall appear in the heavens and on the earth, which terminates in Satan's utter defeat and in God's complete victory and triumph. And at the time of the end this was as of itself to come to pass. So we read in Rev. 20, 11: "And I saw a great white throne, and him that sat on it, from whose face the earth and the heaven fled away; and there was found no place for them."

Whether therefore we consult Isaiah, SS. Peter and Paul or

the Apocalypse, with these exponents of Revelation it always
comes to this, that at the very last the power of Satan shall be
exceedingly overbearing, and then shall suffer final defeat, in
order to give place both on earth and in heaven to an entirely new
state of things. Even the expression that here is chosen is exceedingly significant: "From Whose face (God's) the earth and the
heaven fled away." From the time when in Paradise the first sin
was committed, subsequent to the fall in the angel world, there
had been unholy opposition against God, and God had tolerated
this revolt not only in the demon world but also in the world
of men, yes allowed it to affect even the world of nature, in order
only in the end, when it had vainly spent all its unholy power, to
destroy it in a way that comported with His Majesty. And that
moment had now come. First in the world of men the unholy,
blasphemous power had been thrown down, and now in the end
Satan in his own person is attacked. And at once the absolute
antithesis between God and the satanic commotion loosing ground
strikingly shows itself. Now it is not merely chastisement, but
overthrow, expulsion and utter destruction of the demoniac, so
sudden and so terrible, that all the unholy *flee away* from before
the face of God. Says v. 11: "All have fled away; and there was
found no place for them." The overthrow of the beast, of the
false prophet, and the unholy power in the world of men had
merely been preliminary to the final act of the great tragedy.
After all the lesser unholy powers had been brought low, it now
meant the destruction of the Satanic mightiness. This then leads
to the radical conflict. Now it is the immediate combat between
God and Satan. Humanity plays but a insignificant part in it.
Hence, that in v. 11 suddenly God Almighty Himself appears, unsparingly to force the issue. For suddenly St. John perceives a
brightness on high, and looking up, beheld a great white throne,
which is the throne of God's Majesty. Even Christ as inter-
mediary link loses at this moment His predominant significance.
God Himself from on high shines forth in the omnipotence of
His holiness. And scarcely has God Almighty looked upon heaven
and earth with this finality of judgment, when all things flee
away, and the new world with the new heaven and the new earth
make their appearance.

Immediately, with not so much as a transition, the entirely

modified and changed relation of what was, with what is to come, and shall be, ensues. The depiction of this in v. 12, therefore, is so striking. Judgment is suddenly come. It is not said that it shall come, no preparation for it is made, it is not introduced, it suddenly is there. Also in this again the trying antithesis is strongly evident between what some readers of Rev. 20, 1-10 would make of it and what it reveals. If the content of vs. 1-10 were to cover a period of ten centuries, and in v. 11 without any warning or transition everything were suddenly destroyed and brought to nought, to give place to the new future which will endure to all eternity, the contradiction would be too glaring. To apportion ten centuries to what is merely a transition, and then with a single word dismiss what will endure eternally is no satisfactory relation, yet this is clear, that the content of v. 12 to the end of the chapter leaves no room for doubt but that the turning-upside down of heaven and earth, so to speak, as in the twinkling of an eye begins, goes on and consummates itself.

It is also significant in this connection that in v. 11 God Himself makes His majestic appearance. So we read in v. 12: "And I saw the dead, small and great, stand before God." Every intermediate link is now fallen away. All the children of men now come to stand before God and the books are opened. These books are of two kinds. There is a book with the remembrance of every man's commissions and omissions, which forms the judgment that is to come upon him; but there is also a second book, much smaller than the other, in which are recorded the elect of God by name. The first is spoken of as *books,* in the plural, since in them all the children of men are named by name, and no one book can contain the record of all these many millions. Next to this is the second book in the singular, as it contains exclusively the names of the elect, and hence is considerably smaller. This book is therefore called "the book of life," hence here the number of the dead can not be taken large enough. Even those who by shipwreck suffered death are separately mentioned. Though as a rule presumably they were devoured by monsters in the deep, they thereby did not lose their existence as man, and, in what way soever, they too shall appear again in visible and observable form before God. Moreover they who after death had gained no admission into the Father's house, but as reprobates were immediately consigned to

misery, are not left out, for they too are raised from the dead and
must appear before the holy face of God; which implies the beginning of the dreadful judgment which they must face. Wherefore *hell* is mentioned in the 13th verse: "Death and hell delivered
up the dead which were in them." And then follows the personal
note: "and they were judged every man according to their works."

To consummate the whole representation there is added in v.
15, that if anyone is found, whose name is not written "in the
book of life" he is cast into the lake of fire. Thus nothing more
is said of any further consideration, of protest or excuse. Antichrist and Satan are said to have met their eternal doom in a lake
of fire. And now of lost sinners, also, of those who have rejected every offer of salvation, it becomes known that they likewise are cast into the lake of fire. This statement does not indicate that they were annihilated, but that they entered upon a state
of never ending misery. The 14th verse intentionally calls this
rejection "the second death." The blessed dead entered upon life,
they did not die again, and hence suffer no second death. They
however which in the day of judgment rose from the dead and
appeared before God, and had no part with Christ, had anew to
enter into death, and were to continue in that state of death for
ever. As an aside it should properly here be noted that the saints
that were alive at the time of the end, either did not die but immediately passed over into the state of judgment, or as martyrs were
raised from the dead immediately to enter upon life, so here they
occupy a separate position.

The main concern now, however, is the sudden change of the
world. No particulars regarding this transition are given. Here
we have to do with the entirely natural course of successive
events. There is no room for any interval. Doubtless we cannot
form any clear idea of the last judgment. The numbers of those
upon whom the last judgment shall come are so incalculably great,
that we can not enter into them, especially not, when we note
how in v. 12 the small and great are severally mentioned. Even
if attention had not been called to this, it would of itself have
been obvious that in the judgment the same applies to children
as to those who died in later life. And with respect to children it
must be understood that not only those are counted who have
died in early youth, but also those which in birth, or even before

birth, have forfeited life. Every one who, as a human person, has received life, even though that life remained confined to the mother-womb, appears in judgment. It is inconceivable to us, therefore, how the judgment shall be applied to so many persons in the mass and to so many persons of arrested development. In Rev. 20, 11-15 it all seems to end in scarcely measured time, and we are safest in not entering further into this. God Himself here appears as the judge and passes judgment, and we can never form an adequate idea of God's manner of investigation and passing of judgment. So this aspect of the case also we leave alone. The main concern is the immediate, unlooked-for and sudden coming in of the new condition in which heaven and earth shall endure for ever, and such without transition. And here it must be noted that St. John makes no slightest reference to the way in which this transition is to take place. However quickly a torpedoed boat may go down, eye-witnesses can at least tell something of the way in which it happened. In a great shipwreck or in a large fire particulars are still better known. So we naturally ask how and in what way and with what observable phenomena the transition of the present world into the coming one 'shall take place. Yet the seer says nothing about it. He merely states the fact that the existing world, so to speak, shall suddenly disappear and perish, and shall immediately be superseded—without telling *how*—by a new earth under a new heaven.

Yet what now follows regarding the new world under the new heaven, together with all that precedes, forms one coherent vision. We have demonstrated that here no new vision could possibly have been inserted into the foregoing or have been coupled with it. It could not have been shown more clearly than was done, that here everything concentrates itself in one vision. Neither can one say that with v. 1 in chapter 21 a second vision is attached to the preceding. On the contrary all goes straight on. All forms one whole. And what successively is presented to us is not susceptible of division. So it all comes to this, that the mighty events which are here recorded follow one another *without observable transitions*. Already in v. 10 we saw how Satan joined issue of seemingly long duration with the latest rulers, and how differently it turned out. Scarcely had the two powers clashed, when according to v. 10 then and there, as in one moment, the whole power of Satan was overthrown. All there is said about it is that he was cast into the lake of fire. The same method is followed when the last judgment is executed. Also of this we read in v. 15, that if anyone were found whose name was not written in the book of life, he was cast into the lake of fire. And when we come to v. 1 in chapter 21, we find the same again. Also here the vision at once translates us into the entirely new condition. St. John sees as at the same moment both how the lost children of men perish in the lake of fire and the new heaven spreads itself over the new earth. It all transpires as though unperceived and unobserved. St. John therefore merely says: "And I saw a new heaven and a new earth: for the first heaven and the first earth were passed away," and all he adds is: "and there was no more sea."

Of course he who lives to see the destruction of the world and the unveiling of that which is to endure forever, will naturally tremble at the sight. Intentionally, therefore, one can safely say, all this is here suppressed. All such particulars would divert the attention and the contemplation of these attending circumstances would make us forget the great, the mighty, the supreme event. This must needs be prevented. We are not even informed whether or not there will still be a *transition,* or whether it will end in an *annihilation* of everything that was, and in a new creation of what shall be. It almost seems, as all Bible students acknowledge, as though what was, just sank away, and as though an entirely new world were created; but one feels that such in this absolute sense is not possible. The result of this would be, that the first created world simply vanished, and that now it pleased God to create a second, entirely new creation. But this is out of the question. Already with an eye to the elect and the blessed this would not be possible, for in their resurrection body they will enter upon the blessed life upon that renewed world. But also apart from this, that the first created world would tracklessly disappear is out of the question. This may actually be the case as to its outward form, but not with respect to the core of its existence. The world with its old Paradise is re-created.

If then in 2 Peter even as in Isaiah 65 and 66 expressions occur which seemingly exclude all transition, the fact that believers are translated from the old into the new world postulates the necessity that the identity of the persons be not lost. Just as what happens with the dead, that they go back to the substance of their being, and as disembodied souls continue to exist, yet presently obtain their body back again, must also here be maintained. The creation recorded in Gen. 1 brought a life into existence as a whole, which, however greatly it might be changed and renewed, yet in itself remains identical. One can even say that also the first creation as creation had a soul, and that though the whole body and the whole form of the first creation were to undergo modification, that creation as such would retain that soul.

XXXVIII

THE NEW JERUSALEM*

And I, John, saw the holy city, new Jerusalem, coming down from God out of heaven, prepared as a bride adorned for her husband. Rev. 21, 2.

After the new earth under the new heaven has come, upon that new earth also the tradition of the holy city, of the ancient Jerusalem, is renewed and perpetuated. So St. John testifies: "I saw the new Jerusalem, coming down from God out of heaven, prepared as a bride adorned for her husband." This in the nature of the case excludes identity with the ancient Jerusalem. The name of Jerusalem is retained, but it is no longer the old city. Also in this case everything is become new. Yet not in the sense that herewith every trace of the old city of God has been destroyed. The very retention of the name Jerusalem shows that some relation is still retained between the ancient sanctuary and this new Jerusalem. Also in the past there had always been transitions from place to place, from form to form, from appearance to appearance, without thereby the unity and solidarity being lost. The old sanctuary in Israel did not come from Egypt, but was erected by Moses and Aaron in the wilderness after Israel had crossed the Red Sea. Israel then still wandered from place to place, and so his sanctuary at the time became a tabernacle. As in the wilderness the people dwelt in tents, so the sanctuary had to be a *tent*. It must necessarily be movable with the people, so to speak, and be moved from place to place. Where Israel went, the tabernacle went. But this did not last. When Israel had come into Canaan the holy tabernacle soon obtained a more permanent position in Shilo. And when Jerusalem became the capital city of the whole people, the tent-idea became lost, and on the holy mountain a fixed dwelling was erected, after the tent of Shilo

---

*In the original "The New Jerusalem" covers chapters XXXVIII and XXXIX.

had temporarily been located on the same holy site. By David the transfer, by Solomon the temple. This marked the hour when the holy presence in Jerusalem became bound to this sacred spot. Later the temple was temporarily in ruins, but Zerubbabel soon applied himself energetically to the task of rebuilding the fallen sanctuary, and at last Herod by a reconstruction imparted an even yet more beautiful form to the same. In that temple there was, as of old in the tabernacle, the Holy of Holies, to which sacred place the presence of the Lord bound itself. Not of course as though thereby the omnipresence of the Lord was curtailed, but God had indicated this Holy of Holies for the revelation of His spiritual majesty.

This went on until Christ appeared to reveal God's presence in the spiritual sense, and thus in a far different and richer sense. Christ truly honored the Holy of Holies in the temple, but only for a time. When His Cross drew near, and Jesus with His disciples left the temple, He solemnly announced to His disciples that the hour was at hand, in which the temple was to lose its sacred character, and the fellowship of believers with their God would assume a different form. So the church of the New Testament made its advent. Not that as the presence of the Lord had formerly been bound to the temple of Jerusalem, so henceforth it would be bound to a church building. The tendency indeed has been to perpetuate this idea, and gradually a significance has been attached to the Christian church building as though the presence of the Lord was bound thereto; which at length has led to the altar services of Rome. But this idea has spiritually ever and again been resisted, and especially the Reformers have always insisted that the presence of the Lord should no more locally be bound to a building, but solely to the congregation of believers. So after the earthly Jerusalem with its stone temple had lost its significance, there arose the spiritual Jerusalem that spread all over the world, which is not bound to buildings of wood or stone, but whose spiritual presence is found solely in the congregation of believers wherever it is gathered. Hence there is also now, if you will, a spiritual Jerusalem which is not bound to any locality anywhere, but is found where believers gather, where baptism is the rule, and where the memorial of Jesus' death on Golgotha in bread and wine takes place. But when the old world perishes and gives place to the new earth under the new heaven, also this will be modified. Also then there will be the tie that binds believers together, and all together to God; but that union will bear a form that will befit the new born condition. And this is what the apostle John means when in v. 2 of chapter 21 he declares: "I saw the holy city, new Jerusalem, coming down from God out of heaven." The tie laid of old by God with His chosen people operates also here, but in that new form which is adapted to the new born state. Moses testifies from of old that he had seen the tabernacle in heaven, and that the sanctuary of heaven had come down to this earth. So no one can say that Moses had invented and devised the tabernacle, and that God had taken cognizance of Moses' work. The original was always to be found in God. From God the thought and the form for that thought, through Moses and Aaron, and if you will, also through Aholiab and Bezaleel, had to come down to the people. And when in due time this holy thought of God had found its first embodiment in the tabernacle, the thought of God which it expressed had to remain inspired and inspiring in the spiritual fellowship between God and His people unto the end, while the form that expresses this inspiring thought needed constant reformation and change, according as the spiritual fellowship between God and His people became ennobled, more intimate and sanctified.

So when in Rev. 21, 2 we read of a new Jerusalem, that comes down from God out of heaven, this harks back to what the tabernacle in the wilderness already had offered Israel, and which continued the relation that also locally and formally had existed between Jehovah and His people from the time of their crossing the Red Sea. Yet though the name of Jerusalem is perpetuated, it is here nothing but a name, and it will not do to imagine that the ancient Palestine will continue its existence on the new earth, and that there the ancient Jerusalem will unlock anew the temple for worship. All this in the nature of the case is entirely out of the question. The old is passed away, behold, all is become new. So we read that this new Jerusalem is no reconstruction of the old, but that it comes down from God out of heaven. This does not prevent meanwhile, that there ever is and shall be a spiritual relation between tabernacle and temple on one hand and between the church and the new Jerusalem, that shall come and become manifest on the new earth. What Moses testified, namely that the idea of the tabernacle, the idea of the temple, does not proceed from man, but by 'God is given to man, comes down to him and lays hold on him, also is continued here, and here also makes itself felt. God created man to associate with Him in holy fellowship. Man broke that fellowship. If then there were to be fellowship between God and man at all, it could only be in one people and under a given form. And so it has come to pass. All the other nations had forfeited the fellowship of holiness. What remained of it, was mere semblance. Fellowship with God in a formal way only became established with Abraham's descendants. Moses has been the divinely appointed man, who brought this fellowship to formal expression. And with the consecration of the tabernacle fellowship between God and man, though only for this separated people, became a partial reality. God has lent and given Himself to this reality. First in the tabernacle, then in the temple, until in Christ the Lord our God revealed Himself to His believing people. This gave rise to the breach with the Sanhedrin and so also with the temple of stone on Sion. So the church arose as an auxiliary association. Even this could not be permanent. Also that churchly fellowship is merely an auxiliary means. And when once the old world perishes, to give place to the new earth under the new heaven, the temple shall obtain its full meaning and rich significance. Then there comes a Jerusalem again. In that Jerusalem the presence of the Lord among His people shall be perfect, and that people of the Lord shall no more be a separated Abrahamic race, but the whole reborn humanity. There will be a revelation of the people of God in its several tribes and generations. And on that new earth under a new heaven there will then be no more an Abrahamitish people, that will be distinct from the rest of the nations as the only blessed one, but all the people of the Lord shall enjoy the peace and joy of His holy presence, and all they that do not belong to this new humanity shall have to suffer their own miseries in the lake of fire.

This is the conclusion of the several forms which the sanctuary successively assumed. The tabernacle embodies the rich thought that in our fallen humanity a separation can take place of generations of devout souls that forsake the world and cleave unto God. In the nature of the case this was first an *exception*. The

rest of the nations in the world had forsaken God and had been
forsaken of God, and Common Grace alone afforded them a purpose for continuing their existence in the earth. But the new life
appeared in Israel, though only as an *exception*. Not the world,
but the people of God alone enjoyed the spiritual privilege of the
presence of the Lord, which they found first in the tabernacle,
then in the temple, and eventually in the sacrament and the bond
of believers in Christ's church. But on the new earth under the
new heaven the order is reversed. It is no more a sinful world
with a company of believers as exception. It is become a reborn,
a renewed humanity of believers and saints, all those who by their
unbelief excluded themselves having been consigned to the lake of
fire. Thus it all narrows down to this, and upon this great reality
it all depends. Jerusalem of old was the exception, the new Jerusalem is the whole earth sanctified by God, with her centrum.
What then was exception, now is rule; what then was rule, now
is entirely excluded. Now nothing but Jerusalem, all the rest
sunken away. And therefore this new Jerusalem could not originate in that fallen world. On the contrary it comes down out of
heaven, as a bride adorned for her husband, in order by that
husband to be appropriated as His sole and only one.

This is expressed in the 3rd verse. St. John there testifies:
"And I heard a great voice out of heaven saying, Behold, the
tabernacle of God is with men, and He will dwell with them, and
they shall be His people, and God Himself shall be with them,
and be their God." Though it does not say so, it may be presumed that this was spoken by the angel. It is certainly not a
saying of God and presumably just as little a saying of Christ.
This is not a speech by God, but about God. Yet what here is
spoken by the angel fully confirms our idea of verse 2. Formerly
the tabernacle was not with men, but was with the priests of Levi
among the people of Israel, and was definitely separated from the
rest of mankind. Under the dispensation of the Old Covenant
God did not dwell with the heathen nations, but solely with the
chosen people of Israel. And where Israel time and again and in
great numbers forsook God and apostatized, the fellowship of
God with Israel was bound first to the tabernacle and later to the
temple, so that even though the people at large should become unfaithful, the fellowship of God with Israel would nevertheless be

perpetuated. God did not dwell with the Babylonians or Persians, or with any other people, but solely with Israel, and presently solely with Judah. All this is now changed. Now, so reads the passage, He is with mankind taken as a whole, and He will dwell with that mankind, and all humanity shall be His people; and as under the Old Covenant God sojourned with Israel, and was Israel's God, and dwelt with Israel, so now He shall be the God of all the redeemed and even dwell with them.

Thus nothing is said of a limitation of that dwelling of God to Jerusalem. Here the Jerusalem name occurs solely as the name of the place where fellowship by God is given to His elect. So everything explains itself, provided one does not lose from sight that what can first be an exception, can afterward, with changed conditions, become the fixed rule. The fellowship which God by Moses gave to Israel was of a limited character. The rest of the world had no part in it. The true religion not only had not come to these outside nations, but as St. Paul writes to the Corinthians (1, 10, 20): "What the Gentiles sacrifice, they do not sacrifice to God, but to devils," and as the apostle adds: "I would not that ye should have fellowship with devils." From the first, therefore, a definite *antithesis* expresses itself in Israel's religion. There was not merely a relative, but an absolute difference, yes, more than a difference, even a direct antithesis between what the heathen in matters of religion allowed themselves and what God had instituted in Israel. From the first God places the emphasis upon this. What God created in Israel by way of holy worship and introduced among them, stood un-hewn as conscious antithesis over against heathen public worship. Paganism was not a partial divergence, so that in either case God Almighty was worshipped by Jew and Gentile alike. It was the direct opposite. Afterward, in the dispersion, erring Israel halfway joined themselves to the heathen form, and we see how at length a descendant of Esau builds their temple and as King rules over them. It went by measure. There were Jews in foreign lands, one tenth part of which had wandered off; but the rest remained faithful to the worship of the fathers. Elsewhere there were Jews who denied half of the religion of the fathers, and for the other half affiliated with the Greeks. And finally there were those with whom their old religion had become pure form, and the group's interests really dominated their religion. Yet all this was in direct opposition to the appearance of God in Israel. God's appearance there meant the utter and absolute separation of Israel from the rest of the nations in the earth, and to set them entirely by themselves apart. Israel's Jehovah does not tolerate halfheartedness, which is partly in league with heathen religion. Sharply and decisively rather the antithesis is extended to the very root of Israel's existence. And upon the new earth under the new heaven this antithesis at length gloriously celebrates its triumph. On that new earth indeed Israel gives place to *humanity,* but that whole reborn humanity has taken the Jehovah of the tabernacle and of the temple, or if you will, of Jerusalem, as the One True God to be worshipped. Let this positive statement: "Behold, the tabernacle of God is with men," therefore, not be taken lightly. The very words: "with men" imply the renewal that now comes to pass. Israel was the standard, and they who were inspired by the God of Israel were the believers from *among men* who passed over into the new phase of life. What formerly had been confined to tabernacle and temple on Sion is now become the holy of all mankind. God has first set Israel, separated and apart, over against fallen humanity, and the elect have ended in tabernacle and temple, which is expressed by the saying that the heavenly Jerusalem is come from God out of heaven down to earth.

And this is not all. They, who presently shall enter into the new Jerusalem on the new earth, are, at the moment when this prophecy came to St. John, mostly still in the harrowing and sorrowful days of the martyrs. Tears rather than merry laughter express what fills their mind and heart. They are still under menace of death, they hear the cry of the martyrs, their life is full of woe. Hence that the angel who speaks, at the same time brings to these oppressed Christians and martyrs in the earth the rich consolation of the glorious promise: "And God shall wipe away all tears from your eyes, and there shall be no more death, neither sorrow, nor crying, neither shall there be any more pain · for the former things are passed away" (v. 4). Neither let this be misunderstood. This wonderfully comforting promise is not intended as addressed to those happy ones who have already en-

tered upon the triumph of God's people on the new earth. For
they weep no more and are done with sorrow and crying. That
distress and those tears belong to "the first things," that is to
say to what overtook and troubled the children of God so long
as the old condition on the old earth under the old heaven still
lasted. When on the other hand, the new earth under the new
heaven comes in, all this woe, this sorrow and this grief is forever ended, never to return. If then one asks why nevertheless
this promise is here given, while it seems to refer to conditions on
the new earth, let the double mission of the Apocalypse be recalled. Its purport was to comfort and sustain believers amidst
scenes of cruel persecution in the first Christian century, and also
in a later age, at the approach of the Consummation, to console
and hearten the people of God. Thus it had to be brought to
mind again and again that the Apocalypse was not first to keep us
stedfast amid scenes of apostasy and persecution, but that its first
effect had to come to the good of believers before Constantine,
when again and again it seemed that the cruel emperors would
utterly destroy the faith. So with an eye to these persecuted
Christians of the first three centuries that word of comfort had
to be addressed to believers. The apostle Paul did the same in
his epistle to the Thessalonians, when time and again he reflected
upon the possibility that he might live to see the dreadful persecution. And so it is perfectly natural that, in the days of the apostle
John, when the first Christians were to endure bitterest hardships,
these comforting words were addressed to them, together with
this consoling thought: "the former things are passed away."

Even this is not all. The consoling and heartening message,
which after the Consummation would have no more sense or
meaning, goes still further. The angel now stands aside in reverent silence, and as by way of strengthening the confidence of faith
God Himself resumes the word, even in a way that adds special
weight to it. For the voice goes out from on high: *"Behold, I
make all things new."* Also this in the nature of the case is a
Divine forecast, which can not refer to what shall take place when
the new earth under the new heaven shall have renewed everything and shall bear rule over all things. By that time there is
nothing to be borrowed, as all the old is for ever passed away

and everything is new. Evidently St. John did not grasp at once
the weight and the significance of these words. He heard them
but did not write them down. Hence the word of Divine command: "Write, for these words are true and faithful." And what
is he privileged now to hear? He hears God Himself speak, saying, "It is done. I am Alpha and Omega, the beginning and the
end. I will give unto him that is athirst of the fountain of water
freely. He that overcometh shall inherit all things; and I will
be his God, and he shall be my son." Obviously this can not be
said to him who already dwells on the new earth under the new
heaven, but is addressed to him who longs for it, expects it, centers all his hope upon it, and watches for the approach of the
renewal of life. This is the more strongly evident from what
follows in v. 8, where the warning goes out to all who will not
fully break with sin, and lose themselves in the faith. For now
the Lord speaks what awaits such as are fearful and unbelieving,
and behave abominably, and are murderers, and whoremongers,
and sorcerers, and idolators. None of these have any prospect
of entering into eternal blessedness. Rather the hardest possible
judgment is pronounced upon them. So we read: "Their part is
in the lake which burneth with fire and brimstone: which is the
second death." They have already died once. In the general resurrection they have returned from death into life. But that life is
not their lasting portion. At once they are doomed to death again,
which is expressed by the saying, that their part is "in the lake
which burneth with fire."

Hence this solemn and affecting testimony, first of the angel,
and again that of God Himself, is not meant for ears that are
attuned to the harmonies of the heavenly Jerusalem. There such
a threat, and even such an admonition, can not be in place. When
once it has come to the issue, the old world has passed away, the
new relation has appeared, and transition from unbelief into
faith, of egoism into love, and from licentiousness into godliness
is no more thinkable. The shifting, separating and setting apart
of all that lived into two distinct groups, tarries therefore no
longer, and is not only begun but is now consummated. God's
children will no more be enticed into sin, neither will a luring
voice unto eternal life be heard any more by those whose names

are not written in the Book of life. All this were still possible, and had even to be counted with, so long as temptation by the Devil was still abroad. But now that the old world has passed away and the new earth with the new heaven out of heaven has come down, all indefiniteness is ended. One is either God's or else the lake of fire yawns at his feet to swallow him up. There is no second choice.

XXXIX

THE BRIDE, THE WIFE OF THE LAMB

And there came unto me one of the seven angels which had the seven vials full of the last plagues, and talked with me, saying, Come hither, I will shew thee the bride, the Lamb's wife. Rev. 21, 9.

In verse 9 of chapter 21 we have the last angelic appearance of the whole Apocalypse. This last angel had already appeared to St. John at the outset of the seven vials. Yet this had nothing to do with this appearance of v. 9 of chapter 21. Now the angel has nothing more to say of judgment upon lost humanity, on the contrary he brings a message that exclusively concerns the blessed. Only the careful noting of this fact makes plain the change which this vision undergoes. Now it is again the Lamb that arrests the attention, and the church of the blessed is again *the bride* of Christ, who realizes that from being His bride she is now to become His wife. Already in v. 2 of this chapter the new Jerusalem that came down out of heaven is compared to such a bride. For the text reads: "And I John saw the holy city, new Jerusalem, coming down from God out of heaven, prepared *as a bride adorned for her husband.*" In v. 9 return is at once made again to that bride, and Christ appears in the form of *the Lamb.* This form had been laid aside, when in the further visions the judgment began. When in chapter 5 the great vision began and Christ appeared with the seven seals, v. 13 also presented Him in the form of the Lamb, for St. John heard every creature that is in heaven, and on the earth, and in the sea exclaim: "Unto Him that sitteth upon the throne and *unto the Lamb* be blessing, and honour, and glory, and power for ever and ever." But with the further opening of the seals, the sounding of the trumpets and the outpouring of the vials judgment had come, and Christ did not appear as the Lamb, but as the *Judge* and executioner of the last judgment. Now however as the judgment is consummated and Christ is to deal solely with the blessed and the redeemed, He is seen again in the form of the Lamb, and the blessed make their appearance, as in Ephesians 5, 23 v.v. so here, as His bride.

So it was seen in v. 1 of chapter 21, and so it is observed anew when the last angel appears to show the holy apostle the last vision. Says the angel to St. John in v. 9: "Come hither and I will shew thee the bride, the Lamb's wife". This had been indicated before, as we read in Rev. 19, 7: "For the marriage of the Lamb is come, and his wife hath made herself ready". Thus far that great company of believers that was to become the wife of Christ had always mingled with the unholy earthly life. And even though the honorable title of "bride of Christ" implied that once the unholy mingling would be ended; so long as the process of renewing still went on, the company of believers was still the bride, but could not make her appearance as the wife. That transition from the state of bride into that of wifehood had to be deferred until the judgment had been executed and the sanctified multitude had come to stand by itself. But now indeed it comes to the consummation of the marriage-tie, and with an eye to this in chapter 21, in which the end is told, from the first it is recalled, that the blessed up till now had sustained merely the relation of bride, but that now the hour had come for the consummation of the holy wedlock. Both verses 2 and 9 hark back to this, and in connection with this Christ appears again as the Lamb of God,—that is, in the form of self-surrendering, self-sanctifying and seeking love. The angel here indicates the transition from the provisional into the consummated state by the combination of both names. As v. 9 reads: "Come hither, and I will shew thee the bride, the Lamb's wife." Thus bride and wife are no more separated from one another, but both are included in one sentence; and that combination of both expressions: Bride and wife, indicates the immediate transition. Thus far the congregation of God could only be the bride, and the holy marriage could not be consummated. But now the bride could no longer remain bride. Separation could no more be borne. It must needs give place to the perfect, holy union, and so immediately after the word bride, the angel proclaims the full honorable name of *the Lamb's wife.*

Herewith the glory begins, and the angel gives St. John the inspiring vision of the great city, unparalleled in splendour, which from God out of heaven comes down upon the new earth. And the amazing thing about it is, that what on the old earth was small, on the new earth assumes baffling proportions. Already in Paradise the things of higher order must have been much more beautiful in form and appearance than we have knowledge of after the fall. This original splendour not only returns but now shows itself in its consummation. For what as to splendour and glory was in Paradise but earthly gold, showed only the beginning of things; and from this paradisal form which was susceptible of improvement, consummated glory was destined to develop and in the end exhibit itself. Now, however, the final destiny must at once appear, the consummated glory must immediately become manifest. There would be no more increase, growth, or gradual perfection approaching the final condition. Altogether it must now present itself in its highest, most glorious and most brilliant perfection, and v. 11 expresses this as follows: The holy Jerusalem had "the glory of God: and her light was like unto a stone most precious, even like a jasper stone, clear as crystal." For this reflects the first and general impression, and diffuses the radiating splendour of the heavenly Jerusalem upon us.

It is not in our province to describe the holy city or the new heavenly Jerusalem in all its particulars. This belongs to the exegete, but is no part of the task which we have set ourselves. Accurate exegesis must explain even to particulars the precious stones that are here shown, both in their succession and distinction. For our purpose such a minute description would be inopportune. What interests us here is the striking difference between what the earth now offers by way of precious stones and what shall be her splendour and glory in the hour of the Consummation. The main thought, therefore, is the insignificance of our precious stones now and here, and the unparalleled dimensions of the precious stones of the new Jerusalem. Bear in mind in connection with this that the Jerusalem that came down from above must be distinguished from the rest of the new earth. These two do not coincide. There shall be a new earth, whereon the new Jerusalem shall be the centrum of the then reviving life. It has been made to appear by more than one expositor that in the presently ensuing condition the new Jerusalem shall be the all in all, but this can not be correct. Whatever eminent significance may be attributed to the new Jerusalem that came down upon the

new earth, in distinction from this descending city of Divine
glory there is a new earth, and in chapter 22, 1 there is even
a sketch of a life of nature on it. Still we must limit ourselves
here to the careful study of the description that is given of the
heavenly and now descended Jerusalem. Rev. 21, 21 clearly indicates the relation which the heavenly Jerusalem will sustain to
the surrounding nature. We know a pearl and its small dimensions. But according to the vision in hand: "The twelve gates of
the heavenly Jerusalem were twelve pearls, even that every gate
was of one pearl." It then adds that "the street of the city was
pure gold, as it were transparent glass," but while this could
occur under our present dimensions, what is said of the pearls
could not. This applies equally much to what is said of the
precious stones. Precious stones as we know them are always
very small. There is a difference, and royalty has always proudly
treasured diamonds of unusual size and worn them on state occasions; but even the greatest size of these jewels is as nothing
compared with the precious stones that are here mentioned. As
appears in v. 16 the city was measured with a reed, and measured
twelve thousand furlongs, the length and the breadth and the
height of it being equal, while the wall thereof measured in height
an hundred and forty and four cubits, and the twelve thousand
furlongs extended to all sides. When one thinks of the dimensions of the gates in such walls, and what it must mean that
each gate consists of only one pearl, he realizes what almost immeasurable dimensions have to be considered, even measurably
to form an idea of such a Jerusalem. It is needless for our purpose to enter further into this, to visualize the glory of this completed creation. The most beautiful characteristic of the Paradise
in which Adam dwelt, was plainly but a small beginning of the
glory which shall distinguish the perfected Paradise. Even the
dimensions that are stated, especially of the twelve thousand
furlongs, are so overwhelmingly great, that it is difficult to
imagine such gigantic data. But aside from this, it immediately
appeals, that the precious stones on our earth sink into absolute
insignificance, when compared with the data that are here presented, and whose sole object is to make us realize the presence
of God in this heavenly Jerusalem.

What is told of the names that will stand forth in all their beauty in the foundations and gates of this sacred structure also is of importance. According to v. 12 there will be twelve gates in the wall of the heavenly Jerusalem, and twelve parts of this holy city will each rest upon a foundation of its own. There will be twelve structures, each with a character of its own, and yet mutually connected. As v. 12 reads, in the great high wall, there are twelve gates, and at the gates twelve angels, yet distinguished in this way that on the twelve gates twelve names are written, which are the names of the twelve tribes of Israel. These twelve gates are likewise divided into four groups. There were three gates on the East, three on the North, three on the South and three on the West. This however did not tend to make the inhabitants of that heavenly Jerusalem appear solely to be converted Jews. And to safeguard against this readily intruding error, there immediately follows upon the description of the gates a similar description of the foundations, and of these we read in v. 14: "The wall of the city had twelve foundations, and in them the names of the twelve apostles of the Lamb." Thus Old and New Testament are here placed together as organs of Revelation in their mutual relation, and though what is revealed in Israel lives on in the redeemed humanity upon the new earth, yet there is nothing said to indicate that here we are to think of an Israelitish population. The foundation means yet more than the gate, and the foundation in each part is characterized twelve times as New-Testamentish. Hence that on these foundations we find the names of the twelve apostles, even in such a way, that in v. 14 it is expressly added: "and in them the names of the twelve apostles *of the Lamb.*" Thus also here it does not read of the *Christ,* but of *the Lamb,* in order also here to make one feel that the shifting has been completed, and they alone are reckoned with, who belong to the Messiah, and through the Messiah to God.

In connection with this it must not be overlooked that the names of the twelve apostles, as representatives of the New Testament dispensation, obtain a richer significance than the names of the twelve tribes of Israel. Of the twelve tribes of Israel, which mark the twelve gates, is merely said, that each gate is a pearl. With the presentation of the New Testament— that is, with the twelve apostles, it is entirely different. Not only that the apostles shall see their names written in the foundations,

which of itself is of high significance, but these twelve foundations, as of so much higher significance than the gates, are one
by one separately indicated· Vs. 19 and 20 report that "the
foundations of the wall of the city were garnished with all manner of precious stones"; and then adds specifically and severally
that the first foundation was jasper, the second sapphire, the third
a chalcedony, the fourth an emerald, the fifth sardonyx, the sixth
sardius, the seventh chrysolite, the eighth beryl, the ninth a topaz,
the tenth a chrysophrasus, the eleventh a jacinth, the twelfth an
amethyst. The difference here is very striking. With the representatives of the Old Testament in Israel there is only a brief
mention, that each of them appeared in a pearl of great excellence, while of the apostles it is said, that they were the foundations upon which everything must rest, and that in them all the
most costly treasures that can be found among precious stones
presented themselves in gigantic dimensions. Thus it quite clearly
appears that the prophetical significance of the twelve tribes of
Israel was of a lower order and of one unisonous meaning. The
pearl is of much lesser significance than the diamond. And while
with the twelve tribes the likeness of everything remained equal
to itself and the same, in the New Testament dispensation of the
apostles everything is imaged each in its own distinctiveness, and
for the depiction of the same everything that the treasures of
earth in the richest variation of precious stones, is taken.

Also by this, meanwhile, solely the glory of the creaturely character of the two Revelations of prophets and apostles is indicated,
and the unprecedented glory of this new dispensation in the
heavenly Jerusalem is described in v. 22 f., on one hand by
saying what there will *not* be in this heavenly Jerusalem, and on
the other hand by showing what in this heavenly Jerusalem shall
form the all else excelling glory. One glory shall be missing there
which in the earthly Jerusalem was the highest, namely, the
temple. So reads clearly v. 22: "And I saw no temple therein."
Also no tabernacle. There was no sanctuary any more at all, "for
the Lord God Almighty and the Lamb are the temple of it." All
representation of the holy, heavenly and Divine in earthly form is
here ended. The absolute Divine reality now shows itself and
renders every representation and shadow superfluous. Everything
that from the days of the tabernacle in the wilderness had shown

the Divine in image now has vanished. Even as you put the photograph aside, so soon as you are permitted to welcome in your home the person himself, so it is here. Thus far human life had always been too greatly a commingling of opposite tendencies, too impure and too unholy, immediately and with perfect clearness and purity to let the Divine shine through; but for this at length the moment is now come. This holds good even so absolutely that this new Jerusalem, which out of heaven comes down to earth, has no more need of the sun, neither of the moon; "for the glory of God does lighten it, and the Lamb is the light thereof" (v. 23). In the creation the earth "was without form and void, and darkness was upon the face of the deep," the waking up of life tarried until the word went forth: "let there be light, and there was light." In that creation, however, the shining forth of the light was bound to sun and moon. Hence also the change of day and night. Now, however, these two luminaries disappear, and God Himself enters into His creation and makes His splendor radiate. The bond of unity, the fellowship between God and His creation is now become perfect. Hence that sun and moon lose their significance, the creaturely assistance vanishes, and God Himself in a perfect way immediately diffuses His splendour and majesty in the new world, and among the new population which now is blessed and liberated from all sin. Of course this Divine inshining applies solely and exclusively, as v. 24 testifies, to *the nations of them which are saved.* These, so it reads, shall walk in that Divine light, and all honor and glory of men, even that of the kings of the earth, shall borrow their splendour and lustre from the inshining of that Divine light. And to this Revelation adds: "And her gates"—that is, the gates of that heavenly Jerusalem—"shall not be shut at all by day: for there shall be no night there, and they shall bring the glory and honour of the nations into it." This almost invites the question, why gates that can be closed are thought to be there. This harks back to the practice of those times of protecting cities. Insecurity at large made a city without walls and gates unthinkable; and every gate, sometimes even by day, in any case by night, had to be closed. Thus as the image was naturally taken from the data of those times, there is nothing strange in the reference to gates and walls and of watchers in those walls. Without this addition and further description of the image, it would not have appealed to the Christians of that day. Hence this is not all, and it is intentionally added that the blessed "shall bring the glory and the honour of the nations into" this new, heavenly Jerusalem, where God's glory shall appear, and that there, reversely, nothing shall enter in that defileth and worketh abomination or maketh a lie, but that only and exclusively they shall be admitted into this new Jerusalem, which are written in the Lamb's book of life.

This cuts off the expectation of the possibility of conversion or of another probation after death, which is so frequently held out to unwary souls. On the new earth God's chosen people alone shall drink the cup of heavenly grace, and they who remained strangers to grace, will then have no part in it. Of course this applies to the Father's house previous to the last judgment. He who was not admitted there, because the new life had not been implanted in him before his death, wanders about in unholy spheres and has no part in what at the last judgment makes the names to be written in the Book of Life. The separation does not come only later, but is already effected by the separation of the Father's house from the abode of the other dead. Outside the Father's house there is no place of expectation and no place of transition from the unholy to the holy spheres. And as even before the day of judgment the Father's house effects the shifting and separation, such is the case here. In all the depiction and description of the new Jerusalem there is no single intimation of susceptibility of conversion. They alone whose names are written in the Book of Life have access to that new world and thus obtain access also to that new Jerusalem. It here concerns the immediate fellowship with the living God and with the holy Lamb of God. And that direct fellowship, unhampered, august, and transcendent is possible and thinkable only there, where every obstacle has been swept away, and thus direct fellowship with God Himself has become possible. Therefore the last verse of this chapter puts the Book of Life, as establishing law and order, to the fore again. It will not only be a new *world,* but also a new *world order,* and in consequence of that new *world order* everything that made separation between God and His redeemed shall absolutely be vanquished and fallen away.

XL

THE RIVER AND THE TREE OF LIFE

And he shewed me a pure river of water of life, proceeding out of the throne of God and of the Lamb. Rev. 22, 1.

The prophecy of chapter 22 is taken in the marginal reading of the Dutch Bible in a purely metaphorical-spiritual sense. So runs the marginal reading of v. 1: "This river of the water of life stands for the everlasting blessedness, which both by the operation of the Holy Spirit, and by the vision of God's face on the part of the elect, shall in the future life always be abundant, fresh and pure." This view which was long current, and especially after St. Augustine was quite generally accepted, could upon later consideration not be maintained. There was an element of truth in it, but the explanation was too onesided. The representation in chapter 22 comes down to externals. St. John saw a pure river of the water of life, clear as crystal, proceeding out of the throne of God and of the Lamb. And then follows: "In the midst of the street of it, and on either side of the river, was there the tree of life, which bare twelve manner of fruits, and yielded her fruit every month: and the leaves of the tree were for the healing of the nations." All this has been explained as being purely spiritual; yet the conviction has more and more gained ground that here was a confusion of two distinct spheres of thought, and that the spiritualization of it all does not correspond to the language in which it is clothed, and to the matter which it concerned. Believers that come from the Christian churches are clearly distinguished from later heathen converts, who by missions have been won for Christ. The former enjoy the fruit of the tree of life, and of the latter it is said that they were apportioned the leaves, and hence not the twelve-fold fruit. Here everything depends upon one's idea of what the future is that awaits our human race after the Consummation, and thus upon the new earth under the new heaven. To presume that the condition that now prevails in the Father's house shall be continued, is plausible enough; but it ignores the real meaning of the Revelations and of the entrance upon a new earth under a new heaven, and in that case everything in the Father's house is to remain as it has always been.

If one feels that this cannot be so; that the Father's house merely bears a *provisional* character; that the last judgment, and the appearance of the new earth under the new heaven will create an entirely modified condition, it directly follows that the onesided spiritual conception of chapter 22, 1 is untenable. Rightly, therefore, in later days this onesided spiritual exposition has been abandoned, and now almost universally justice is done to the practical meaning of what is here foretold. Evidently here two things must be distinguished. There is the spiritual state of the elect upon the new earth under the new heaven, which state is unconditionally admitted to be a spiritually perfect one. In the new humanity, on the new earth under the new heaven there will be no more trace of sin. Nothing shall mar their holy character. They will have been translated into an absolutely holy state. No sinful inclination will ever make itself felt in them. No impulse and ardour that wells up in them from their inner being shall ever resist God, but shall wholly and solely be effected in them by God. This can not clearly and strongly enough be impressed upon the mind. In the humanity that shall dwell on the new earth under the new heaven before God, nothing shall oppose God. No remnant of the former unholy life is thinkable in them. Every motion of the soul, every spiritual action that is at work in them, can not and will not operate in them otherwise than from God. Satan has no more power over them, for his case has been settled for ever. From the sinful world no influence of whatever sort shall any more act upon them, for they are absolutely and forever separated from it, and indeed that world no more exists. In no particular do they live any longer from their own selves, which, in any way whatever should be apart from God, and therefore should turn against God. Now they are God's. The urge of life springs up in them from God alone. The tie that binds them to the holy God operates in them unweakened from moment to moment. From Him proceeds all life in them, both of body and of soul. What was originally intended but miscarried, in Paradise, here appears in full operation. As the organ has no other significance than the artist, who plays on it, can elicit from it, so also man on the new earth under the new heaven will not be able to emit any sound but what God elicits from the inward life of his soul. As regards the spiritual state, the harmony between what goes on in man and what God wills and purports will be perfect, perfect from the very first, and without a single moment of divergence—ever continuously perfect.

In so far as this was referred to St. Augustine, our marginal Commentators, and all who consider mainly the spiritual relation between God and man, had to confess, as is also incumbent on us, that on the new earth under the new heaven the new humanity shall not only live by God's hand but also by God's spirit. That the Holy Ghost should for one moment not wholly govern them, were unthinkable. Not a single exception shall here be possible; and therefore, it is so expressly stated in v. 3; "There shall be no more curse against anyone." Exception to the fixed and positive rule of the new life will be entirely out of the question. Not only will apostasy or any sin be no more possible, but in the most absolute sense there will be no *inclination* to any sin whatever. Nothing shall have power to operate in a human heart, save what springs from the direct harmony with the Holy God and thus is worked therein by God Himself. There will be no more question of any struggle against sin, or of any compulsion of unholy inclination; and all action that arises in the soul of the Redeemed and effctively works in them, shall unto all eternity never be anything else than what God Himself works in them and brings to pass. And verse 1 of chapter 22 is the depiction of that new state. The apostle sees a pure river, that is to say, a stream of human life, without taint or contamination, and its waters bring life to every human being. That it says additionally that this "water of life" here shows itself to be "clear as crystal," emphatically indicates that now there can be no more sinful inmingling or sinful inclination, and that this is not owing to man, but solely to the fact that this stream of the new life does not originate in man, and moves towards God, but that it proceeds out of the throne of God to inspire human life, and such indeed in connection with the action of the Lamb, that is to say, under the saving action that goes out from the Lamb upon us sinners, for

the absolute destruction of every connection with anything that
is sinful and unholy in the new humanity, which then will dwell
on the new earth. So to this extent we must admit that the old
exposition of this sentence was correct. What shall spiritually
operate in man on the new earth under the new heaven comes
from God alone, operates from its Divine origin and is not an
action that proceeds from man toward God, neither is it a spiritual
action which from man, seeking God, goes out toward God, but
an action that reaches out towards man and inspires his inner
being with the holy. The source is in God and not in man. Thus
in behalf of the reborn humanity it is a stream of life that proceeds from God that now enters into the reborn humanity and
there maintains the absolute purity of life with such heavenly
effulgence that, clear and pure as crystal, it overflows from God
into man, and thanks to the salvation which the Lamb offers, is
never more susceptible of desecration. So we detract nothing
from the absolute character of this invulnerable holiness. On the
new earth there is no motion toward God. except as it first comes
from God to man. God is now again in the fullest sense the
Creator and man again the *creature*. There is nothing independent
in man thinkable, by which in praise or adoration or consecration
he could enrich God's life. God always is and shall be the sun,
whose spendour and glow reflect themselves in man. From God
it shines out in man, from man that Divine splendour scintillates
back to God. That in this first verse of chapter 22 there is mention of a river, tends to take life in the reborn humanity, not individually, but collectively. The whole reborn humanity stands
before God as a holy unity that is athrob with life, and therefore is compared to a stream of living water which does not proceed from man, as though man could bring anything to God,
but proceeds from God, radiates from God in all of the new
humanity, from God shines in her and from her back to God.
Only, and here observe the mistake in the former exegesis,
while the life of God very really radiates thus in the then living
humanity and is reflected therefrom back to God, this but notes
one aspect of the matter. That reborn humanity does not remain
on its knees in uninterrupted worship of God, but shares all sorts
of mutual relations as nation, family and household, which new
relations in the second place imply new callings, new life-tasks,

new commissions, in which collectively it has to glorify its God, and the followers of St. Augustine have utterly overlooked the accomplishment of the new life-task. The new life of the reborn humanity on the new earth will not be one of mere religious reveries, but *will be a full human life* which will exhibit all the glory that God in the first creation had purposed and appointed for the same, but which by us was sinned away. At present piety as a guiding and inspiring principle is still antithetical with the promptings of our sinful life. Hence that its beginning is individual, and can only partly govern our personal and our communal life. But in the new condition which on the new earth God shall effect in the reborn humanity, everything, in conformity to the new principle of life, shall richly develop itself anew. There will not merely be devout and pious people, but it will be an absolutely new existence which permeates and embraces the renewed human life in all its articulations and appearances.

So this new humanity must not be imagined as in every way alike, but as diversified by everything that characterized believers at the time of their death and of their entrance upon the new life. This even applies to a person's age. Great multitudes have died before they knew anything of this life. The newly born, or scarcely so much as born, who, as God's elect, immediately entered upon the higher life, have in the nature of the case not known our rich development of life. This of course did not involve any loss as regards their spiritual being; for that is animated by the Spirit, yet of necessity they who presently so come back to human life on the new earth, lack what others have obtained. But also apart from this, in the new life the difference between man and man, as regards the gifts and talents wherewith each has been endowed will continue to exist. This detracts nothing from our blessedness. He who is least mentally endowed can enjoy the nearness of his God as richly as the most talented. Nor is this all. In the future that awaits us on the new earth, all of life is renewed and with all its rich destiny returns. The striking difference of talents and intellectual powers therefore shall there be perpetuated. Not just for one moment, but permanently, for God did not create men of perfectly equal magnitudes, but rather of endless variety. Human nature itself accounts for the difference of aptitude. Education and practice may modify this difference to some extent, but as actual fact one has talents and gifts, which the other lacks, and the men of genius, whose brilliant gifts it is difficult to explain, are few. This applies to all departments of life, to art and science, to agriculture and commerce. Everywhere this difference presents itself and in every way, and when according to their various talents we divide people into groups or classes, the lower classes are always the most numerous, and the men of genius and leading spirits are for the most part mere exceptions. These differences do not depend upon our life in God or upon God's life in us. The most devout worshippers are found rather all to frequently among the humbler classes, while the men of genius, and such as are born leaders, depart from their God. But it shall not be so on the new earth and under the new heaven. Everything shall there be animated by God alone, every one shall stand up for God; but the differences will nevertheless be evident. The nature and divisions of humanity have their rise in God's ordinance, and on the new earth also shall unfold themselves accordingly.

Only when this is kept in view, can justice be done to the close of v. 2, which reads: "the leaves of the tree are for the healing of the heathen" (Dutch ver.). It can not mean that in this final scene, the Christians of the heathen world should be of lower standing as respects their calling than the older members of the Christian church; or that the latter should enjoy the glorious fruits of the Tree of Life, while heathen converts should only receive the leaves of that tree. All this is unthinkable. In God's sanctuary on the new and sanctified earth dwell exclusively God's children who spiritually are animated by God. The only particular in which the heathen that have last been brought to God are less favored than the others is, that in almost no single respect have they enjoyed the richer racial development which was accorded to the members of the Christian churches. The former are spiritually mature. Here on the other hand is a backwardness that must still be made up. To this the leaves of the Tree of Life tend as means. Thus nothing is said of a gift that should come to them from the culture of the world; the spiritual comes to them also altogether from God; and the Tree of Life, which from Paradise brought the memory with it of a spiritual culture now appears, here not only in its fruit, but even also in its leaf, able to effect an inspiring and elevating operation. These later converts lacked something, not because of sin or unholiness, but simply a deficiency in holy development, and which is not made up by chastisement, but by the leaves of the Tree of Life. Otherwise the twelvefold fruit of the Tree of Life alone would be reckoned with, while here even the leaf of that tree is of service. And so the latest converts from the heathen nations are doubly favored. They not only enjoy the fruit of the Tree of Life, but also the inner virtue of its leaves is their profit. This is still more clearly indicated in v. 3, which reads: "And there shall be no more curse against anyone" (Dutch ver.). This plainly implies that what the last converts from the heathen nations still lacked was not anything negative, nor unholy, nor sinful, but was merely a deficiency in development. Otherwise the curse of God must have rested upon the remnants of sin in them. But there is no such sinful remnant there. The latest converts from the heathen world also have absolutely broken with Satan and sin. Their life too therefore springs solely from what God has worked in them. Only, what God purports to be in a converted and sanctified sinner can already have been effected *entirely* or merely yet *in part*. And this is what will come to pass with the last converts from the heathen world to bring about a stronger development of the holy in them, in order, so to speak, to make good their backwardness.

If now we look away from this exception in the case of the latest converted heathen nations, the representation in hand is very plain. In the first place God does not endow all men equally. Some are more favored than others. Men of genius are rare. And this will not be different in eternity, but will continue even as the Divine ordinance has been from the beginning. Moreover in our earthly life all too many, by accident or misfortune or by lack of means on the part of their parents or of themselves, fail of bringing out what is in them. Many a talented man has been carried out to the grave, who, had his life been spared, would have enchanted the world with the display of his rich gifts, and which gifts, in amounts of immeasurable magnitude, have been lost to the world. Fire, murder or misfortune might be the cause, though it might equally be the result of an early death, as consequence of a weak constiution or of the sin of parents. In the nature of the case this works no *spiritual* harm, for God is wonderfully able to implant even in a young infant all the fulness of His grace. But it makes a difference with respect to the intellectual and practical development. A nation or a person has developed richly along cultural lines, while others are either backward or entirely lacking in this respect. So on the new earth this backwardness and loss should necessarily be made up. Hence the difference that will be observable on the new earth. Yet though this must be noted and be counted with, it must not be overlooked that this backwardness is merely temporary. Presently it shall have been made up. This difference however must be reckoned with, because the Scripture does, but it is a difference that passes away.

Only let no one think that the degree of development, which may be attainable in this life, is the highest within human reach. Nothing intimates that on the new earth, age upon age, human life shall become numb with monotony and endless uniformity. As a slave in the heart of Africa can not form the least idea of what rich development a professor, a poet, an artist in Europe can attain unto, so it is not given us to know the ever richer culture to which the redeemed humanity on the new earth can mount. We do not know the form of that new and higher life. Possibly the forms of our present life will there be unrecognizable, but in any case what is of lower standing here, will upon its arrival in that new life quickly unfold itself to perfect ripeness, and what will fully have matured will pass over into the culture of eternity, which will very far surpass all the culture that our life here has ever had at command. Always "the water of life, proceeding out of the throne of God and of the Lamb, *clear as crystal.*"

As we already observed there can be no question in connection with this of the confinement of all of the new life within the gates of the new Jerusalem. The new earth must be distinguished from the holy city in which Almighty God, yet now without temple or tabernacle, spiritually chooses His abode. Whether this absolute change will confine itself exclusively to the sun, moon and this earth, so that the rest of the universe will retain its original form, is not revealed. Whatever questions can be asked regarding this are undoubtedly very interesting, but Revelation here does not concern itself with them, any more than it did in the narrative of the creation. He who would exhibit the revelation of the Apocalypse is safest not to trouble himself with such matters. Obviously St. John received his higher communications in a form that was adapted to what in those days, and thus to himself and to his readers, was the common world view; even with respect to sun, moon and stars. By itself this was most natural and, therefore, did no harm, since the revelation of the mystery of the future concentrated itself entirely upon the new center for all creaturely life in the new, spiritual Jerusalem. The main purport was to show clearly and severally that spiritually now everything was free from stain, had become new and was to the good of every child of God, but that the external life had to present itself in an entirely new form. This had already been so clearly understood by Ezekiel and Micah, Zechariah and Daniel, and especially by Isaiah that, in the reading of their prophecies it is still surprising how clearly and intelligently they peered into the presently coming eternity. Two things in the end were at stake. In the first place a fellowship with the Eternal, such as had truly been foreshadowed in tabernacle and temple, but had never yet been enjoyed to the full; and in the second place, a possession of the created world, such as for one moment this had been foreshadowed in Paradise, but in its reality could only here be known and enjoyed. This is what these chapters (21 and the first part of 22) portray in brilliant, figurative language, to both of which therefore also in the exegesis of chapter 22, 1-5, full justice must be done.

XLI

THE RENEWAL OF HEAVEN AND EARTH

The wolf and the lamb shall feed together, and the lion shall eat straw like the bullock: and dust shall be the serpent's meat. They shall not hurt nor destroy in all my holy mountain, saith the Lord. Isaiah 65, 25.

The tendency to spiritualize the prophecy of "the new earth," in Rev. 22, 1-5, is undoubtedly encouraged by the similar predictions to Israel in the Old Testament. In Hosea 2, 18 we read: "And in that day I will make a covenant for them with the beasts of the field, and with the fowls of heaven, and with the creeping things of the ground: and I will break the sword and the battle out of the earth, and will make them to lie down safely." Ezekiel 34, 25 reads: "And I will make with them a covenant of peace, and will cause the evil beasts to cease out of the land; and they shall sleep in the woods." And much more definitely we read in Isaiah 11, 6-9: "And the wolf shall dwell with the lamb, and the leopard shall lie down with the kid; and the calf and the young lion together; and a little child shall lead them, and the cow and the bear shall feed, their young ones shall lie down together: and the lion shall eat straw like the ox. They shall not hurt nor destroy in all my holy mountain: for the earth shall be full of the knowledge of the Lord, as the waters cover the sea." And so we read in the last verse of the last chapter but one of Isaiah: "The wolf and the lamb shall feed together and the lion shall eat straw like the bullock: they shall not hurt nor destroy in all my holy mountain, saith the Lord"; a prediction which is yet more worthy of note, because in v. 22 of the last chapter of Isaiah in connection with this is likewise spoken of a "new heaven and a new earth," where sin shall no more be known. Zechariah in the last chapter of his oracles points to an equally holy future, in which sin and the results of sin shall once and for all be ended, when in v. 6 *f.* he writes this holy prophecy: "And it shall come to pass in that day, that the light shall not be clear,

nor dark: but it shall be one day which shall be known to the
Lord, not day, nor night: but it shall come to pass, that at evening time it shall be light. Also it shall be in that day, that living
waters shall go out from Jerusalem."

The writers of our marginal notes understood these vigorous
Old Testament passages also to be prophecies of what spiritually
was to come. Of the living waters that should go out from
Jerusalem, the marginal reading observes: "By this must be
understood the gift of the Holy Ghost which Christ was abundantly to pour out upon His church." Already this single instance
shows that the writers of the marginal readings have entirely
spiritualized the eschatological sayings of the Old Testament, and
thereby from the first have betrayed the tendency to attribute
significance almost exclusively to the spiritual enjoyments. This
naturally prepared the purely spiritual conception of the first part
of Rev. 22; and plainly no justice has been done to this final part
of the great prediction, either by the writers of the marginal
readings or by those who with them paid homage to a similar
exposition. Read the marginal notes on chapter 22, and the only
possible conclusion is that here we have to do with figurative
language only, and that this last prophecy purports merely to make
sure the *spiritual* glorification of the people of the Lord, to fix
the attention solely upon the single individuals, and to limit itself to the ascertainment of the holy relation in which the elect
would forever stand to the Truine God. The prophecies which
we have quoted from the Old Testament have undoubtedly co-
operated in the process of giving currency to this exposition. It
was peculiarly characteristic of the Old Covenant, even in Isaiah,
Micah, Ezekial and Zecheriah, that it always went out from the
Jerusalem in Palestine and ended with the coming of the Messiah. Even in Isaiah there is no compelling indication of the great
middle period, that has already elapsed after the Ascension of
Christ in the course of history. And when the reason is asked
for this hiatus in Old Testament prophecy, let it be said that
he who here posits contrary demands shows that he really does
not understand the character of the holy prophecy in Israel. For
then obviously one deems that this Old Testament prophecy was
a verbal and literal whispering in the ear of the history that is
to be awaited, and this betrays an utter want of appreciation of

the exalted character of ancient prophecy. There was no prophetical office, as many ever yet imagine, which merely required
ability to hear words that were whispered in the ear. Unspiritual
persons would have been capable of lending themselves to this.
In that case the prophets would have been mere copyists, without
the addition of anything more. And the direct opposite of this
took place. The prophet was trained for his exalted task by God
Himself. The prophet's whole life was designed with an eye to
that high calling. And all that the prophet could do was but
the result of God's action upon his mind, that had thus been
tuned and prepared. As a result of this, all that could loom up
before the prophetical imagination regarding the coming of the
Messiah and regarding the consequences of that coming, could
only be, what was directly connected with Jerusalem, and would
concentrate itself in the coming of the Messiah. The New Testament alone therefore could show what, after the coming of the
Messiah, would develop from His appearance and disappearance, and so only could the apocalyptical doctrine regarding last
things present what actually is to come.

The attempt of later date to interpret, in connection with this
exposition of Old Testament prophecy, also what presently for
ever is to come mainly spiritually, hung together with this wrong
conception and was in part a result of it. Only it was entirely
overlooked that in this way the Father's house was undervalued
in order to perpetuate the condition that presented itself in the
same. It was based upon the, by itself, accurate conviction that
the spiritual is of higher significance than the visible and corporeal. God is Spirit; the angels are spirits; in the Father's house
there were none others than redeemed spirits; and so the conviction forced itself upon one that also for us as men, the spiritual
is the highest and only blessed state, and that the formal and
corporeal were of too low an order to be renewed and perpetuated
together with the spiritual. Since, however, the Scripture in all
manner of ways continually also emphasizes this corporeal, external and formal of the eternity that is to come, this spiritualization could no longer satisfy one; and so of itself the appreciation
of what also externally would be our portion in eternity has come
back.

A backward look upon the story of the creation confirms one's confidence in the accuracy of this insight. In the Genesis narrative of the creation, the spiritual undeniably comes in only at the end, after all the formal and material has preceded. In the creation story there is no intimation that man should stand at the head, that he should occupy the foreground and from the first should be in command of the whole creation. Rather everything that is not spiritual comes first. In the five creative days all the rest of the creatures are mentioned, but not man, and only at the end the exponent of God's image also appears. Even the whole animal world has the precedence. First comes the dust of the earth, and only after that we read, that of this dust of the earth God formed man; and this even in such a way that man came first as regards the body, and that only after that the breath of life was breathed into his nostrils. Thus it is not first the spiritual man that makes his appearance in the Universe, so that only afterwards an earth was created for him; but that the earth with everything that belongs to it had come first and, when all this was ready, only then on that material earth was man bodily,—that is, in visible form, created; and only after that was the higher spiritual breath breathed into him. In the creation of man this alone is of surpassing significance, namely that God said: "Let us make man in our image and after our likeness"; so, however, that at once there is added: "And let him have dominion over the fish of the sea, and over the fowl of the air, and over cattle, and over all the earth, and over every creeping thing that creepeth upon the earth." And then follows: "So God created man in His image, in the image of God created He him." And not only this, but also in the blessing which God pronounced upon man the temporal and the earthly is equally much included. As we read in Gen. 1, 28: "And God blessed them, and God said unto them, Be fruitful, and multiply, and replenish the earth, and subdue it: and have dominion over every living thing that moveth upon the earth." Such was the original creation, and of that creation it is said in Gen. 1, 31: "And God saw everything that He had made, and, behold, it was very good." And when such was the procedure in the creation, when there was no mention yet of sin or of curse, how then in connection with this entirely onesided work of God, which was decisive with respect to the whole future, can one look upon all the sensual, visible and formal as having no place in the eternal blessedness, in order to retain nothing save the spiritual? This in fact would place humanity in that eternal future on a par with the angels, and would nullify the entirely unique significance of the human race as "exponents of God's image." Surely, by the fall, a breach has taken place in the work of creation, which forced itself into man's spiritual mode of being; and in connection with this breach man's social life has been radically modified. Yet in all this lapsed state of things God has taken no measures to impart a purely spiritual existence to man. This could at once have been effected. Rather the plan, the object and effort of the work of Redemption has been to restore what was lost, and even so to restore it that it never could be lost again. This however necessarily demanded, that fallen man, when finally restored, should appear as the perfected and henceforth inviolable Image of God, in entire conformity to the fundamental lines of the same which were given in the creation. Hence a purely spiritual conception of what is to come, is directly contradicted by the opening pages of Holy Scripture. He who is thus minded takes, upon his own authority, as purely spiritual, what from the first page of Holy Scripture to the last is put forward as claim for the human being; to wit, that spiritually he should appear as a child of God, and at the same time, as the exponent of God's Image, he should be a ruler in a *visible creation*. In keeping with this Isaiah, Ezekiel and Zechariah also emphasize the *externality* of our human life, and together with us the world, that has been subjected to us, looks forward to a new future that has been prepared for it.

This detracts nothing from the unique worth of the spiritual, in the eternally redeemed humanity. We readily confess that they that have been saved unto the life eternal find the kernel of their being, of their destiny and of their future, in their holy sonship; but in addition to this the claim must equally readily apply that man remains *man*, that he does not become an angel, and that, as man, he shall forever occupy that position which in the creation and in the recreation has been assigned to the "flesh", if we may say so—that is, to man. The whole Mediatorship stands or falls therewith. When the apostle writes: "And the Word became flesh and dwelt among us," he does not make the Mediator appear

in a temporary pseudo-form, but this Mediatorship is His glory
which accompanies Him in dying, is now maintained in His
heavenly state, and in His return to judgment shall perpetuate itself. It is emphatically told that after His crucifixion no bones
of Christ were broken, but that intact He was carried to His
grave; that He rose in bodily form and thus entered upon the
glorification which He on Tabor had momentarily enjoyed in
advance. Thus it is out of the question that it has anywhere been
prophesied, that the soul of Christ has taken flesh upon itself in
our behalf, and still dwells in that Mediatorial form, but that in
the end this Mediatorial appearance is to be abandoned and laid
aside again. Rather it is repeatedly emphasized that the Mediator
shall come down to this earth in a visible observable form, and,
as the exponent of the human form that shall be observable with
the eye, shall here execute judgment. So there is no indication,
however remote, that after His coming to judgment the Incarnation and what is connected with it shall be considered closed.
Rather His Incarnation and His appearance in the form of Mediator is ever in the foreground. We ourselves will not be summoned to judgment as pure spirits, as the "resurrection *of the
flesh*" is, as expressly as possible, emphasized; and so the new
unfolding of life on the new earth is always depicted as *externally*
observable, even in the form of the original creation, but which
form now is no more changeable, but abiding, so as to make the
richness of life that originally was apportioned us of God, in fulness of existence, come to its permanent and richer unfolding.

The original world was a creation of God in a higher sense
than the world of angels. In Adam was expressed the holy and
all else surpassing thought: "Let us make man *in our image* and
after our likeness." Creative power could reach no higher than
this, and from the first that creation of man in God's image and
after God's likeness, as Gen. 1, 26-31 shows, was connected with
all of our earthly life. Both the creation of man in God's image
and the rich unfolding of everything that was earthly in this creation, corresponded fully to one another. Hence sin corrupted
both the spiritual and the bodily life. And again, in necessary
connection with this all Scripture shows that, for the salvation of
our race, the coming down of God to us men, only became pos-

sible by the assumption on the part of the Son of God of *our flesh,* and that therewith He became subject to all our human needs, subject even to death, and that only as Son of man, and therefore in the human form, He could rise again from the dead, for ever to occupy His dominant position in all our human race. There was not the slightest degradation of Deity in the fact that the Son of God, as Son of man, ate and drank, slept and awoke, labored and rested. Jesus has never repelled the human on account of its human form (everything sinful and defective of course excluded). Rather He is entered upon everything that is human, and such even in the given form, which the human had been accorded in the original creation. It was culpable onesidedness, therefore, as often as with respect to the eternal life that awaits us, the spiritual alone was considered, and the former visible, observable and formal were not only put aside, but counted as of secondary importance, in order presently, as utterly unworthy of continued existence, to destroy it. Of course, also here one has to be on his guard against onesided exaggeration. The modification which as a result of the fall this visible earth and our human life underwent, is very considerable. Hence accurately to sketch an image of the future world is not given us. What here presents itself can in the hereafter disappear, and again from the data of creation can come forth what in the original Paradise tarried to appear. It is our desire therefore to watch against all onesidedness and exaggeration. Only the undeniable fact, which must suffer no loss by reason of spiritual onesidedness, is, that the original creation of Paradise shall be maintained even in such a way and in such a form, that the reborn Paradise shall in its visible form shine forth eternally and resplendently to the glory of God.

So there is nothing mysterious or strange in the fact that, at the close of the Apocalypse, we have the prophecy of a *city,* in distinction from the surrounding country. The distinction between city and country proceeds from the data which in the great work of creation governed the Lord's thoughts and will. If we believe that on the new earth the data of the original creation shall be perpetuated in a higher form, also the distinction between the agricultural and the central municipal life is bound to characterize the hereafter. The question we here face is: whether when our old world passes away to make room for the new earth under the new heaven the modification will exclusively affect our sun and planetary system, or whether this will involve the whole starry world. They who have a deeper knowledge of the starry heavens find it almost inconceivable that our little earth should be the center of God's infinite Universe. And yet all depends on this. All revelation regarding the Consummation confirms the impression that what happens with our world concerns the lot of the whole visible kingdom of heaven. Meanwhile our earth, including our solar and planetary system, is, when compared with the whole starry world, so small and insignificant, that such a future can scarcely be imagined. Hence the attempt that has so frequently been made to distinguish the lot of our solar system from that of the cosmic system as a whole, and to ask whether our solar system might not be set apart from the rest of the universe, and to assume for that rest of the same an entirely different existence, and an entirely different future, from that which applies to our earth. Yet Holy Scripture does not countenance this assumption. What is told of the future of this earth and of this solar system is all-embracing and predominant and affords no room in God's holy doing for a Consummation alongside of and entirely apart from our world. Not that we could allow ourselves to deem that what is here revealed of the Consummation particularizes things down to the smallest detail, which in every way links itself to our present life; yet though we grant in this respect the possibility of indirect modifications and divergences, in the fundamentals of summarized human life nothing can be changed. It is, and always shall be, the world which God Almighty has created, which He, in spite of all the sins of angels and of men, has in its broad dimensions upheld and maintained, and which at the time of the end He will so bring out to a perfect form of life, that it will perfectly correspond to His purpose of creation, and which, in spite of the sins of angels and of men shall make His original plan—now no more susceptible of corruption—shine forth resplendently in fulness and richness of form.

The glory that is manifested diverges at the end of the Consummation, therefore, entirely from our present world order. They that shall be privileged to live in glory, and to live for ever, shall then not merely be permitted to worship God, and call upon Him, but shall be the recipients of such a heightened glory that they, as v. 4 of our chapter says: "shall see God's face and shall bear God's name in their forheeads." From the moment that this glory appears, God Himself shall give them light, and they shall reign as kings, that is to say, they shall enjoy a royal majesty, and such to all eternity. Hence is added in v. 6: These sayings are faithful and true; and the Lord God of the holy prophets has sent His angel to shew unto His servants the things which must shortly be done." This announcement v. 7 concludes with the words: "Behold, I come quickly: blessed is he that keepeth the sayings of the prohpecy of this book." With this the presentation of the Consummation terminates, and there is no need of entering further upon the closing part of Revelation. For while the Consummation has truly been sketched as in an image, as an event it only takes place when the conclusion comes to an entire and perfect execution. He who lives in faith and hope waits for this, but the Image of the Consummation itself does not depend upon this. The features of this image can no further be outlined than here they are presented in vs. 1-7. What comes after this, must, even minutely, be considered by him who undertakes an exposition of the whole Apocalypse; but with respect to the Consummation this can be passed by in silence. When once the new earth shall be resplendent under the new heaven, and upon that new earth the holy city, which shall all be a temple of God, shall reveal God's holy presence, and such as the center of the blessed life, which then shall give the whole world a setting in glory, the final object of God's original creation as well as of His saving grace shall have been reached.

XLII

NO RESTITUTION OF ALL THINGS

And cast ye the unprofitable servant into outer dark-
ness: and there shall be weeping and gnashing of teeth.
St. Matth. 25, 30.

If then herewith we have come to the final word in our study
of the Consummation, a last objection calls for special notice.
Throughout our exposition it always, and in every way, appeared,
that the salvation that is to come shall be the portion of true believers alone, and that all the rest of mankind shall be apportioned eternal misery. With the exception of Origen and a few
mystics and the Anabaptists, this always was, and still is, fully
accepted among all believers in the church of Christ in the world.
Thus as a rule it was but little questioned and was still less written about, and one acquiesced in this end of the lost, which is so
clearly indicated in God's Word. Yet though this acquiescence is
a demand of God's Word, and though we can not temper the aw-
fulness of this dreadful tragedy, with every exposition of the
end and Consummation, it is always something that profoundly
stirs the emotions and affects one very painfully. This emotion is
the more keenly aroused when others present the case, as though
they had it in their power to undo this greatly distressing fact,
even in such a way that leaders and influential figures in the
Christian world warmly advocate the actual salvation of all mankind, and accept it with complete assurance. This doctrine of
universal salvation is called "Apocatastasis pantone", a term that
is borrowed from St. Peter's discourse in Acts 3, and which in
v. 21 testifies of Christ: "Whom the heaven must receive until
the times of restitution of all things, which God hath spoken by
the mouth of His holy prophets since the world began." Though
this saying does not warrant what is inferred from it, to speak
of the "Apocatastasis pantone" has become more and more
general, and is understood to mean that the apostle here has fully
assured us that in the end all men shall attain unto blessedness.

Especially Schleiermacher took the lead in this. In his *"Christliche Glaube"* and in his valuable treatment of the *Doctrine of Election* he indeed expressed himself with exceeding care, yet definitely in favor of the milder conception in the spirit of Origen. The Swiss Dr. A. Schweizer, author of the *Christliche Glaubenslehre der Evangelisch-Reformirten Kirche* (1884) sympathizes with Schleiermacher in this, and is even more outspoken. In England Schleiermacher's representation found favor with Dr. Rurt, Bishop of Dromore. Though Dr. Martensen had a leaning towards this view, he always accepted the possibility of an eternal doom. And however much Dr. Ritschl personally favored Schleiermacher's representation, he too admits very frankly, that the possibility of an eternal retribution is not excluded. In fact there has been doubt about this matter even from the days of Origen, and the inclination to exclude all idea of eternal punishment has become prevalent. The mystical and very subjective heretics among the Anabaptists encouraged this conception. Yet in the Christian world the Church's idea of a blessedness in which believers and elect alone have part, has almost universally been maintained. Only when liberalism gained the upper hand in theology, a turn came in this respect, which especially through Schleiermacher obtained a mighty impulse. And without exaggeration it can now be said that, fairly generally among the more free-thinking Dogmatists Schleiermacher's view has both gained an entrance and become prevalent.

This was possible only when, on one hand, the authority of Holy Scripture and, on the other hand, the spiritual authority of Christ and His apostles was so bitterly attacked, that they actually became nugatory. One now deals at will with Holy Scripture, especially with the Old Testament; the Divine authority of Christ is almost entirely set aside, and the apostolic writings are subjected to individual criticism, rather than accorded the submission of the mind to the authority of the apostles. So again it can be said without exaggeration that from the first until now the church of Christ has been true to the conviction, that merely a part of the dead enter into the Father's house, and that in the day of judgment many even of the baptized shall be excluded from the blessed life on the new earth under the new heaven. And as in this closing chapter we deal with this grave subject, in the nature of the case, and in keeping with the practice that has been observed throughout this work, we do not criticize the liberal writers, nor anyone who attacks the authority of the prophets and the apostles, but take our unqualified stand by the sayings of Christ and His apostles.

Let us then turn to the positive sayings of Christ, and before all else let us refer to the oft repeated word in His lips, that at the end of the last judgment there *shall be weeping and gnashing of teeth,* which characterization obviously indicates absolute misery. Before Christ, the Baptist had already taken this uncompromising stand, when he preached the Messiah who was to come, whose fan would be in His hand, and who would purge His threshing-floor, and gather His wheat into His barn, and what proved to be chaff He would burn with unquenchable fire. Likewise our Lord, in keeping with this, and confirming this positive saying, in His exposition of the parable of "the tares of the field" (Matth. 13, 40-42) has definitely testified: "As therefore the tares are gathered and burned in the fire; so shall it be in the consummation of this world. The Son of man shall send forth His angels, and they shall gather out of His Kingdom all things that offend, and them which do iniquity, and shall cast them into a furnace of fire; *there shall be wailing and gnashing of teeth."* In precisely the same manner He expressed Himself in the parable in Matth. 22, 1-14. Here we have the story of the man who had been invited to the marriage-feast, and had come, but without the wedding garment, and in connection with this Jesus says: "Bind him hand and foot, take him away, and cast him into outer darkness; *there shall be weeping and gnashing of teeth."*

We learn the same lesson from Matth. 24, 51, in what Christ there says of the unfaithful servant: "The Lord of that servant shall come in a day when he looketh not for him, and in an hour that he is not aware of, and shall cut him off, and appoint him his portion with the hypocrites: *There shall be weeping and gnashing of teeth."* And again Christ utters the same equally definite testimony in Matth. 25, 30 where, regarding the unprofitable servant who did not prepare himself for the coming of his lord, He says: "Cast ye the unprofitable servant into outer darkness:

there shall be weeping and gnashing of teeth." This positive say-
ing of Jesus is recorded four times. From this it does not appear that Christ did not also say it at other times; for surely not
a tenth of what Jesus has spoken has been recorded in the Gospels. But from what has been recorded and handed down, it
appears, that this conclusive saying of Christ: "There shall be
weeping and gnashing of teeth," undoubtedly belongs to the
habitual manner of speech which Christ constantly inculcated on
His disciples and hearers. This imposes the solemn obligation
upon us all in preaching, in catechetical or confirmation classes,
continually to point to this incisive word of Jesus, and to inculcate
it on the rising generation and those who hear or read us. Our
Lord evidently intended that this hard saying, which cuts off
every way of escape, should deeply be impressed upon our mind,
and this not only justifies, but demands the attempt in every way
of placing salvation and reprobation antithetically over against
each other. It plainly shows that in the days of His earthly ministry Christ constantly perceived the inclination to soften the
absolute antithesis, as was indeed the case with the Greek Jews.
Far from encouraging this sparing and softening way of treating
this matter, Christ has, as appears from every pertinent saying,
refuted the same with utmost positiveness of speech, has insisted
ever anew upon the inexorable and distinct drawing of the divid-
ing line, and impressed upon the hearts of His disciples and His
hearers that they should never minimize their expectation regarding the judgment with respect to the absolute antithesis between
those that are destined to be eternally saved, and the reprobates
who have no prospect save that of eternal doom.

The absolute finality of these sayings of Christ makes it imperative that a deaf ear be turned to all those appeals that are so
frequently made to certain apostolic sayings in support of the
modern theory of the Apocatastasis. For instance appeal has
been made to I Tim. 2, 3-4 where we read: "For this is good and
acceptable in the sight of God our Saviour, who will have all
men to be saved, and to come to the knowledge of the truth";
which taken by itself, can be said of all preaching of the Word,
for no preacher ever thinks of excluding any of his hearers from
the Gospel call, but zealously urges them all to surrender themselves to God and to turn to Christ. In 2 Peter 3, 9 we read:

"The Lord is not slack concerning His promise, as some men count slackness; but is longsuffering to usward, not willing that any should perish, but that all should come to repentance," which saying, as appears from the context, does not refer to all hearers, but solely to those who will come to conversion, as the designated means for making them enter upon eternal life. The same applies to I John 2, 2, where the apostle testifies of "Jesus Christ the righteous," that "He is a propitiation for our sins, and not for ours only, but also for the sins of the whole world." He who is familiar with the writings of St. John well knows that he did not expect an ingathering of all mankind. He merely says that the atonement is not limited to those with whom he was in constant touch, but extends to all mankind, to all that are brought to the faith. Hence to appeal to such expressions is useless, as though indeed the apostles would so glaringly have contradicted themselves. Rather it must be acknowledged that their positive conviction regarding the blessedness which awaits believers only, gave them freedom in the exposition of the truth to make use of more liberal terms. This is the more significant because this question does not concern exclusively those who lived after the coming of Christ and knew His Gospel, but all that have lived from the days of Cain and Abel, to men of all nations under both Old and New Testaments, and from now on to the end of the world. And the contention is, that no single human being of the present, past or future shall be lost, but that every one that is born as man shall once be partaker of the perfect glory.

Three views must here be carefully distinguished. One is that only they who were truly converted before death shall be saved. The second is, that they who have lived under the Christian dispensation and spiritually have remained strangers to Christ and have died in their unconverted state, will in the hereafter have another chance of being initiated into the mystery of salvation and of conversion to Christ. And the third, which is held by those who have utterly abandoned the orthodox confession, is, that they who both before and after Christ have been estranged from the holy, and have wandered off into forbidden paths, will in the hereafter undergo a new training and a much higher education; that this higher training is not at once effective in every case, so that even a second or a third period of sanctification may be required; but that in the end every man will be inspired by the holy, and be it after long ages, every human being will attain to spiritual purity and be incorporated in the higher spiritual community. When these three views are placed side by side, it is interesting to note that the first has been held almost universally by Christian theologians; that the second view has gained little popularity, except among the anabaptists, until Schleiermacher made it more acceptable in the eyes of many; and that the third view was first held by the theologians who had fallen away from Christ, and now prevails almost everywhere among modernists and those that have wandered still further off from the truth.

Between these three views the choice is wholly controlled by the *Person of Christ*. If according to modernists Christ is only a man, and distinguished merely because of His deeply religious endowment, we can grant that the nations in all parts of the world, which have lived before Christ and have taken part in the general development, have from age to age made advances on higher or lower levels, and, if need be entirely apart from Christ, have reached the standpoint they now occupy. If the modernists, in question here, still believe in a life after death, there is nothing to prevent them from cherishing the belief that the dead continue their development in the other world in like manner as here. If however one can not accept this view, then death ends all, and the former generations have ceased to exist. Only the modernist who still believes in a future life can admit a continuous development after death, though it be of age-long duration, even as to this day it still goes on among many nations in the earth that are entirely apart from Christ, and only for so far as the peoples have come in contact with the Christian religion together with the spiritual influence of Jesus. So this presupposes the possibility of a continuous development after death on the part of the vast multitudes which from times immemorial have lived apart from Christ, and, for so far as Jesus would exercise influence upon them, that influence would merely be the action of His genial religious highness.

The followers of Schleiermacher occupy an entirely different standpoint. According to them the human race has always been divided into two parts, the greater of which has never been in touch with Christ, and thus has never come under the power of the Gospel; while the incomparably much smaller part of humanity has by revelation become subject to grace. This dispensation of grace began with Seth, continued in ever lessening measure until Noah, propagated itself in Shem, and partly in Japhet, until in Abraham it became exceptional, and Israel became a nation, was enriched first by prophecy and then in Bethlehem's manger by Immanuel, and so passing over into the Christian church has overshadowed our human life. Thus at this standpoint the sphere of faith limits itself to everything that has made preparation for the coming of the Lord, that has appeared in Him, and now as aftermath of His appearing lives on in the Christian church. And be it, that the Christian religion occasioned disappointment almost everywhere, this makes no difference, since from Schleiermacher's standpoint there is no final judgment after death, but the development that is here begun perpetuates itself in the heavenly sphere. Even after death this can again lead to reaction; but higher leading again takes hold of the backslider, and so the cultivation of spirits can go on to all eternity. The last judgment, the Return of Christ and the conclusion of the dispensation of our lot thereby actually entirely fall away.

Finally over against the modernists and the Schleiermachians stands the Christian confession which retains the twelve articles of faith, tolerates no departure from the Holy Scriptures, and stedfastly holds to the peculiar and entirely independent dispensation of Divine Revelation; worships Christ, as, with the Father and the Holy Ghost, a unique triune God; promises eternal blessedness to those only who have received His fellowship and continue life therein; and who do not withdraw themselves from the solemn confession, that they who are not elected, not regenerated and not implanted in Christ, are forever lost. So only does there come a Consummation; so only does that Consummation bring the final issue; and so only is the rich Revelation of both Old and New Testaments verified.

Here too all depends upon whether one bows to Christ's authoritative speech, or sets it aside in favor of his own representation. In His deeply-stirring word to the lawyer Christ has not put the love of neighbor on a par with the love we owe to God, but very far below it. In Matth. 22, 36 the lawyer asks Jesus: "Master, which is the great commandment?" And Jesus' answer is twofold; we should in the first place love God with all our heart, all our soul and all our mind, which He says is "the first and great commandment": and secondly, which in devotion is like unto it: "Thou shalt love thy neighbor as thyself." But note, this is the *second;* the other is *the first;* and must precede it, and only when justice is done to the first will the second apply. Without the first, which must precede, the second is without merit. Yet as a rule unbelievers place these two commandments indiscriminately side by side, as though the second without the first had any sense. Utterly subversive of this are the striking words of Psalm 139, where the chief musician in vs. 21 and 22 testifies: "Should not we hate, O Lord, them that hate thee? I hate them with perfect hatred." So in the blessed eternity there will be no hint of pity for the lost. There all love concentrates itself in and upon God, with all the heart and soul and mind; and thus of itself what resists and rejects God can no more be the object of our love. This is only possible and tolerable so long as sentence is still pending, while this will absolutely be impossible after the judgment has been pronounced. Were this otherwise, there would be no blessedness in the new Jerusalem. Sorrow and pity for the lost would distress us unto all eternity.

It goes without saying that this implies great sorrow of heart, so long as the sentence is not yet passed, and hope is still alive that he who is against Christ will turn to Christ, and we feel solemnly obligated to lend our aid in this direction. But if we confess, and this is what counts, that finally the moment comes in which judgment is executed and the Consummation follows, then it results of inexorable necessity that there is no more possibility of conversion, and that the last judgment decides the lot of all. Thus every attempt to give conversion a place in the hereafter is a direct denial of the teachings of Scripture and the Christ regarding the end of things in the last judgment. And as a matter of fact, every modernistic or ethical theologian who seeks to win our approval of this representation is bound to begin anew with detracting from the word of Christ. To give free rein to one's own insight the first and great commandment is then abandoned; and in the face of Old and New Testaments, yes, in the face of the positive sayings of the Christ of God, one posits a world order of his own.

Already in the days of Origen it was remarked, that we have no warrant to set final decisions and the last judgment aside, because this would sacrifice all positiveness regarding the course and the unfolding of the world and of mankind. In the last instance this would make Almighty God dependent upon human choice, both as regards the process of the world which He has created and the work of grace which He has devised; and such not with respect to mankind as a whole, which in a mammoth mass meeting might pass a final judgment, but with respect to each individual separately. This could only end in unlimited division and in chaotic confusion, rendering a final conclusion of the world forever impossible. Rather than the rational mind of God, the emotional outburst of sinners would then pass judgment upon the ever newly forming centuries. In that case God would have abandoned judgment regarding His Universe to the arbitrariness of human feeling; not man would receive the disposition of his lot from God Almighty, but God Almighty would passively have to look on and see, how human individuals play the game of arbitrariness with His Universe. So this comprehensive study of the Consummation could not be brought to a close, without having uncompromisingly disputed a widely propagated representation, which at every application pitifully proves its absolute untenability. For however much one may contend that in the end the persistent love of God will allure and draw the most unwilling ones unto Himself, life here on earth furnishes abundant and most convincing proof of the utter helplessness of tenderest love in the face of the malignity of the heart.

INDEX

I. NAMES AND SUBJECTS

INDEX

INDEX

INDEX

Return of Christ, twofold interpretation of — (entirely unexpected or prepared) 19; beginning of the upheaval before the—25 separation between believers and unbelievers at the—199; the — to judgment 249, 256, 262.

Revelation, God's ordinary—73; — to John views the end of the world and the church, 17; the— points to the transition state 20, 49; the real apocalypse in the— begins with chapter 4, I or 6, I, 25; no chronological connection in the—38, 39; in the—we have the divine representation of the world process, 37; division into four parts of the—41; the seven churches in the—41; the—and the apostolate 50, 53; the—and the church life 42; 53; the—is clothed in the Jewish national form, 62; construction of the— 84; three apocalypses in the— (chapter 14) 112, 121, 127; in the—the parousia is presented as close at hand and as far off in the future 271.

Ritschl, Dr. 347.

River, the pure—of the water of life 330.

Roman Empire, the—is the last world empire 224, 229; the—and law (Recht) 229, 232.

Rurt, Dr. 347.

Satan, work of—to oppose the return of Christ 204, 234;—at the parousia 279; binding of—274; victory over—by Michael 280; the binding of—lasts perhaps but a few days 292; final punishment of—and other demons 299, 304.

Schleiermacher 347, 351, 352.

Schweizer, Dr. A. 347.

Scorpions, image of the—in Rev. 98.

Sea of glass, the—163.

Seal, the—of God on the foreheads of believers 101.

Seals, the seven—view the end and are opened directly one after the other 74, 79; the—evidently not large 74; the four at the opening of the—75; beasts the first

four—75, 79, 82; the fifth of the —77, 82; the sixth—80, 82, 91; the seventh of the — embraces Revelation 8-22, 8, 82; and has no content of its own 85. See also: **Book.**

Song of victory, Rev. 19, 1-10, 249.

Souls of the martyrs under the altar, 77.

Sun, change in the action of the —at the parousis 183.

Tabernacle, idea of—310, 314, 325; See also: Temple.

Temple, the—of the tabernacle in Rev. 15, 169; that—is closed at the outpouring of the vials 172; purpose of the—173; no more reconciliation in the—174, 175; idea of the—311, 314, 325.

Throne of God, the — in Rev. 15, 169.

Time, the cessation of—233.

Transition state, the—between the old and the new heaven and earth 192; twofold report of the—199; separation between believers and unbelievers in the—199.

Tree of life, the—on the new earth 328; the leaves of the—334.

Trumpet, significance of the — in Israel 87, 88; the seven—s in the Rev. of St. John 84; why seven —? 86; the seven—follow each other quickly 89, 91; the first— 89; the second—91; the third—94, the fourth—96; the fifth—98; the sixth—105; the seventh—105.

Vials, significance of the word— 120; content of the revelation of the seven — 132; time of the— 132; handing out, material and carriers of the seven—169; with the—grace comes to an end 174; the—are the last historical events 175; the first three—176; the fourth, 185; division of the— 184; fifth, 185; sixth, 186; seventh—189.

Vision, the heavenly—in Rev. 14, 112, 134, 159.

Witnesses, the two—85, 110.

Woes, the three—85.

Wood, 27.

INDEX

II. BIBLICAL PASSAGES

INDEX